D0163148

THE KENNEDY FAMILY
OF MASSACHUSETTS

THE KENNEDY FAMILY
OF MASSACHUSETTS

A BIBLIOGRAPHY

Compiled by
Dorothy Ryan
and Louis J. Ryan

GREENWOOD PRESS
Westport, Connecticut • London, England

Library of Congress Cataloging in Publication Data

Ryan, Dorothy.
  The Kennedy family of Massachusetts.

  Includes index.
  1. Kennedy family—Bibliography. I. Ryan, Louis J.
II. Title.
Z5315.K4R9   [E843]   016.973922'092'2 [B]   81-6672
ISBN 0-313-23189-3 (lib. bdg.)   AACR2

Copyright © 1981 by Dorothy Ryan and Louis J. Ryan

All rights reserved. No portion of this book may be
reproduced, by any process or technique, without the
express written consent of the publisher.

Library of Congress Catalog Card Number: 81-6672
ISBN: 0-313-23189-3

First published in 1981

Greenwood Press
A division of Congressional Information Service, Inc.
88 Post Road West, Westport, Connecticut 06881

Printed in the United States of America

10 9 8 7 6 5 4 3 2 1

To Mary Beth, Martha, and Rosemary

CONTENTS

INTRODUCTION

Legends and myths as well as folklore and facts hold particular fascination for all people who would understand the world about them. Myths as collective beliefs beget realities through those who successfully pursue those beliefs. Legends and folklore may embroider, obfuscate, or preserve the myths in terms of facts. Careful recording of the facts as legends develop ensures preservation of the legitimate beliefs without corruption of the myths.

Twin preoccupations with folklore and fact prompted the compilers to undertake the present bibliography on the Kennedy family of Massachusetts and the presidency and Congress of the United States in a particular time in history. No responsible social scientist would dispute the great impact of the Kennedy family on the history of the second half of the twentieth century. As professional scientists we were intrigued by the abundance of published materials of the 1950-1980 period—some formulating hypotheses and recording facts, and others creating, controverting, or combating myths or legends such as Camelot, for example. Our academic interest in gathering materials for this collection was accentuated as our poetic selves became fascinated by the romance and tragedy—and sometimes comedy—of this familial phenomenon.

The books, articles, and writings recorded here form a bibliographic record of our personal collection and are annotated and arranged by us. Some of the titles make brief reference to the subjects of this bibliography, yet in our judgment have overall significance. Obviously the collection is not inclusive, but we believe it to be representative and fair. Some polemics are omitted because we feel they are so lacking in objectivity as to be unworthy of advertisement; some are included as examples of the "opposition."

There are 4,082 items in this bibliography distributed thus: 1,469 hardbound items, 1,865 periodicals, 442 miscellany, 263 conventional paperbacks, and thirty-eight recordings. The miscellany includes signed letters, monographs, photogaphs, reports, reprints, brochures, flyers, critiques, and other materials not easily classified.

Because of the abundance and interrelationships of materials and the limitations of space, the categories are not completely discrete. Numerous titles in the John F. Kennedy section include Robert F. Kennedy and Edward M. Kennedy as well as other members of the Kennedy family. Conversely, many listings in the RFK and EMK sections refer back to JFK.

The outline of this work as indicated in the contents gives precedence to the office of the United States presidency by placing the names of John F. and Jacqueline Bouvier Kennedy first among the Kennedys. Genealogical family data are included under this heading. Sections on the Robert F. and Ethel Skakel Kennedy and Edward M. and Joan Bennett Kennedy families follow. A section on other members of the Kennedy family concludes this material.

This collection of items by and about members of the Kennedy family includes works dealing wih their impact on the social, economic, artistic, religious, and political worlds. It contains enumerations of original works by the Kennedys, general biographies, and works about the Kennedys categorized into specific time periods and topics.

Section One on John F. and Jacqueline Bouvier Kennedy contains, in addition to their autographs, writings, ancestries, general biographies, art and musical interests, attraction of media, incidents of youth, marriage and children, social activities, portraits, photographic collections, and recordings, items on JFK's geographical background, the Harvard University and United States Navy years, his various political campaigns, his election to the presidency in 1960 and the inauguration, public opinion surveys, his relations with the economic, professional, religious, ethnic, and political communities (including the liberals and the Right), and his relations with young people. There are also listings on his personal health, and on cartoons and other humor about him. The literature on President John F. Kennedy's administration includes a general category as well as others on foreign affairs in particular countries, United States defense policies, domestic affairs, and the assassination and its aftermath. The not inconsiderable literature by and about Jacqueline Bouvier Kennedy Onassis is also represented. Other nations whose relations with the Kennedy administration are examined in detail are: Africa, Arab-Israel, Canada, Finland, India and Pakistan, Japan, Latin America, NATO countries and the Common Market, the Peace Corps and the Third World, Russia and China, Cuba, and Vietnam. The items on United States defense policies refer to the nuclear test ban, flexible response, trade expansion, CIA espionage, the diplomatic establishment, and the United Nations, as well as more general works. Domestic affairs include an examination of the genesis of the antipoverty program, the arts, business and labor, civil rights in general and in specific regions, the March on Washington for Jobs and Freedom and civil rights for women, the Congress, the Departments of Agriculture and Interior, the economics of the New Frontier (inflation held to 1%-3%), education and health, fallout shelters, the FBI, the Secret Service, the judicial system, mental health and mental retardation, the post office, presidential politics and regional political studies, and the space program.

Section One also has twenty pages of titles on the assassination of John F. Kennedy and the aftermath. Special mention should be made of the comprehensive historical and legal bibliography *The Assassination of John F. Kennedy*, compiled by DeLoyd Guth and David R. Wrone. This covers the 1963-1979 years and includes maps.

Section Two presents the literature on Robert F. and Ethel Skakel Kennedy. In addition to writings, speeches and interviews, and general biographies and particular studies in the pre-1960 period, RFK's record as United States Attorney General is scrutinized, as well as his period as United States Senator of New York. The campaign for the presidential nomination that led to his death in 1968 is covered in 234 items.

Writings, speeches, and interviews of Edward M. and Joan Bennett Kennedy are reported in Section Three, along with EMK's books, autographs, and recordings. General biographies, the Senate years of EMK, the 1980 presidential campaign, and works of and about Joan Kennedy conclude this section.

Section Four contains a brief list of writings by and about other members of the Kennedy family.

The writings by the Kennedy family members are listed in chronological order. Books about them are alphabetical by author or editor. In the few instances where no author or editor is named, the title is used for alphabetical arrangement. First editions are specified. Variant editions are placed under major title headings.

Major magazine articles are listed under the authors' names. Brief articles are arranged in chronological order under the title of the magazine. Some magazine articles are difficult to title. For example, *Life* often used three headlines for one story: the first on the cover, the second in the index, and the third in the heading of the article. We have used the one that best describes the content of the article.

In the interest of space, publishers' names and newspaper and periodical titles have generally been abbreviated.

Where the periodical item appears in a separate issue of the magazine, the symbol (−) is used to indicate that it is disbound. If the item is bound in with other issues of the magazine, the symbol (+) is used.

One cannot experience a survey as extensive as this without appreciating the simplicity amidst the complexity of the presidency of the United States. The Adams family—with father and son both becoming presidents, and their descendants continuing the family tradition by writing or being active in politics—is an early example of a familial endowment of statesmanship; an aristocracy of genetic but not inherited succession.

In the twentieth century the Kennedys of Massachusetts furnished a contemporary illustration of family contributions to American social and political life. The presidency, it seems reasonably clear, was the ambition of Joseph P. Kennedy. When circumstances of the Franklin Roosevelt era made realization of that goal impossible, the eldest son, Joseph, was chosen to prepare for the role. When he was killed in an Allied foray into Europe in World War II, the mantle fell to John, who was initially more given to literary endeavors. After the sorrowful interlude following Dallas, Robert sought a Senate seat and the presidency. His assassination pointed a new direction for the youngest son and senator, Edward. That this familial tenacity will end with Ted Kennedy seems unlikely, considering the political involvement already shown by the next generation of the Kennedy clan.

Our study, resulting in the bibliography of our collection, has enabled us to appreciate better the people involved, the presidency, and the electoral process. We are happy, through our publisher, to share our research with others.

ABBREVIATIONS

AAPSS	*American Academy of Political and Social Science Annals*	Betts & Mir.	Betts and Mirror Press
		biblio.	bibliography(ies)
		bk. rev.	book review
		bk(s).	book, books
A&B	Allyn and Bacon	B-M	Bobbs Merrill
		bull.	bulletin
A-C-C	Appleton, Century Crofts	c.	copies, copyright
ALA	American Library Association	Chap.Hill	Chapel Hill
		C.McC	Coward McCann
ALS	Autograph letter signed	C.McC.&G	Coward McCann and Geoghegan
AMA	American Medical Association	co.	company
		Col. Jrnl. Rev.	*Columbia Journalism Review*
Anti-Def.	Anti-Defamation League	comm.	committee, commission
ARA	Area Redevelopment Administration	Comm.Ch.	Communication Channels, Inc.
Assn.	Association Press	comp.(s)	compiler(s)
		Cong.	Congress, Congressional
A-S	Abelard Schuman	Contemp.	Contemporary Books
Athen.	Atheneum		
Atl.	Atlantic Press	CQ	*Congressional Quarterly*
Bal.	Ballantine Books	C.U.E.	Center for Urban Education
Berkeley-Med	Berkeley Medallion		

D'day	Doubleday	HR&W	Holt, Rinehart and Winston
distr.	distributer	ibid.	the same
D-M	Dodd Mead	illus.	illustrated, illustrator, illustration
DS&P	Duell, Sloane & Pearce		
ed.	editor, edited, edition	int'l.	international
Ency. Brit.	*Encyclopedia Britannica*	intro.	introduction
		Ives W.	Ives Washburn
Ency.		J. Hopkins	Johns Hopkins
Enterp.	Encyclopedia Enterprises	jr.	junior
		jrnl.	journal
enlarg.	enlarged	LB	Little Brown
F&F	Faber and Faber	Ldn.	London
		L.H.J.	*Ladies Home Journal*
F&W	Funk and Wagnalls	lib.	library
fdn.	foundation	Lipp.	Lippincott
ff.	following	ltd.	limited
FS&G	Farrar, Straus and Giroux	MacF.	MacFadden
		MacF-B	MacFadden Bartell
fwd.	foreword	Macm.	Macmillan
geog.	geography	mag.	magazine
GPO	Government Printing Office	M.C.	Mason Charter
		McD.	McDonald
G&D	Grosset and Dunlap	McG-H	McGraw Hill
		M&M	Marzani and Munsell
H&H	Herder and Herder	M.I.T.	Massachusetts Institute of Technology
Harp.	Harper		
H&R	Harper and Row	ms.	manuscript
H&S	Hodder and Stoughton	NAL	New American Library
H&W	Hill and Wang	NAL-W	New American Library-World
HB&J	Harcourt, Brace and Jovanovich	nat'l.	national
		n.d.	no date
HB&W	Harcourt, Brace and World	NEA	National Education Association
H-M	Houghton Mifflin		
hq.	headquarters	no.	number

NLRB	National Labor Relations Board	rev.	revised
N.P.	No publisher	R.McN	Rand McNally
NYT	*New York Times*	RNS	Religious News Service
O&D	Outerbridge and Dienstfrey	S&D	Stein and Day
op.cit.	already cited	S&S	Simon & Schuster
OSU	Ohio State University	S&W	Sheed and Ward
photo(s)	photographs, photographer	St.M.	St. Martin's
p.,pp.	page, pages	Sat. Rev.	*Saturday Review*
Pere Marq.	Pere Marquette	Scrib.	Scribner's
P-H	Prentice Hall	Sen.	Senator
POAU	Protestants and All Other Americans United (for separation of Church and State)	S.E.P.	*Saturday Evening Post*
pt.(s)	part, parts	sess.	session
Pres.	President	S-F	Scott, Foresman
prtg.	printing	soc.	society
pseud.	pseudonym	Spec.Publ.	*Special Publications*
publ.	published, publisher	sr.	senior
Publ.Exp.	Publishers' Export Co.	TLS	Typed letter signed
Quad.	Quadrangle	U.	University
qtly.	quarterly	U.N.	United Nations
R.D.Press	Readers' Digest Press	Univ. Bks.	University Books
		U.P.I.	United Press International
		U.S.	United States
		vol.(s)	volume(s)
		W&T	Weybright and Talley
		Wash. Sq.	Washington Square
		West. Isl.	Western Isles

SECTION ONE

JOHN FITZGERALD KENNEDY

JACQUELINE BOUVIER KENNEDY ONASSIS

PART ONE. JOHN F. KENNEDY

THE WORKS OF JOHN F. KENNEDY

Signed Letter, Photographs, Card, Telegram

TLS, Oct.18, 1960. Seven lines expressing gratitude for interest in candidacy. From Nat'l HQ U.S.Senator John F. Kennedy for President. Signed: John Kennedy

Presentation photograph, March 2, 1962. Signed: "To Mrs.
Lucy Ryan with my best wishes, John Kennedy."

Presentation photograph, April 10, 1963. Signed: "To George
J. Aitken with my good wishes, John F. Kennedy."

Printed card, five lines "grateful for support and confidence"
re missile crisis. Signed John F. Kennedy. Envelope
postmarked November 19, 1962.

Telegram, March 9, 1962. To Mrs. Lucy Ryan: "I would like to
wish you a very happy 75th birthday. May you have many,
many more. John F. Kennedy."

Books, Reviews, Articles, Interviews, Published Letters

WHY ENGLAND SLEPT. Wilfred Funk (1961). Originally published
in 1940 and based on JFK's senior honor thesis at Harvard.
Dolphin, wrs., 1st ed.

A NATION OF IMMIGRANTS. Anti-Defamation League of B'nai B'rith
(1958). Wrs. As a Senator JFK sponsored and guided through
the Senate the only major amendment to the Immigration and
Nationality Act of 1952.
Rev. and enlarg. Harper & Row (1964) Intro. RFK
Harper Torchbook (1964) wrs. Intro. RFK
Popular Library, 1964. 1st ed. wrs. Intro. RFK

PROFILES IN COURAGE. Harper (1956). This book awarded Pulit-
zer Prize - only time for a member of U.S.Senate. JFK's
theory of the motivation of these men "...it was precisely
because they did love themselves - because each one's need
to maintain his own respect for himself was more important
to him than his popularity with others..." p.239
Cardinal ed. Pocket Books, March, 1957. Wrs.
Harper & Row (1961). Inaugural ed.
Popular Library. March, 1961, 1st ed., wrs.
Harper & Row (1964). Memorial ed. Fwd. RFK
Perennial Library, 1964. 1st ed., wrs.
H&R Young Readers' Memorial Ed. abridged. (1961, 1964)
Scholastic Book Services, 1964. 1st prtg. wrs.

THE KENNEDY FAMILY OF MASSACHUSETTS

<u>Books</u>, <u>Reviews</u>, <u>Articles</u>, <u>Interviews</u>, <u>Published</u> <u>Letters</u>

"How Should Cadets Be Picked?" N.Y.T.MAG. Aug.19, 1951: 16ff.

"Social Security: Constructive If Not Bold." NEW REPUBLIC
Feb.8, 1954: 14-15, chart. +

"A Great Day in American History." COLLIER'S, Nov.25, 1955:
40-43ff. Daniel Webster's speech March 7, 1850.

"The Man Who Saved a President: Ross of Kansas." HARPER'S
Dec., 1955: 40-44. READERS' DIGEST 40TH ANNIVERSARY TREASURY
1961: 66-77.

"Brothers, I Presume?" THE WORLD OF VOGUE. Viking, 1963: 323-
325. First published VOGUE Apr.1, 1956: 117,142. On the current "hostility between the political and literary worlds."

"Take the Academies Out of Politics." SEP, June 2, 1956:36ff.

"Politics in America." HARVARD ALUMNI BULLETIN, Dec.7, 1963:
259-261. Reprint of 1956 article.

"Unemployment: How Government Will Help." Interview with JFK.
U.S.NEWS AND WORLD REPORT, Jan.11, 1957: 133 +

"Democrat Says Party Must Lead Or Get Left." LIFE, Mar.11,
1957: 164-166ff. Photo in color of JFK on cover.

"Algerian Crisis: a New Phase?" AMERICA, Oct.5, 1957 -

"A Democrat Looks at Foreign Policy": 349-364 in AMERICA'S
FOREIGN POLICY ed. H.K. Jacobson, Random, 1960. 1st prtg.
First published FOREIGN AFFAIRS Oct. 1957.

"A Woman of Courage" (Jeannette Rankin, Republican Congress-
woman from Montana.) McCALL'S, April, 1976: 43-44, illus.
Reprinted from January 1958 issue.

"The Fate of the Nations." NEA JRNL., Jan.1958: 10-11 +

"When the Executive Fails to Lead." REPORTER, Sept.18,1958:
14ff.

"General Gavin Sounds the Alarm." REPORTER, Oct.30, 1958:
35-36. Review of James M. Gavin's WAR AND PEACE IN THE
SPACE AGE. Harper, 1958

"Kennedy's Reform." NEW REPUBLIC, Mar.2, 1959: 5. Concerns
Sen. Kennedy's proposal for revision of the immigration and
naturalization laws. JFK's reply and editor's rejoinder
in Mar.30, 1959: 3,24.

WORKS OF JOHN F. KENNEDY

Books, Reviews, Articles, Interviews, Published Letters

"Labor Racketeers and Political Pressure." LOOK, May 12, 1959: 17-21, illus.

"Let's Get Rid of College Loyalty Oaths." CORONET. Apr.,1960 88-94, illus.

"What Senator Kennedy Says:" interview on WRC-TV, May 14. U.S. NEWS AND WORLD REPORT, May 30, 1960:122-123 -

"Issue Is Whether the Power of U.S. Is Increasing." U.S.NEWS AND WORLD REPORT. June 13, 1960: 49-50, illus. +

"Disarmament Can Be Won." BULLETIN OF THE ATOMIC SCIENTISTS. June, 1960:217-219.

"'We Must Climb to the Hilltop.' The National Purpose Discussion Is Resumed." LIFE. Aug.22, 1960: 70B-72ff. illus.

"A Day I'll Remember." LOOK. Sept.13, 1960:51-54, illus. The memorable day after JFK had won the Democratic Presidential nomination - and his account of the choice of LBJ for V.P.

"Kennedy on the Issues." U.S.NEWS AND WORLD REPORT. Oct. 10, 1960: 84 -

"As Kennedy Foresaw the Presidency; Although What Follows Was Written in January, 1960, It Represents the Views of the Presi-dent-elect Today." U.S.NEWS AND...Nov.28, 1960: 76-78 -

"An Interview with John Kennedy." BULLETIN OF ATOMIC SCIENT-ISTS. Nov. 1960: 346-347. Answers by JFK to a series of quest-ions submitted by the editorial board to both presidential candidates. Nixon sent a policy statement instead of answers.

"New Frontier; An Exclusive Interview." CATHOLIC WORLD. Nov., 1960: 80-86, illus. Interrogator, Patrick Donaghy. Front cover: photo of JFK and Nixon. -

"Sport on the New Frontier: The Soft American." SPORTS ILLUS-TRATED. Dec.26, 1960: 14-17, illus. Also "Jack Kennedy Prac-tices What He Preaches": 18-23, with facsimile of his hand-written sailing history. Cover in color of JFK and JBK.

"Why Go Into Politics": 59-67, autobiography. In James M. Cannon, ed., POLITICS, U.S.A. 1st ed. Doublday, 1960. "In looking back, I have never regretted my choice of profession, although I cannot know what the future may bring." p.66

"A View of the Presidency" in THE PROGRESSIVE. Jan., 1961: 14-16, illus. Address to Nat'l Press Club in 1960.

THE KENNEDY FAMILY OF MASSACHUSETTS

Books, Reviews, Articles, Interviews, Published Letters

"The New President Answers Ten Major Questions Facing America."
By Pat Frank. THIS WEEK. Jan.15, 1961: 6-9, illus. -
Cover: The Kennedy Family - in color by Jacques Lowe.

"Commendation of Miss Helen (Missy Adams) Teacher of the Year."
LOOK, May 23, 1961: 19, illus. -

"Every Citizen Holds Office." NEA JRNL. Oct., 1961: 18-20,
illus. in color by Norman Rockwell. +

"An Urgent Letter to All Americans." LIFE. Nov.15, 1961: 95.
Cf. also "Fallout Shelters, a New Urgency..." 96-108, illus.
and editorial "Let's Prepare...Shelters." Oct.13, 1961: 4.

"Message on Behalf of Magazines." LIFE. Dec.22, 1961, illus.
full page of JFK at desk in color. -

Brandon, Henry. AS WE ARE: 17 CONVERSATIONS BETWEEN THE AMERI-
CANS AND THE MAN FROM THE LONDON SUNDAY TIMES. 1st ed., illus.
Doubleday, 1961. Sen. JFK: 177-191.

"The Next 25 Years." LOOK. Jan.16, 1962: 17.

"Kennedy's View of the Presidency: A Leader Must Lead."
BUSINESS WEEK. Mar.17, 1962: 25-27 illus.+

"Essential Nourishment;" statement on National Library Week.
PUBLISHERS' WEEKLY. Apr. 16, 1962: 76.

"Letter dated March 7, 1962, from President Kennedy addressed
to Chairman Khrushchev"; "Message dated March 10, 1962, from
Chairman Khrushchev to President Kennedy." UN REVIEW. April,
1962: 37-39. On exploration and uses of outer space.

Editorial: "Businessman's Letter to JFK and His Reply." LIFE.
July 6, 1962: 30-34 illus.

"The Strength and Style of Our Navy Tradition." (FDR collection
of naval art.) LIFE. Aug.10, 1962: 79-81ff. illus.

"Great Performances;" JFK interview on TV with Max Ascoli,
Dec.17, 1962. REPORTER. Jan.,3, 1963: 12,14.

"The Arts in America" (the role of the Federal government in
encouraging cultural activities): 4-8 in CREATIVE AMERICA, the
Ridge Press, 1962.

"Creative America: The Arts In America." LOOK. Dec., 1962:
104-118, illus. Adaptation of the book. -

WORKS OF JOHN F. KENNEDY

Books, Reviews, Articles, Interviews, Published Letters

Kurland, Philip, ed. OF LAW AND LIFE and Other Things That Matter. Papers and Addresses (of Felix Frankfurter) 1956-1963. Belknap Press of Harvard Univ., 1965. Exchange of letters between Frankfurter and Pres.JFK: 246-250.

"Where We Stand." LOOK, Jan.13, 1963: 18-19ff., illus.

Deindorfer, Robt.G. ed. "The Private Letters of John F. Kennedy." GOOD HOUSEKEEPING, Feb.,1963: 74-75ff. Full page color sketch of JFK by Gundel Finger.

"Physical Fitness: A Report of Progress." LOOK, Aug.13, 1963: 82-83, illus.

"What Business Can Do For America." NATION'S BUSINESS, Sept. 1963: 29-31ff., illus. +

"What Women Can Do Now For Peace." McCALL'S, Nov.,1963: 102-103ff., illus.

THE PRESIDENT SPEAKS OUT ON UNIONS. Flyer, wrs., illus. 4pp. N.P., n.d. Support for organized labor rights.

"President Kennedy in Germany." BERLINER ILLUSTRIRTE, special issue, 1963. JFK on front cover in color. 79pp. folio on JFK's presence and words in Germany, illus. in color. Includes his talk "the message of freedom."

O'Hara, Wm.T., ed. JOHN F. KENNEDY ON EDUCATION. Columbia,U., 1966. Group of speeches and writings from 1947 to 1963.

"Peace and Freedom Walk Together." WAY: CATHOLIC VIEWPOINTS, Jan.-Feb., 1964: 13-17. - The substance of the Commencement Address at American University, June 10, 1963.

AMERICA, THE BEAUTIFUL in the Words of John F. Kennedy. Color plate of JFK tipped on, illus. in color and b/w. Country Beautiful Foundation, 1964. On man, the land, the arts, dignity.

Tourtellot, Arthur Bernon, ed. THE PRESIDENTS ON THE PRESIDENCY. 1st ed. Doubleday, 1964. From the public and private writings of our presidents from Washington to Kennedy.

David, Jay (pseud) ed. THE KENNEDY READER. BM, (1967). Collection of writings by and about JFK on domestic and foreign affairs, memorabilia.

McCarthy, Joe. "A note from President Kennedy." LADIES HOME JRNL., Dec., 1972: 66, illus.

THE KENNEDY FAMILY OF MASSACHUSETTS

Speeches and Public Statements, Quotations, Recordings

JOHN FITZGERALD KENNEDY; A COMPILATION OF STATEMENTS AND
SPEECHES MADE DURING HIS SERVICE IN THE UNITED STATES SENATE
AND HOUSE OF REPRESENTATIVES. Wrs. 88th Cong., 2nd sess.,
Senate Document No. 79. GPO, 1964. Period 1947-1960. An
appendix includes additional speeches, articles and statements
of JFK which appeared in the Congressional Record. Most of
this latter material presented outside the Halls of Congress.

"America's Stake in Vietnam;" address, June 1, 1956. VITAL
SPEECHES, Aug.1, 1956: 617-619 +

"Comity and Commonsense in the Middle East. Suez, boundaries,
arms, refugees and economic development." VITAL SPEECHES,
Apr.1, 1957: 359-361. Delivered to 1957 Brotherhood Obser-
vance of Nat'l Conf. Christian and Jews, Feb.24, 1957.

"The World and God..." CATHOLIC DIGEST, Jan.1965: 21-23. Condensed from RNS Aug.28, 1964 - An address by JFK on Sept. 7,
1957, at the Columban Fathers' Seminary, Milton, Mass. Previously unpublished.

Harrison, Selig S. ed. INDIA AND THE UNITED STATES. 1st prtg.
Macm., 1961: "The Dollar Gap:" 63-64; "The Politics of Foreign Aid:" 111-112. Washington Conference of May, 1959 with
88 leading Indian and American authorities.

Nevins, Allan, ed. THE STRATEGY OF PEACE. 1st ed. Harper 1960.
Selection of speeches and public statements of JFK as Senator
from Massachusetts.
Harper, wrs., 1960. Includes 13pp. on foreign policy added.
Popular Library 1st prtg. 1961.
Maloney, Jos.F. Review of STRATEGY OF PEACE. BEST SELLERS:
May 1, 1960: 61 -

"Disarmament Can Be Won." BULLETIN OF THE ATOMIC SCIENTISTS,
June, 1960: 217-219. A slightly abbreviated version of a
speech delivered by JFK at Univ. of New Hampshire March 7,1960.

"I Am Not the Catholic Candidate for President;" full text of
an address to the American Society of Newspaper Editors in Washington, D.C. May 20, 1960. U.S.NEWS, May 30, 1960: 122-123+

"Kennedy and Johnson Open the Campaign; full text of Senator
John F. Kennedy's speech of acceptance as presidential nominee
to the Democratic National Convention on July 15, 1960."
U.S. NEWS...July 25, 1960: 100-102, illus. +

"The Democratic National Convention - Acceptance Address."
VITAL SPEECHES, Aug.1, 1960: 610-612

WORKS OF JOHN F. KENNEDY

Speeches and Public Statements, Quotations, Recordings

Boykin, Edw. ed. THE WIT AND WISDOM OF CONGRESS. F&W, 1961.
Three excerpts from JFK.

"History Will Be Our Judge;" address to Mass. Legislature,
Jan.9, 1961. VITAL SPEECHES, Feb.1, 1961: 227-228 +

"Balance of Payments and Gold." Special Supplement No.31,
U.S. Information Service, Embassy of the U.S. - Rome. Feb.7,
1961.

"Executive Order 10925" establishing the President's Committee On Equal Employment Opportunity. Wrs. March 7, 1961.
GPO, 1962.

Tillett, Paul, ed. THE POLITICAL VOCATION. "Special Message
on Conflicts of Interest:" 443-453. Basic Books, 1965.
Submitted to Congress April 27, 1961.

Evans, Rowland, Jr. "That Wit in the White House," SEP,
Sept.,2, 1961: 16ff., illus. JFK's use of banter as tool.

Gross, Franz B. ed. THE UNITED STATES AND THE UNITED NATIONS.
"An Address to the United Nations," Sept. 25, 1961: 277-288.
U. of Oklahoma Press, 1964.

The President's Panel on Mental Retardation. REPORT TO THE
PRESIDENT: A PROPOSED PROGRAM FOR NATIONAL ACTION TO COMBAT
MENTAL RETARDATION. "Statement of the President Regarding
the Need for a National Health Plan in Mental Retardation,
Oct. 11, 1961:" 196-201. Wrs. GPO, 1962.

JFK quotation ALA BULLETIN, Jan. 1962: cover feature. Pictures
of JFK and Eisenhower with their respective quotes on the ex-
treme positions of ultra-rightists. JFK quotation is from his
speech in Los Angeles, Nov.18, 1961.

Gardner, John E. ed. TO TURN THE TIDE: A Selection from Pres.
Kennedy's Public Statements from His Election Through the 1961
Adjournment of Congress, Setting Forth the Goals of His First
Legislative Year. Fwd. Carl Sandburg. Intro. JFK. 1st ed.
Harper, 1962.
Popular Library, wrs., 1st ed., 1962

"The State of the Dollar. A Free World Problem." VITAL
SPEECHES, Oct. 15, 1962: 7-8.

"Arms Quarantine of Cuba." VITAL SPEECHES, Nov.15, 1962:66-68.
Delivered over TV and radio, Wash.D.C., Oct.22, 1962.

Foreign Policy Assn. Fact Sheet No.8. "United States: New Dir-
ections in Foreign Policy" Illus., wrs. 1962.

THE KENNEDY FAMILY OF MASSACHUSETTS

Speeches and Public Statements, Quotations, Recordings

"The President Informs the People." A learning program on Presidential press conferences with focus on Nov.20, 1962. Wrs. John F. Kennedy Library, Waltham, Mass., n.d. Cassette of the press conference included.

"The State of the Union. Tax Reduction Proposed." VITAL SPEECHES, Feb.1, 1963: 226-230.

Office of the White House Press Secretary for Immediate Release March 13, 1963. "Remarks of the President." 19th Washington Conference The Advertising Council.

A MEMORY OF JOHN F. KENNEDY. Dublin: Wood Printing Works n.d. illus. in color. Visit to Ireland June 26-29, 1963. Includes his speeches of the four days as well as witty asides.

"A Moral Imperative. Equality of Treatment." VITAL SPEECHES, July 1, 1963: 546-547. Delivered over TV and radio June 11,1963

Goldwin, Robt.A. ed. WHY FOREIGN AID? Wrs. R. McNally, 1963. JFK's foreign aid messages of 1961 and 1963: 1-9, 131-140.

"Executive Order 10980" establishing the President's Commission on the Status of Women in REPORT: AMERICAN WOMEN 1963. Wrs. GPO, 1963: v. This report includes JFK's directive to executive agencies in July, 1962, widening Federal employment opportunities for women.

McClelland, Grant S. ed. U.S.POLICY IN LATIN AMERICA. Wilson, 1963. JFK: "Cuba, Russia and the U.S." 176-180; "The President Proposes the Alliance for Progress:" 213-217.

Boykin, Edw. ed. U.S. PRESIDENT. STATE OF THE UNION. F&W, 1963. JFK: 482-488.

PUBLIC PAPERS OF THE PRESIDENTS 1961-1963. National Archives and records service. Wash.D.C., 1962, 1963, 1964. Three vols. The Presidential proclamations, messages and reports to Congress of JFK as well as important public speeches and statements.

Nevins, Allan, ed. THE BURDEN AND THE GLORY. The Hopes and Purposes of Pres. Kennedy's Second and Third Years in Office as Revealed in His Public Statements and Addresses. Fwd. LBJ. 1st ed. Harper & Row, 1964.

Gardner, Gerald, ed. THE SHINING MOMENTS; the Words and Moods of John F. Kennedy." Wrs., illus. Pocket Books, 1964.

Filler, Louis, ed. THE PRESIDENT SPEAKS; From Wm. McKinley to Lyndon B. Johnson. Putnam, 1964. JFK: 374-408.

WORKS OF JOHN F. KENNEDY

Speeches and Public Statements, Quotations, Recordings

Adler, Bill, ed. THE KENNEDY WIT. Illus. Citadel (1964).

Muirhead, Peter P. "The Kennedy Legacy." HIGHER EDUCATION, Jan.-Feb., 1964: 5-7, illus. + JFK's words on youth and education, equal educational opportunity, The National Education Improvement Act of 1963.

Harris, Leon A. THE FINE ART OF POLITICAL WIT. Dutton,1964. JFK: 255-276.
Review of THE FINE ART OF POLITICAL WIT. NEWSWEEK, Sept. 14, 1964: 92ff., illus. -

Madow, Pauline, ed. THE PEACE CORPS. H.W.Wilson, 1964. JFK on the Peace Corps and Youth Services: 17-25; 96-99ff.

Chase, Harold M. and Allen H. Lerman, eds. KENNEDY AND THE PRESS. Crowell, 1965. The texts of 64 news conferences and eight special interviews.

Singh, Ram and M.K. Haldar eds. KENNEDY THROUGH INDIAN EYES. (Delhi) Vir Publ., 1965. A selection of JFK's speeches and writings relating to the peoples of the developing countries.

Adler, Bill, ed. MORE KENNEDY WIT. 1st ed. Citadel, 1965.

Meyersohn, Maxwell, comp. MEMORABLE QUOTATIONS OF JOHN F. KENNEDY. 1st prtg. Crowell, 1965.

Schneider, Nicholas A. comp. RELIGIOUS VIEWS OF JOHN F. KENNEDY IN HIS OWN WORDS. 1st ed. B. Herder, 1965.

Settel, T.S. ed. THE WISDOM OF JFK. 1st ed. Dutton, 1965. Culled from his speeches.

Adler, Bill, ed. THE COMPLETE KENNEDY WIT. 1st ed., illus. Citadel Press, 1967. Includes humor known to have been uttered publicly by JFK as a young man.

Goldman, Alex J. ed. THE QUOTABLE KENNEDY. 1st ed. this format. Belmont, 1967.

WORDS TO REMEMBER. Illus. in color. Hallmark, 1967. Fwd. RFK.

International Business Machines Corp. NOT SUBJECT TO CHANGE. 1969. Quotation of 11 lines from JFK on success or failure in the eyes of history.

GREAT WORDS OF OUR TIME. Illus. in color. Hallmark, 1970. Six quotations from JFK and RFK.

* * * * * * * * * *

and Public Statements, Quotations, Recordings

ton Ministerial Assn. TAPE OF REMARKS TO THE MIN-
JSTON WITH QUESTION AND ANSWER PERIOD. Sept.12,1960

✓Challence Records. THE WIT OF JOHN F. KENNEDY AT THE PRESS
CONFERENCES. UHF618.

Continental Record Co. JOHN FITZGERALD KENNEDY - A Memorial
Tribute. Oath of office, inaugural address, speeches.

✓Council for United Civil Rights Leadership. WE SHALL OVERCOME.
The March on Washington, Aug.28, 1963. UCR1A-1B. JFK Press
Conference.

Diplomat Records. JOHN FITZGERALD 1917-1963. Words of JFK.

Documentaries Unlimited Inc. JOHN FITZGERALD KENNEDY: May 29,
1917-Nov.22, 1963. Vol.1. Includes words of JFK and JBK.

✓Ebony Magazine (recording). JOHN F. KENNEDY AND THE NEGRO.
XCTV-96558-9. "Civil Rights Statements from JFK's Great
Speeches."

Longines Symphonette. THE KENNEDY YEARS 1956-1963. LW 125-
126-127. Three 12" records. Major speeches of JFK.

Miller International Co. ACTUAL SPEECHES OF FRANKLIN D. ROOS-
EVELT AND JOHN F. KENNEDY. Album P-16100

Philips. KENNEDY IN GERMANY. Monaural PCC210. Speeches.

Pickwick International, in cooperation with N.Y.TIMES. JOHN
FITZGERALD KENNEDY - THE PRESIDENTIAL YEARS 1960-1963.
Excerpts from speeches - a documentary. DLP169A,B

Powertree Records Inc. PRESIDENT KENNEDY IN IRELAND in cooperation with Eireann Radio. Speeches there. PLP5007

Premier Album Inc. JOHN FITZGERALD KENNEDY. A MEMORIAL ALBUM.
Highlights of speeches of JFK.

Spoken Word Inc. THE FOUR KENNEDY-NIXON DEBATES. The 1960
campaign. Debates complete and unabridged. Four 12" records.
SW-9407-9408- 9409-9410.

20th Century-Fox Records. JOHN FITZGERALD KENNEDY: A DOCUMENT-
ARY. The Presidential Years 1960-1963. TFM-3127. Some of
JFK's key words.

WORKS OF JOHN F. KENNEDY

Forewords and Introductions

Eds. of YEAR. HISTORIC DECADE 1950-1960. Year, 1960. Fwds.
JFK and Henry Cabot Lodge. 1 p.

Donovan, Robt. J. P.T. 109: JOHN F. KENNEDY IN WORLD WAR II.
1st ed. McGraw-Hill, 1961. Intro. letter JFK: 15.

Josephy, Alvin M. ed. AT CLOSE QUARTERS: P.T.Boats in the
U.S.Navy. Naval History Division, Wash.: 1962. Errata sheet.
JFK fwd.: vi-vii.

Davidson, Bill. PRESIDENT KENNEDY SELECTS SIX BRAVE PRESIDENTS.
H&R, 1962. JFK fwd.: v.

President's Comm. on Equal Employment Opportunity. REPORT ON
THE COMMUNITY LEADERS' CONFERENCE, May 19, 1962. GPO, 1962.Wrs.
Fwds. JFK and LBJ.

U.S. Dept. of Labor. AMERICA IS FOR EVERYBODY. Wrs. GPO, 1962.
JFK fwd. statement: vii.

Athearn, Robt. G. THE HISTORY OF THE UNITED STATES. THE NEW
WORLD. Vol. 1. American Heritage-Dell, 1963. JFK fwd.: 4-7.
Reprinted in AMERICAN HERITAGE Feb., 1964, under title "Presi-
dent Kennedy on History:" 2-4.

Horn, Calvin. NEW MEXICO'S TROUBLED YEARS. The Story of the
Early Territorial Governors. 1st ed. (Albuquerque) Horn and
Wallace, 1963. JFK fwd.: 9-10.

Sorenson, Theodore. DECISION-MAKING IN THE WHITE HOUSE: The
Olive Branch or the Arrows. Columbia, 1963. JFK fwd.: xi-xiv.

Stevenson, Adlai. LOOKING OUTWARD: Years of Crisis at the United
Nations. H&R, 1963. JFK preface: xi-xii.

Udall, Stewart L. THE QUIET CRISIS. HR&W, 1964. JFK intro. xi-
xiii

U.S. Congress. ECONOMIC REPORT OF THE PRESIDENT Transmitted to
the Congress Jan. 1962 Together with the Annual Report of the
Council of Economic Advisers. Wrs. GPO, 1962: 3-27. Ibid.
1963: ix-xxviii.

Bibliographies Listing JFK Writings

Crown, James Tracy. THE KENNEDY LITERATURE. N.Y. Univ., 1968
Gropp, Arthur E. "A Kennedy Bibliography" in THE BOOKLOVERS'
   ANSWER, May-June, 1964: 14-15. Re Latin America affairs.
Sable, Martin H. A BIO-BIBLIOGRAPHY OF THE KENNEDY FAMILY.
   Scarecrow Press, 1969.
U.S. Library of Congress. JOHN FITZGERALD KENNEDY 1917-1963. A
   Chronological List of References. 1964. Supplement, 1964.Wrs.

WORKS ABOUT JFK

Ancestry: Ireland

Coogan, Tim Pat. "Sure, and It's County Kennedy Now." N.Y.T.
MAG., June 23, 1963: 7-9ff. illus. - Photographic cover:
County Wexford, Ireland.

Corry, John. GOLDEN CLAN. The Murrays, the McDonnells and the
Irish American Aristocracy. 1st ed. H-M, 1977.

Corry, John. "Golden Clan: How the Irish Arrived in Society."
N.Y.T. MAG., Mar. 13, 1977: 16-19ff. illus.

Roddy, Joseph. "Irish Origins of a President." LOOK. Mar.14,
1961: 17-25, illus.

Slevin, Gerard. "The O'Kennedys." IRELAND OF THE WELCOMES.
Jan.-Feb., 1968: 29-31, illus. -

Woodham-Smith, Cecil. THE GREAT HUNGER. Ireland 1845-1849.
H&R, 1962. The famine in Ireland that sent Patrick Joseph Kennedy of County Wexford to Boston. Bostonian reaction to desti-
tute emigrants.

Ancestry: Patrick Kennedy and John F. Fitzgerald

Ainsley, Leslie G. BOSTON MAHATMA. Humphries (1949). Biography of Martin M. Lomasney. Includes John F. Fitzgerald.

Curley, James M. I'D DO IT AGAIN. A Record of All My Uproar-
ious Years. P-H, 1957. John F. Fitzgerald one of the principals
with vignettes of Pat Kennedy, his son Joseph and grandson JFK.

Cutler, John Henry. "HONEY FITZ." THREE STEPS TO THE WHITE
HOUSE. The Life and Times of John F. (Honey Fitz) Fitzgerald.
B-M, 1962.

Dinneen, Joseph F. THE KENNEDY FAMILY. L.B., 1959. History of
three generations.

Hennessy, Michael E. MASSACHUSETTS POLITICS 1890-1935. Illus.
Norwood Press, 1935. Includes the career of John F. Fitzgerald.

Russell, Francis. "Honey Fitz." AMERICAN HERITAGE, Aug., 1968:
28-31ff.

Writings of Joseph P. Kennedy

I'M FOR ROOSEVELT. Reynal & Hitchcock (1936).
Twelve page introduction to THE THREE KEYS TO SUCCESS, by Sir
Wm. M. Beaverbrook. 1st ed. D.S. & P., 1956.

Ancestry: Works About Joseph P. Kennedy

Baille, Hugh. HIGH TENSION. Harp.(1959). Chaps. 11 and 12: remarks of Ambassador P. Kennedy re W.W.II and England-U.S.A.

Birmingham, Stephen. REAL LACE. AMERICA'S IRISH RICH. H&R, 1973. Includes early years of Joseph P. and Rose Kennedy.

Cameron, Gail. "The Kennedy Nobody Knows" (Ann Gargan). LADIES' H.J., June, 1966: 70ff.-

Cramer, C. H. NEWTON D. BAKER: A Biography. 1st ed. World, 1961. Brief account of Joseph Kennedy's enlistment of W.R. Hearst's influence to secure nomination of F.D. Roosevelt in face of threat of Baker's candidacy.

Dallas, Rita, with Jeanira Ratcliffe. THE KENNEDY CASE. Putnam, 1973. With Maxine Cheshire "My Eight Years as Jos. P. Kennedy's Private Nurse." LADIES' H.J., Feb., 1971: 77ff.; Mar., 1971: 106ff.

Douglas, Wm. O. GO EAST, YOUNG MAN; The Early Years. 1st ed. Random, 1974. Autobiography. Friendship with Jos. P. Kennedy who appointed Douglas to the Securities and Exchange Commission. Description of visits to the Kennedy family home in early years.

Farley, James A. JIM FARLEY'S STORY. The Roosevelt Years. McG-H., (1948). Presentation copy with ALS. Numerous mentions of Jos. P. Kennedy "whom he (FDR) never liked." p.198.

Hudson, Richard and Raymond Lee. GLORIA SWANSON. Castle, 1970. Reference to Gloria's partnership with Jos. P. Kennedy.

Josephson, Matthew. THE MONEY LORDS. The Great Finance Capitalists 1925-1950. Weybright & Talley, 1972. Traces Jos. P. Kennedy in Wall St. through his "prudence" in conducting S.E.C.

Kennedy, John B. "Joe Kennedy Has Never Liked Any Job He's Tackled," in THE AMERICAN DREAM: A Half-Century View from AMERICAN MAGAZINE. 1st ed. D'day, 1964: 189-199. Article written in 1928, explains financial success of Jos. P. Kennedy.

Koskoff, David E. JOSEPH P. KENNEDY: A Life and Times. 1st ed. P-H, 1974. Many details with pejorative adjectives.
Review by Martin F. Nolan, N.Y. T. BK. REV., Mar.31, 1974:1,14.

Lee, Gen. Raymond E. THE JOURNAL OF... 1940-1941. Jas. Leutze ed. 1st ed. L-B, 1971. Unsympathetic portrait of Ambassador Kennedy's role.

LIFE. "Joe Kennedy Book: Private." Feb. 26, 1965: 38B - Re anthology planned by EMK. "Joe Kennedy Dies at 81." Nov. 28, 1969: 36.

THE KENNEDY FAMILY OF MASSACHUSETTS

Ancestry: Works About Joseph P. Kennedy

Marcus, Sheldon. FATHER COUGHLIN. 1st ed. L-B, 1973. Extensive biblio. Describes Jos. Kennedy's friendship with Coughlin and as Coughlin-Roosevelt liason.

Miller, Merle. PLAIN SPEAKING. An Oral Biography of Harry S. Truman. Berkeley, 1974. Strong dislike of Jos. P. Kennedy reflected in Truman's attitude to JFK.

Moffat, Jay P. THE MOFFAT PAPERS, ed. by Nancy H. Hooker. Harvard U., 1956. Diplomatic history of years 1931-1943. Reports words and actions of Kennedy as Ambassador to England.

Mosley, Leonard. LINDBERGH. A Biography. 1st ed. D'day, 1976. 1st ed. Includes correspondence with Ambassador Kennedy.

Potter, Jeffrey. MEN, MONEY AND MAGIC. The Story of Dorothy Schiff. C., McC. & G., 1976. With Joseph P. Kennedy as friend from younger years - many stories of the Kennedys.

Roosevelt, Elliot and James Brough. A RENDEZVOUS WITH DESTINY: The Roosevelts of the White House. Putnam, 1975. Includes 15 anecdotes of Jos. P. Kennedy Sr.

Russell, Francis. THE PRESIDENT MAKERS: From Mark Hanna To Joseph P. Kennedy. 1st ed. L-B, 1976.

Sherwood, Robt.E. ROOSEVELT AND HOPKINS. An Intimate History. Harp.,1948. Portrays Joseph P. Kennedy as defeatist about Britain's chances in the war.

SOCIAL JUSTICE. "Joseph Kennedy and Family." Feb.6,1939: 20.

Tull, Chas.J. FATHER COUGHLIN AND THE NEW DEAL. Syracuse U., 1965. Considers Kennedy Sr. as intermediary between Roosevelt and Coughlin.

U.S.NEWS... "The Amazing Story of Joseph Kennedy." Jan.1, 1962: 47 -

Whalen, Richard J. THE FOUNDING FATHER: The Story of Joseph P. Kennedy. A Study in Power, Wealth and Family Ambition. NAL-World, 1964.
Reviews: Margaret Coit in SAT. REV. Dec. 19, 1964:20-22. -
Frank Freidel in N.Y.T. BK. REV. Nov.29, 1964: 28,30. -
Wm. V. Shannon in NEW REPUBLIC, n.d. -
Excerpts: READER'S DIGEST, Oct., 1963: 150-158 -; SEP Pt. One: Oct.10, 1964: 26-29ff.
"Joseph P. Kennedy: a portrait of the Founder." FORTUNE, Jan. 1963. 111-118ff. "How Joe Kennedy Made His Millions." LIFE, Jan. 25, 1963: 59-60ff.-

WORKS ABOUT JFK

Ancestry: Works About Joseph P. Kennedy

YEAR - 1951. An Annual Record of Current Pictorial History. Under "National Affairs:" former Ambassador to Britain Joseph Kennedy suggestion U.S. should withdraw from commitments in Europe and Asia, concentrate on protecting its own shores.

Ancestry: Writings of Rose Kennedy

McCALL'S. "Rose Kennedy Talks About Her Life, Her Faith and Her Children." Dec., 1973: 74-75ff.

"Believing in America Is Making It Work." LADIES' H.J., Jan., 1974: 88-89. Also: "Fashions With Meaning" - Rose, Ethel and Kathleen Kennedy from N.Y. Bedford-Stuyvesant: 86-87.

TIMES TO REMEMBER. 1st ed. D'day, 1974. Contains much of genealogical interest. Printed card Sept. 20, 1974, facsimile signature.
Review: N.Y.T. BK. REV. Mar.31, 1974 by Martin F. Nolan: 1ff.
Excerpts: Parts 2,3,4. WOMAN'S DAY. Mar.1974: 52-60ff.; April 1974: 72-75ff.; May, 1974: 58-61ff.

"On Being a Grandmother" in BEST OF OUR LIVES, E.S.Newman ed. Hallmark (1975): 5-6.

Tillett, Leslie. AMERICAN NEEDLEWORK 1776/1976. 1st ed. N.Y. Graphic Soc., 1975. Fwd. Includes Rose Kennedy's piano bench cover made by her mother; and American Rose pattern. (Jacqueline Kennedy Onassis asked Mrs. Kennedy to write this forward.)

Ancestry: Writings About Rose Kennedy

Berquist, Laura. "A Visit with the Indomitable Rose Kennedy." LOOK, Nov.26, 1968: 25-34. Photo of Rose in color on cover.

Cameron, Gail. ROSE: A Biography of Rose Fitzgerald Kennedy. Putnam, 1971. Also: Berkeley Medallion, 1972. Wrs.
Excerpts: LADIES' H.J. July, 1971: 87-89ff.; Aug., 1971: 67-69 ff. Aug. cover painting of Rose.

Emerson, Gloria. "How Rose Kennedy Survived." McCALL'S, Aug., 1975: 68ff.

Faber, Doris. THE MOTHERS OF AMERICAN PRESIDENTS. NAL (1968) Rose Fitzgerald Kennedy: 14-28.

Hershey, Lenore. "How Rose Keeps Growing." LADIES'H.J., May, 1972: 83ff.

LIFE. Photograph, June 15, 1962: 44C-. "Rose Kennedy at 80" by Sylvia Wright, July 17, 1970: 20-25. Photo on front cover.

THE KENNEDY FAMILY OF MASSACHUSETTS

Ancestry: Writings About Rose Kennedy

Roosevelt, Felicia Warburg. DOERS AND DOWAGERS. D'day (1975).
Conversations with 20 women. Rose Kennedy: 83-104.

Cf. JFK Writings for "Family Fugue: Variations on the Joseph
Kennedys" by Lesley Blanch in 1933-1934 section WORLD IN VOGUE
op.cit.

JFK Biographies

Amory, Cleveland ed. CELEBRITY REGISTER. 1st ed. H&R, 1963.
In addition to John, Joseph Sr., Rose, Jacqueline, RFK, Ethel,
EMK.

Associated Press. TRIUMPH AND TRAGEDY. The Story of the Kennedys. AP, 1968. From the famine in Ireland to death of RFK.

Bassett, Margaret. PROFILES AND PORTRAITS OF AMERICAN PRESI-
DENTS AND THEIR WIVES. Bond, Wheelwright (1969). JFK and JBK:
383-401.

Burns, James MacGregor. JOHN KENNEDY: A POLITICAL PROFILE.
H.B.&W. (1961). Also Avon, 1960. 1st ed. wrs.
Review by Joseph Maloney, BEST SELLERS, Mar.1, 1960: 424 -

Carr, Wm.H.A. JFK: AN INFORMAL BIOGRAPHY. Lancer, 1962. Wrs.
JFK: A COMPLETE BIOGRAPHY 1917-1963. Lancer, 1964. Wrs.
Ibid. Magnum Easy Eye Bks. n.d.

Clinch, Nancy. THE KENNEDY NEUROSIS. G&D, 1973. So-called
"psycho-history." Revisionist interpretation.
Review by Robt. Claiborne, N.Y.T.BK. REV., Feb.25, 1973:36ff.
Review by A.L. and J. George in PSYCHOLOGY TODAY, June, 1973:
94ff.

Considine, Bob. "No Stranger To Courage" in ENCYCLOPEDIA YEAR-
BOOK. Grolier, 1958: 104-106. Sen. JFK at forty.

ENCYCLOPEDIA BRITANNICA. Book of the Year - 1962: 69 references to Kennedy family; Ibid. 1963: 60 references.

Fay, Paul B. Jr. THE PLEASURE OF HIS COMPANY. H&R (1966). The
story of a twenty-one year friendship with JFK.

Hirsch, Phil and Edw. Hymoff, eds. THE KENNEDY COURAGE. 1st
prtg. wrs. Pyramid, 1965. Examples of JFK and family members.

Jensen, Amy LaF. THE WHITE HOUSE AND ITS THIRTY-THREE FAMILIES.
McG-H., 1962. Chap. 15: "A New Frontier."

THE KENNEDYS. Ideal Publ., 1962: wrs.

16.

WORKS ABOUT JFK

JFK Biographies

McCarthy, Joe (Weston). THE REMARKABLE KENNEDYS. Wrs. Dial,
1960. Chap.I. an interview with Joe Sr. and John.
Popular Giant. 1st prtg., wrs. 1960.
Excerpts: "Jack Kennedy" LOOK, Oct. 13, 27, Nov.10, 1959.

O'Donnell, Kenneth and David F. Powers. "JOHNNY, WE HARDLY
KNEW YE." 1st ed. L-B, 1972. Insights of these first hand
observers. Poignant, informative, humorous. Little known
campaigning activities of JBK. ALS Dave Powers, Sept.22, 1972.
Excerpts: McCALL'S. Sept., 1972: 75-77ff.
Review by Chas.L.Mee, Jr. N.Y.T.BK.REV. Jan.21, 1973: 6-7

THE PRESIDENTS AND THEIR WIVES FROM WASHINGTON TO KENNEDY.
Wrs. (Wash.D.C.) Haskin Service, 1961.

Schlesinger, Arthur M. Jr. A THOUSAND DAYS. John F. Kennedy
in the White House. 1st prtg. H-M, 1965. Penetrating study.
Excerpts: LIFE. July 16, 23, 30, Nov.5, 12, 19, 1965 -
Discussion: by Geo. Kateb. COMMENTARY, June 1966: 54-60.
Review: by Raymond Moley. NEWSWEEK, Dec.20, 1965: 108.
Review: TIME. Dec.17, 1965: 54-56ff.

Sidey, Hugh. JOHN F. KENNEDY, PRESIDENT. 1st ed. Atheneum,
1963. From 1958 through White House years.
Revised edition. 1st prtg. Atheneum, 1964
 Crest. 1st prt. wrs., 1964

Sorenson, Theodore C. KENNEDY. H&R (1965). Important for facts
and for Kennedy the man.
Excerpts: LOOK. Aug.10, 24, Sept.7, 21, Oct. 19, 1965. Illus.
in color by Bernard Fuchs, two page drawing by Austin Briggs.
Review by Stewart Alsop. SEP, Oct. 9, 1965: 14.
Review by Murray Kempton. ATLANTIC, Oct.,1965: 71-74.
Review: NEWSWEEK. Oct.11, 1965: 34-34; "Sorenson as JFK's
Alter Ego" Jan.27, 1966: 16-17 -
Review by Raymond Moley. NEWSWEEK, Nov.8, 1965: 20. -
Review by Robt.E. Burns. CRITIC, Dec. 1965-Jan. 1966: 69-70.
Discussion: by Geo. Kateb. COMMENTARY, June 1966 op.cit.

Vidal, Gore. "The Holy Family." ESQUIRE, April, 1967: 99-102ff.
JFK, RFK, EMK and a grown-up John on front cover in color.

Wicker, Tom. KENNEDY WITHOUT TEARS: The Man Beneath the Myth.
Morrow (1964). JFK and the pursuit of excellence.
Excerpts: ESQUIRE, June, 1964: 108-111ff. Portrait Shikler. -
Excerpts repeated in ESQUIRE Oct. 1973 - 40th Anniv. Issue.
Reviewby James MacGregor Burns. N.Y.T. BK. REV. Oct.11, 1964 -

Recording: JOHN F. KENNEDY AS WE REMEMBER HIM. Columbia Records
Legacy Collection. Illus. vol.,two LP records L21-1017.
 Joan Meyers ed.

JFK's Favorite Books

Collection of some of JFK's favorite books according to Rose Kennedy (TIMES TO REMEMBER op.cit.); Hugh Sidey ("The President's
Voracious Reading Habits," LIFE, Mar.17, 1961:55-56ff.) and JFK
exhibit at New England Book Festival week of Sept. 12, 1970.

Childhood: ARABIAN NIGHTS; BLACK BEAUTY (Sewell); BILLY WHIS-
KERS series; MOTHER WEST WIND series; CHILD'S GARDEN OF VERSES,
KIDNAPPED, TREASURE ISLAND (R.L.Stevenson); KIM (Kipling); BAMBI
(Salten); STORY OF A BAD BOY (Aldrich); WING AND WING (J.C.Cooper)
UNCLE TOM'S CABIN (Stowe); PILGRIM'S PROGRESS (Bunyan); KING
ARTHUR AND THE ROUND TABLE; Scott's WAVERLEY NOVELS.

Adulthood: MELBOURNE (David Cecil); THE RED AND THE BLACK
(Stendahl); THE HEMINGWAY READER; GUNS OF AUGUST (Tuchman); THE
AGE OF JACKSON (Schlesinger); "The Great Democracies," (Vol.4 of
THE HISTORY OF THE ENGLISH SPEAKING PEOPLE, Churchill); PIL-
GRIM'S WAY (John Buchan, Lord Tweedsmuir). This latter book JFK
gave to JBK during their courtship. FROM RUSSIA WITH LOVE by Ian
Fleming was quoted by Sidey as one of JFK's ten favorites - er-
roneously as it later turned out. John Pearson in THE LIFE OF
IAN FLEMING (McG-H, 1966) described a casual encounter with JFK
that played a part in Fleming's last years (295-301).

Youth

Berkman, Edw.O. THE LADY AND THE LAW (Fanny Holtzman). 1st ed.
L-B,1976. Includes John and Joe Jr. as young men in pre-war
Britain helping penniless refugees get to safety.

Davies, Marion. THE TIMES WE HAD. Life with Wm.R.Hearst. 1st.
B-M, 1975. Jos.P.Kennedy and escapade of "Joe Jr. or Jack."

Day, Dorothy. LOAVES AND FISHES. 1st ed. H&R, 1963. 30 years as
leader of Catholic Worker. Joe Jr. and Jack who came one night to
Mott Street and talked until the small hours with her.

Lader, Lawrence. "His Excellency Joseph P.Kennedy..." ESQUIRE,
Sept. 1961:82-85. Candid photo of JFK at dance May 29, 1938.

Prescott, Peter S. A WORLD OF OUR OWN. Notes on Life and Learning in a Boys' Preparatory School. C-McC,1970. JFK at Choate.

TIME CAPSULE 1939-1945. 6 vols. Time-Life, 1968. JFK in 1939,
1940, 1943, 1944 and 1945 among others.

Wiley, Irena. AROUND THE GLOBE IN TWENTY YEARS. An Artist at
Large in the Diplomatic World. 1st ed. McKay, 1962. Memories of
a Polish artist-wife of an American Foreign Service officer.
Anecdote: how JFK posed as a child for an angel in a wood sculp-
ture panel now in the Vatican. Glossy print of JFK as angel
laid in.

WORKS ABOUT JFK

Boston, Massachusetts

Adams, Russell B., Jr. THE BOSTON MONEY TREE. 1st ed. Crowell, 1977. Including Joseph P. Kennedy.

Amory, Cleveland. THE PROPER BOSTONIANS. Dutton, 1947. Social and economic snobbery of Boston and Harvard.

Bacon, Edwin M. revised by LeRoy Phillips. BOSTON: A Guide Book Ginn, 1928. includes Brookline where RFK was born in 1925.

Beebe, Lucius. BOSTON AND THE BOSTON LEGEND. Illus. Suydam. A-C, 1936. A character study of Boston. The North End of the Fitzgeralds and Kennedys with episodes of past and present.

BOSTON. The Official Bicentennial Guidebook. Wrs. Dutton,1975 Mentions historic sites of Kennedy family.

Howe, Helen. THE GENTLE AMERICANS 1864-1960: Biography of a Breed. H&R, 1965. 1st ed. The literary and social life of some remarkable Bostonians. Author's brother moderated the last pre-election TV debate between JFK and Nixon.

Morison, Samuel Eliot. ONE BOY'S BOSTON 1887-1901. H.M., 1962 Cf. chapters 3 and 10 for attitudes towards the Irish.

Richardson, Elliot. "Poisoned Politics: the Real Tragedy of Massachusetts." ATLANTIC, Oct. 1961: 77-81.

Thernstrom, Stephan. POVERTY, PLANNING AND POLITICS IN THE NEW BOSTON. Basic Bks., 1969. Boston's 1961 anti-poverty program which became the prototype for similar programs. JFK's and RFK's active roles in the demonstration project.

Whitehill, Walter M. BOSTON IN THE AGE OF JOHN FITZGERALD KENNE-DY. U. of Okla., 1966. Portrait of the city with JFK as reference point.

Cape Cod - Palm Beach

Damore, Leo. THE CAPE COD YEARS OF JOHN FITZGERALD KENNEDY. P-H, 1967.

Hunt, Richard P. "The Ship of State Rocks Hyannis Port." N.Y.T. MAG., May 26, 1963: 30-31ff.

LOOK. "Palm Beach," Feb. 13, 1962: 26-48. Includes Rose.

Ney, John. PALM BEACH. The Place, the People, Its Pleasures and Palaces. 1st ed. L-B, 1966. Past and present of one of the homes of America's "Royal Family" (the Kennedys), by the Republican neighbor who lives across the street.

Cape Cod - Palm Beach

Plimpton, George. "Newport Notes: the Kennedys and Other Salts." HARPER'S, Mar., 1963: 39-47.

Spencer, Wilma Bell. PALM BEACH. A Century of Heritage. 1st ed. Mount Vernon Publ., 1975. Kennedys included in chapter 5.

JFK Harvard Years

Bissell, Richard. YOU CAN ALWAYS TELL A HARVARD MAN. McG.-H., 1962. Chapter 16. "One Minute to Play, or Jack at Harvard."

Kahn, E.T., Jr. HARVARD: Through Change and Through Storm. Norton, 1969. Much Kennedyana.

JFK Navy Years

Bulkley, Capt. Robt. J., Jr. AT CLOSE QUARTERS. PTBoats in the United States Navy. Naval History Division, GPO, 1962. JFK experience in the Solomons: 120-128. JFK foreword op.cit.

Donovan, Robt.J. PT 109: John F. Kennedy in World War II. 1st ed. McG-H, 1961. Introductory letter by JFK op. cit.

Farley, Edw. I. PT PATROL. Wrs., 1st prtg. Popular Library, 1957. Includes author's own adventures and exploits of Lt. JFK.

Hersey, John. "Survival" in HERE TO STAY: Studies in Human Tenacity. Knopf, 1963: 87-106. First published in NEW YORKER June 17, 1944.
READERS' DIGEST condensation, Aug., 1944: 75-80.

Lord, Walter. LONELY VIGIL. Coastwatchers of the Solomons. 1st ed. Viking, 1977. First complete account behind Japanese lines. Includes JFK's PT109 from this viewpoint.

Tregaskis, Richard. JOHN F. KENNEDY: WAR HERO. Wrs., 1st prtg. Dell, 1962. Expanded edition of a Landmark Book published under another title. Approx. 20,000 words added.

Whipple, Chandler. LT. JOHN F. KENNEDY - EXPENDABLE. Wrs. Universal Publ., 1964. Account of JFK's years in U.S. Navy.

Marriage

LIFE. "LIFE Goes Courting with a U.S. Senator. John Kennedy and His Fiancee Enjoy an Outing on Cape Cod." July 20, 1953: 96-99. Cover photo. "The Senator Weds. Young John F. Kennedy Takes Pretty Photographer for Bride." Sept. 28, 1953: 45ff.

Marriage

LOOK. "An Informal Visit with Our New First Family," by Laura Berquist.Feb.28, 1961: 100-101ff. Illus. R. Avedon. Cover photo in color.

MacPherson, Myra. THE POWER LOVERS: An Intimate Look at Politicians and Their Marriages. Putnam, 1975. Includes the three Kennedy brothers and their wives.

TIME. "An American Genealogy." Sept. 28, 1962: 38-39. Concerns the late Louis L. Blauvelt's THE BLAUVELT FAMILY GENEALOGY (1957) - basis for nation-wide campaign of anti-Kennedy innuendo.

Children

Considine, Bob. IT'S ALL NEWS TO ME. 1st ed. Meredith, 1967. Eyewitness accounts of news events, incl. the death of Pres. Kennedy's infant son, Patrick Bouvier, and other memoirs of the Kennedy family.

GOOD HOUSEKEEPING. "Bringing Up the Kennedys." Luella Hennesey as told to Margot Murphy. Aug., 1961: 52-57ff. Cover photo. "Caroline's Wonderful Little White House School," by Helen Thomas. Oct.,1963: 84-85ff. "Caroline Kennedy: the Charm Is Familiar". May, 1975: 84-85. Cover photo in color. "Caroline Kennedy Turns 18," by Lester David. Oct., 1975: 96-97ff. Photo report "John Kennedy Jr. 16 and Grown-up." Oct., 1976: 112-116.

Kennedy, Caroline. "Graceland: a Family Mourns." ROLLING STONE Sept. 22, 1977: 40. Feature on Elvis Presley, unsigned.

LADIES HOME JOURNAL. "Caroline and John Kennedy Jr.: The Happy Years Are Now," by Gail Cameron, June, 1968: 54ff. "Caroline Kennedy Turns 16," by Maud Shaw with Peter Whittle. Nov.1973: 76-77ff. Cover photo. "JFK,Jr." by Winzola McLendon. Oct.1975: 88-89ff. "Caroline Kennedy: Adventures of an Innocent Abroad," by Willi Frischauer. Feb.1976: 90ff. Cover portrait in color.

LIFE. "Son of the President-elect Has His First Picture Taken in the Baptismal Dress Worn by His Father 43 Years Ago." Dec.19 1960. Cover photo in color. "On a Warm Spring Morning, a Warm Reaction." April 14, 1961. (Caroline chasing playmate. This photo gave rise to new restrictions on use of long-lens pictures) "The Children's Homecoming." Nov.3, 1961: 55. Photograph: "Lots of Fun in Italy for Mother and Me." Aug.24, 1962: 34. "Caroline Becomes a Celebrity at Age 4." Sept.7,1962: 32-35. Photograph: "Two Glen Ora Youngsters Halve Their Birthday." Dec.7, 1962. "Luck with Your Locks, Young John," by Miguel Acoca. May 24, 1963. "The Hospital Shades Come Down and Vigil Starts Over Patrick Kennedy..." Aug. 16, 1963: 28-30. Cover photo.

THE KENNEDY FAMILY OF MASSACHUSETTS

Children

LOOK. "Caroline," by Laura Berquist. Sept.26, 1961: 76-82ff.
Color photo on cover - Avedon. "Caroline's Wonderful Summer."
Aug.14, 1962: 82-86ff. "The President and His Son," by Laura
Berquist. Dec. 3, 1963: 26-34ff. Color photo on cover. The
Kennedy Children," Berquist. Oct. 5, 1965: 28-33.

McCALL'S. "In the White House News," by Dr. John Wm. Walsh.
Aug., 1963: 34ff. The doctor who delivered the infant Patrick.
"Oh, To Be a White House Pet!" Nov.,1963: 216, by Marianne
Means . "How Caroline and John Remember Their Father," by Dave
Powers. Nov., 1973: 84-87ff. "Caroline Kennedy: Living Down a
Legend, " by W. McLendon. Nov. 1974: 42ff. Cover photo.

NEWSWEEK. "Caroline in the White House." May 15, 1961: 65-66.
Cover painting. "With a New Kind of Loneliness; Birth and Death
of the Kennedy Baby." Aug. 19, 1963: 17-18. - "Old School Tie."
Aug. 26, 1968: 50. John Jr. at school.

Shaw, Maud. WHITE HOUSE NANNY. My Years with Caroline and John
Kennedy. NAL (1966). 2nd copysubtitle: "My Seven Momentous Years
with Caroline and John Kennedy Jr."Ldn. Leslie Frewin, 1966.
Signet. 1st prtg., wrs. 1966.
Excerpts: "Now, John F. Kennedy's Children Go On Without Him."
L.H. JRNL., Feb., 1966: 68ff. Jackie and Caroline on cover.-

U.S.NEWS... "Education of Caroline." July 9, 1962: 59-61. -
"A Time of Tragedy for the Kennedys." Aug., 1963: 8. A baby
specialist explains Patrick's fatal illness. "A Look Inside the
White House School." Oct. 7, 1963: 70-72. -

WOMAN'S DAY. "Caroline Kennedy and Her Pets," by Hilda Cole
Espy. July, 1962: 26ff. Cover painting of Caroline.

Election 1946-1952

Blair, Joan and Clay. THE SEARCH FOR JFK. Wrs. Berkeley Medal-
ion, April, 1977. Focus on years 1935-1947. Putnam, 1976.

Goldman, Eric F. "The 1947 Kennedy-Nixon 'Tube City' Debate."
SAT. REV., Oct.16, 1976: 12-13. A forgotten bit of Americana.

Gorman, Jos. B. KEFAUVER: A POLITICAL BIOGRAPHY. Oxford, 1971.
Includes 1952 victory over JFK.

Key, V.O., Jr. POLITICS, PARTIES AND PRESSURE GROUPS. Crowell,
1967. Describes some of JFK's campaign techniques for congressional elections and other references.

LIFE. Editorial: "We Agree Mr. Kennedy." Aug.25, 1952: 22. The
1952 Massachusetts senatorial race. "Row over Massachusetts Pen-
sions Encourages G.O.P." Sept. 22, 1952: 34-39.

WORKS ABOUT JFK

Election 1946-1952

LOOK. "A Kennedy Runs for Congress." June 11, 1946: 32ff.
First campaign for House of Representatives. Produced by Henry
Ehrlich, photographed by Hy Peskin.

Martin, Ralph and Ed Plaut. FRONT RUNNER, DARK HORSE: A Political Study of Senators Kennedy and Symington. 1st ed. D'day,1960.
Good account of JFK's race for the House.

Phillips, Cabell. "Case History of a Senate Race." N.Y.T.MAG.
Oct.26, 1952: 10-11ff. JFK campaign for Senate seat of Henry
Cabot Lodge Jr. +

Election 1956-1958

Bell, Jack. THE SPLENDID MISERY. The Story of the Presidency
and Power Politics at Close Range. 1st ed. D'day, 1960. In part
an interesting first-hand account of JFK's bid for VP in 1956.

Brown, Stuart G. CONSCIENCE IN POLITICS; Adlai Stevenson in
the 1950's. 1st ed. Syracuse U., 1961. Includes 1952, 1956,
1960 presidential campaigns.

Harris, Eleanor. "The Senator Is In a Hurry." McCALL'S, Aug.
1957: 44-45ff.

Knebel, Fletcher. "Can a Catholic Become Vice-President?" LOOK
June 12, 1956: 33-35.

LIFE. "The Emergence of a New Democratic Party." Aug.27, 1956:
20-35. Includes JFK near win over Kefauver.

Louchheim, Katie. BY THE POLITICAL SEA. D'day, 1970. 1st ed.
The 1956 convention and others. Her poem to JFK "A Time to Keep."

Martin, Ralh G. BALLOTS AND BANDWAGONS. McNally (1964). Selected conventions: Republican 1900, 1912, 1920; Democratic 1932,
1956. JFK's defeat that made him President.
Signet. Wrs., 1st prtg., 1964.

Moos, Malcolm and Stephen Hess. HATS IN THE RING: The Making
of Presidential Candidates. Random (1960) Reference to 1956.

Rischin, Moses. "OUR OWN KIND." Voting by Race, Creed or National Origin. Wrs. Report to the Center for Study of Democratic Institutions, 1960. Reactions to Catholic Presidential nominee
1940, 1955, 1956. Also cf. "Bailey memorandum" p.7.

TIME. "Primaries." Sept.22, 1958: 20. JFK vs. Vincent J.
Celeste in Massachusetts.

Election 1956-1958

Turner, Russell. "Senator Kennedy, the Perfect Politician."
AMERICAN MERCURY, Mar. 1957: 33-40. Cover portrait in color.+

UAW SOLIDARITY. Nov.10, 1958. Front page photo of JFK and
JBK re Senate win in Massachusetts.

U.S.NEWS... "The Kennedy Brothers: Off to a Fast Start." Apr.12,
1957: 77-79.+

Van Camp, John. "What Happened to the Labor-Reform Bill?"
REPORTER, Oct.2, 1958: 24-28. Kennedy-Ives labor-reform bill.

Wildavsky, Aaron B. PRESIDENTIAL ELECTIONS: Strategies of
American Electoral Politics. 1st ed. Scribner, 1965. JFK vs.
Kefauver, Nixon, Stevenson, the debates.

Election 1960

Abels, Jules. THE DEGENERATION OF OUR PRESIDENTIAL ELECTION: A
History and Analysis of an American Institution in Trouble. 1st
prtg. Macm. 1968. 1960 campaign.

Agranoff, Robt. ed. THE NEW STYLE IN ELECTION CAMPAIGNS. Wrs.
Holbrook Pr., 1976. "Kennedy campaigning" - JFK, RFK, EMK, Nixon.

Alexander, Herbert E. FINANCING THE 1960 ELECTION. Wrs. Citizens' Research Fdn. Study No. 5, n.d.

AMERICA. State of the Question (letters to the editor). Apr.4,
1959: 30ff. Sen. Kennedy: Catholic candidates discussed.
Current Comment: "Kennedy Wins." "A Catholic President."
July 23, 1960: 466, 470. Robert G. Hoyt "Opinion Worth Noting:"
Digest of an article on the religious issue published in CATHO-
LIC REPORTER Oct.28, 1960: Nov.5, 1960: 171-175. "The Peoples'
Choice;" "Busy President-elect;" Vicente Andrade "Latin America
and Mr. Kennedy;" Mary McGrory "Welcome and Tactful Beginning;"
Nov.19, 1960: 257, 284, 288, 289. -

Anderson, Walt. CAMPAIGNS: Cases in Political Conflict. 1st
prtg. Goodyear, 1970. 14 political campaigns. JFK in W.Va.:
163-176.

Ashbolt, Allan. AN AMERICAN EXPERIENCE. 1st Amer. ed. Eriksson,
1967. Australian's experience 1958-1961. Includes 1960 campaign.

ASHLAND AVENUE BAPTIST (Lexington Ky.). "Why I Am Afraid of a
Catholic President" by Wm. E. Burke. May 6, 1960:1. "Religious
Freedom - the Church - the State and Sen. Kennedy" by W.A. Cris-
well. Aug.5, 1960: 1-3. "Why I Cannot Vote for Sen. Kennedy"
by Clarence Walker. Sept. 16, 1960: 1-3. Zerox copy of letter
from Clarence Walker, pastor and editor, n.d.

WORKS ABOUT JFK

Election - 1960

AVE MARIA. Michael J. Kirwan: "Vote for Kennedy;" Wm. E. Miller
"Vote for Nixon." Oct. 22, 1960: 6-10ff. JFK and RMN on cover.-
"A Wrap-Up of the Election's Effect on the Understanding between
Catholics and Protestants..." by John J. Kane. Reprint from Dec.
17, 1960, by Nat'l Conf. Christians and Jews.

Barrett, Patricia. "An Assessment of American Pluralism in the
Light of the 1960 Presidential Election." Address at Marysville
College, St. Louis. Mo., Jan. 27, 1961.- RELIGIOUS LIBERTY AND
THE AMERICAN PRESIDENCY. Herder & Herder, 1963. Provides fine
bibliography of articles re the religious factor in the campaign.

Bartley, Numan V. FROM THURMOND TO WALLACE. Political Tenden-
cies in Georgia 1948-1968. Johns Hopkins, 1970. Analysis of
JFK vote in 1960 and Jimmy Carter vote in 1966.

BIBICAL RECORDER. A Declaration of Conscience for Baptists to
Consider: Oct, 8, 1960. (Flyer) Signed by 28 Baptists.

Blanshard, Paul. GOD AND MAN IN WASHINGTON. Beacon Pr., 1960.
Argues responsibility of Catholic candidate to declare position.
Review by John J. O'Connor in THE CRITIC, Apr-May, 1960: 61.
Review by Jos.J.Snee in BEST SELLERS, Mar.1, 1960:417 -

Bloom, Melvyn H. PUBLIC RELATIONS AND PRESIDENTIAL CAMPAIGNS: A
Crisis in Democracy. 1st ed. Crowell, 1973. 1960: 73-112.

Bruno, Jerry and Jeff Greenfield. THE ADVANCE MAN. An Offbeat
Look at What Really Happens in Political Campaigns. Morrow:1971
With JFK from Wisconsin in 1960 to Dallas in 1963.

BUSINESS WEEK. "How Humphrey, Kennedy Line Up in Wisconsin
'Beauty Contest'." Mar.26, 1960: 162-164ff. "The Democratic
Victory" with editorial comment: Nov.12, 1960: 25-34ff. +

Campaign Release: HIGH HOPES AND ALL THE WAY. 45 rpm 2077,2078

Campbell,Angus. "Has Television Reshaped Politics?" COLUMBIA
JOURNALISM REVIEW. Fall, 1962: 10-13. Includes additional articles on 1960 election. "Following Up" Winter, 1963. With
Philip Converse et al. ELECTION AND THE POLITICAL ORDER. Wiley,
1966. Chaps. 5 and 6 on 1960 presidential election.

Carney, Francis M. and H.F. Way, Jr., eds. POLITICS 1960. Wad-
sworth, 1960.

CAROLINA ISRAELITE. July-August, 1960: 1. Endorsement of JFK.

Roper, Elmo. "The Myth of the Catholic Vote." CATH. DIGEST,
Feb.1960:31-32. From SAT REVIEW Oct.31, 1959. -

THE KENNEDY FAMILY OF MASSACHUSETTS

Election - 1960

CATHOLIC WORLD. Sheerin, John B. "Catholic Candidates." Oct., 1958: 9-10. Fuchs, Lawrence H. "The Religious Vote, Fact or Fiction?" Oct., 1960: 9-14.

Chalmers, David M. HOODED AMERICANISM: The First Century of the Ku Klux Klan -1865-1965. D'day , 1965. 1st ed. Influence on Kennedy-Nixon campaign: 367, 368.

Congressional Quarterly Service. POLITICS IN AMERICA 1945-1964. Wrs. CQ, 1965. Summary of JFK election and ff.: 32-48.

Cox, Claire. THE NEW-TIME RELIGION. P-H, 1961. Church positions on the issue of a Catholic as President.

Danzig, David. "Bigotry and the Presidency." COMMITTEE REPORTER May, 1960: 20-21ff.

David, Paul T. ed. THE PRESIDENTIAL ELECTION AND TRANSITION 1960-1961. 1st prtg. Brookings Institution, 1961.

Demaris, Ovid. CAPTIVE CITY: CHICAGO IN CHAINS. Stuart, 1969. The 1960 presidential vote fraud claim touched on.

Democratic Nat'l Comm. Research Division. THE 1960 DEMOCRATIC FACT BOOK. Wrs. Fact Sheet RD-60-16, "Two Platforms, Two Parties and Four Men," Aug., 1960. "Memorandum: Areas of Concern About Which Questions Are Frequently Asked With JFK's Answers." N.d. Reprint "Religion and the Presidency" Nat'l Conf. Christians and Jews, n.d.

Democratic Nat'l Convention, Los Angeles CA. OFFICAL PROGRAM, 1960. Wrs.

The Democratic Platform, "The Rights of Man," July 12, 1960. Wrs.

De Toledano, Ralph. ONE MAN ALONE. F&W, 1969. Biography of Nixon w draws on relationship with JFK.

Eaton, Herbert. PRESIDENTIAL TIMBER; A History of Nominating Conventions 1868-1960. Free Press, 1964.

Fair Campaign Practices Committee, Inc. Report "The State-by State Study of Smear: 1960." Wrs. Feb, 1962.

Felknor, Bruce. DIRTY POLITICS. Norton, 1966. Includes ethics and tactics in JFK-Nixon 1960, RFK and Keating 1964.

Fenton, John. MIDWEST POLITICS. H.R.& W., 1966. Contains analysis of the Kennedy vote in 1960.

26.

WORKS ABOUT JFK

Election - 1960

FORTUNE."A New Mask for Big Government" by Max Ways. READERS'
DIGEST June 1960: 43-48. From FORTUNE April 1960. - "The
Economics of the Candidates" by John Osborne. Oct. 1960: 136-
141ff. + "What Business Wants from Lyndon Johnson" by Edmund K.
Faltermayer. Feb. 1965: 122-125ff. Includes executive voting 1960.

Friedrich, Carl T. THE PATHOLOGY OF POLITICS: Violence, Betrayal,
Corruption, Secrecy and Propaganda. 1st ed. H&R, 1972. Election
of JFK in the face of vicious propaganda at times.

Glock, Chas. Y. and Rooney Stark. CHRISTIAN BELIEFS AND ANTI-
SEMITISM. 1st ed. H&R, 1966. Cf. Table 69.

Gorman, Ralph. Editorial: "The New President." SIGN, Jan. 1961:
6. - JFK and JBK on cover.

Greenstein, Fred I. THE AMERICAN PARTY SYSTEM AND THE AMERICAN
PEOPLE. Wrs. P-H, 1963. Twelve year period.

Haley, J. Evetts. A TEXAN LOOKS AT LYNDON. A Study in Illegit-
imate Power. Palo Duro Pr. 1964. LBJ-JFK competition in election.

HARPER'S. "The Next Election Is Already Rigged" by Richard L.
Strout. READERS' DIGEST Jan. 1960: 117-120. From HARPER'S
Nov.1959. "Hard Questions for Sen. Kennedy" by John Fischer.
Apr.1960: 16ff.+ "The Choice" (between JFK and Nixon) by Fisch-
er. Oct. 1960: 14ff. +

Henderson, Chas. P. Jr. THE NIXON THEOLOGY. 1st ed. H&R, 1972.
Chap.8"Martyrdom -Campaign 1960."

"Highlights of Sen. Kennedy's Legislative Achievements as a Memb
er of the Senate." N.P. n.d.

HUMAN EVENTS. "The Great Forand Hoax. Part 5: Con Man in the
White House?" July 7, 1960. "Kennedy for President? A Roman Catholic Priest Says 'No,'" by Juniper B. Carol. July 28,1960:313-4.
"20 Questions About Jack Kennedy." Sept.29, 1960: 461-462.

Huttlinger, Joseph and Cronan Carey. "JFK's Chances of Obtaining
Presidential Nomination." JUBILEE, May, 1959: 2-4. -

THE INSIDER'S NEWSLETTER. July 18-Aug.15, 1960. "The Presidential
Campaign." 9 issues. (note: this newsletter is published in two
sections, one for men and one for women. Aug.15th lacks one for
women.)

Jennings, M. Kent and L. Harmon Ziegler eds. THE ELECTORAL PRO-
CESS. P-H, 1966. Essays, especially Herbert Alexander, John H.
Kessel, Donald R. Mathews and Jas. Prothro, and D.G. Sullivan.

Election - 1960

Johnson, George. RICHARD NIXON. 1st ed. wrs. Monarch, 1961. Two chapters on the race with JFK.

Judah, Chas. and Geo.W.Smith. THE UNCHOSEN. C-McC. (1962). Johnson vs. Kennedy: 299-332.

Kerwin, Jerome G. POLITICS, GOVERNMENT, CATHOLICS. Wrs. Paulist Press, 1961.

Key, V.O.Jr. THE RESPONSIBLE ELECTORATE. Rationality in Presidential Voting 1936-1960. Harvard U., 1966. Chap.5 on Kennedy.

Kiernan, Gene E. "Test Your Memory on '60 Kennedy-Nixon Debates." DAYTON LEISURE, Sept.5, 1976: 19.

Knebel, Fletcher. "Pulitzer Prize Entry - John F. Kennedy" in CANDIDATES 1960 edited by Eric Severeid: 181-215. Basic, 1959.

Kraus, Sidney, ed. THE GREAT DEBATES. Background, Perspective, Effects. Peter Smith, 1968. Orig. publ. Indiana U. in 1962.

Ladd, Everett C. Jr. with Chas. D. Hadley. TRANSFORMATIONS OF THE AMERICAN PARTY SYSTEM. Political Coalitions from the New Deal to the 1970's. 1st ed. Norton, 1975. JFK in 1960.

Lasky, Victor. JOHN F. KENNEDY. What's Behind the Image? Wrs. Free World, 1960.

Levin, Murray B. with Geo. Blackwood. THE COMPLEAT POLITICIAN. Porlitical Strategy in Massachusetts. 1st ed. B-M, 1962.

LIFE. "John Kennedy's Lovely Lady." Aug.24, 1959: 75-81. JBK on cover. "Should a Catholic be President?" by James A. Pike. Dec.21, 1959: 78-80ff. Also - editorial re Pike: 30. "Letters to the Editors" re Pike's article. Jan.18, 1960: 12."Voters' Image of the Ideal President," by Daniel Yankelovich. Mar.21, 1960: 124-126ff. (Notes how the top candidates measure up.) "Strategic Warpath in Wisconsin..." March 28, 1960: 22-30."Night Watch on Wisconsin," Apr. 18, 1960: 26-27. "A Small State Takes the Limelight" (W.Va.) May 9, 1960: 24-29 - "A Young Man Now Really On His Way," May 23, 1960: 62. "Top Men Roll On to the Convention," July 4, 1960:25-27. "The Nixon-Lodge Ticket," Aug. 8, 1960: 16-25. "Our Resolve Is Running Strong," by Richard M. Nixon. Aug.29, 1960: 86-88ff. "The Drama of the Issues." Sept. 19, 1960: 35. Also editorial "What About Quill, Mr. Kennedy?" "That Fancy Fashion Fuss...Pat vs.Jackie," Sept.26, 1960: 18-22. Also "A Catholic Faces His Protestant Clerical Questioners:"42. "Two Brooding Men in a Dazzling Duel," Oct.10, 1960:26-29. Also "Lovely Aspirants for Role of First Lady:"150-158. "The Second Nixon-Kennedy Debates Starts with Another Fuss Over Lights:" Oct. 17, 1960: 117.

Election - 1960

LIFE continued. Editorial: "Nixon's Domestic Program and Philosophy Are Far Better than Kennedy's:" Oct.17, 1960: 40.
"Of Two Able Candidates, Nixon Inspires More Confidence on Cold War Policy:" Oct.24, 1960: 36. "Ike's Record Laid on the Line," Nov.7, 1960: 26-34. Also Letters to the Editor re LIFE'S endorsement of Nixon, and "We Are Electing a President of the World," by Billy Graham: 109-110. "A Family Man with a Big New Job To Do" (the victorious young Kennedys). Nov.21, 1960: 32-40. Family color photo on cover. Also, editorial: "The 1,461 Days: Kennedy Has Best Wishes of All and a Chance to Earn Mandate He Missed," Nov.21, 1960: 42.

Lipset, Seymour M. "Religion and Politics in the American Past and Present:" 69-126 in RELIGION AND SOCIAL CONFLICT, ed. by Robt. Lee and Martin E. Marty. Oxford U., 1964.

LOOK. "The Rise of the Brothers Kennedy," Aug.6, 1957: 18-24ff. Produced by Laura Berquist. "Lyndon Johnson: Can a Southerner Be Elected President?" Aug. 18, 1959: 63-64ff. Entire issue of April 26, 1960, on insider's view of nation's capital. "A Protestant View of a Catholic for President." May 10, 1960:31-34ff. By Dr. Eugene Blake and Bishop G. Bromley Oxnam. "1.4 Million in Poll; Nixon and Kennedy Lead," July 5, 1960: 26-27. "The Kennedys: a Family Political Machine:" July 19, 1960: 43-46. "Campaign Turn: Things Are Jumping for Jack," Oct.31, 1960: 22-23. "How To Steal an Election," by Richard Wilson. Feb.14, 1961: 57-61. "...no organized national conspiracy to steal 1960..."

McCarthy, Max. ELECTIONS FOR SALE. 1st prtg. H-M, 1972. How campaign costs have tripled from 1960 to 1970.

McInerney, T.J. "To Keep or Not to Keep the Electoral College." ST. ANTHONY M., May 1961: 16-19 - Electoral, popular vote 1960.

McLendon, Winzola. "The Unsinkable Pat Nixon." McCALL'S, Oct., 1973: 84-85ff. Includes reactions to 1960 election.

Mailer, Norman. "Superman Comes to the Supermarket." ESQUIRE, Nov. 1960:119-127. - 1960 Democatic convention. SOME HONORABLE MEN. L-B (1976) Political conventions 1960-1972.

Maurois, Andre. FROM THE NEW FREEDOM TO THE NEW FRONTIER. McKay, (1963). JFK's presidential campaign and numerous quotations.

Mazo,E and Moos, M. et al. THE GREAT DEBATES. Wrs. Center for the Study of Democratic Institutions, 1962.

MEDICAL TIMES AND RESIDENT PHYSICIAN. Sept., 1960. 4p. zerox. Presidential straw poll: Nixon 68.6%, Kennedy 25.7%.

THE KENNEDY FAMILY OF MASSACHUSETTS

Election - 1960

Michener, James A. REPORT OF THE COUNTY CHAIRMAN. 1st prtg.
Random, 1961. JFK presidential campaign at precinct level.
Bantam, 1961. 1st prtg. wrs. Condensation: "Inside Kennedy's
Election." LOOK, May 9, 1961: 56-60ff. cover photo in color.
Review: N.T.T.BK.REV., July 9, 1961 by Samuel Lobell: 12.

Mullen, James J. "Newspaper Advertising in the Kennedy-Nixon
Campaign." JOURNALISM QUARTERLY, Winter 1963:3-4ff. Zerox copy.

NATION. "Debating the Great Debate; a Symposium." Alan Harrington et al. Nov.5, 1960: 324-347. +

NBC MEET THE PRESS. Guest Richard M Scammon, Nov.13, 1960.
Merkle Pr. Analysis of voting patterns of 1960 campaign.

Nat'l Comm. for Civic Responsibility. "Hate: The Voice of Ex-
remism," n.d. Quotations from "hate JFK" literature. 4p.

Nat'l Kennedy for President Committee. "Kennedy Wins Smashing
Victory in Wisconsin - 106,000 Vote Margin" Apr. 1960. 4p.

NEW REPUBLIC. "A Catholic for President?" Pts. 2 and 3. Nov.25,
Dec.2, 1957, by Helen Miller. "The Kennedy Strategy," Feb.15,
1960:3-4. "Catholics in America," by J. Pelikan, A. Schlesinger,
March 21, 1960: 11-15. "Kennedy and the First Ballot" by Theodore
Lowi. Apr.11, 1960:13-15. Kirkpatrick, Jean: "How Wisconsin Vo-
ted." Apr.18, 1960:8. "Bigotry in W.Va." by Joseph Alsop. May 2,
1960: 11-12. "Kennedy as President" by Selig Harrison. June 27,
1960: 9-15.

NEW YORK TIMES ELECTION HANDBOOK 1964, Harold Faber ed. McG-H.
1964. On JFK,Tom Wicker and Warren Weaver. 1960 voting patterns.

N.Y.TIMES MAGAZINE. "Election Cry: 'Win with Harvard.'" by Grace
and Fred M. Hechinger. Oct.9, 1960: 26ff. - "Why There Are Bigots
by Jas.A.Pike. Oct.30, 1960:12ff. "'Washington Would Have Lost a
TV Debate." by Henry S. Commager. Oct.30, 1960: 13ff. - "'Why I
Am Voting For - and Against - ' The Case for Nixon," by Russell
Kirk: 19ff. "The Case for Kennedy," by Arthur Schlesinger Jr.:
19ff. The case against Kennedy and the rebuttal by Russell Kirk:
116. Schlesinger replies:116-117. Nov.6, 1960.- cover photo.

Nimmo, Dan. THE POLITICAL PERSUADERS. The Technique of Modern
Election Campaigns. Wrs. P-H, 1970. JFK strategies.

Nixon, Richard M. THE CHALLENGES WE FACE. 1st ed. McG-H, 1960.
One reference to JFK - accused of criticising Eisenhower.

Pike, James A. A ROMAN CATHOLIC IN THE WHITE HOUSE. 1st ed.
D'day, 1960. "...questions you should ask before you vote."
Written with the assistance of Canon Richard Byfield. Review by
J.J.Clarke, BEST SELLERS, May 1, 1960: 64-65. -

WORKS ABOUT JFK

Election - 1960

Polsby, N.W. and A.B. Wildavsky. PRESIDENTIAL ELECTIONS:
Strategies of American Electoral Politics. Scribner's, 1964.

Reichley, Jas. STATES IN CRISIS: Politics in Ten American States,
1950-1962. U. of N. Carolina, 1964.

REPORTER. "The Cool Eye of JFK" by Douglas Cater. Dec.10, 1959:
27-32. "Humphrey vs. Kennedy" by Sander Vanocur. Mar.17, 1960:
28-30. "A Tide in the Affairs of JFK" by Douglas Cater. Aug.4,
196016-18.+ "The Clergy Faces Mr. Kennedy" (Houston-Sept.12,
1960). Oct.13, 1960:32-34.

Reuther, Walter. SELECTED PAPERS. H.M.Christman ed. 1st prtg.
Macm.1961. In "Mike Wallace Interview" Oct.17 and 18, 1960,
Reuther defended JFK's presidential candidacy.

Richter, Edw.J. and Berton Dulce. RELIGION AND THE PRESIDENCY:
A Recurring American Problem. 1st prtg. Macm.1962: 122-221.

Robinson, Lloyd. THE HOPEFULS: The Presidential Campaigns. D'day
1966. The last ten campaigns through the eyes of the losers.

Roseboom, Eugene H. A HISTORY OF PRESIDENTIAL ELECTIONS. 1st prt.
of 2nd ed. Chap.32 added: "The Kennedys Take Over": 543-72.

Rovere, Richard. "Letter From Washington." NEW YORKER, Nov.19,
1960. Analysis of 1960 presidential election.

Ruff, Elson. "In Conclusion": Catholics and Protestants Are
Bound Together...THE LUTHERAN, Oct.5, 1960. Reprint 1p.

Ryan, L.A. Outline of Presidential Campaign Clinic for 1960 for
members of the Introductory Sociology course at the College of
Mount St. Joseph, Cincinnati. Sept.-Nov.,1960. Mimeo. Report on
the analysis of LIFE and SATURDAY EVENING POST coverage of the
1960 presidential campaign with excerpted articles (College of
MSJ). Response of 21 theology students: an evaluation of JFK's
speech to the ministers in Houston - after hearing the tape recording of it. Original papers. Sack for Democratic campaign
material from Democratic National Committee - 1960. Contains
tape of Sen. Kennedy's address to Protestant ministers in Houston
and discussion, op.cit.

SATURDAY EVENING POST. "The Battle of Wisconsin: Kennedy vs. Humphrey." Apr.2, 1960: 16ff. "Kennedy's Magic Formula." Both by
Stewart Alsop. 2nd art. Aug.13, 1960: 26-27ff. "The Quandary of
Henry Cabot Lodge."Feb.8, 1964: 70-73, by Stanley Karnow. With
anecdotes of 1960 campaign.

Election - 1960

Schlesinger, Arthur Jr. KENNEDY OR NIXON? Does It Make Any Difference? 1st prtg. Macm. 1960. Review by Francis P. Canavan AMERICA, Oct.15, 1960: 97 -

Selden, Harry L. "The Electoral College: Does It Choose the Best" in AMERICAN HERITAGE, Oct., 1962:12-18ff. 1960 election.

Sherrill, Robt. and Harry W. Ernst. THE DRUGSTORE LIBERAL: Herbert H. Humphrey in Politics. 1st prtg. Grossman, 1968. Saga of H.H.H. in critical vein. Includes 1960 primary fight against JFK.

Sorenson, Theodore. "Election of 1960:" 437-457, in THE COMING TO POWER, edited by A.M. Schlesinger Jr. 1st ed. Chelsea House,1972.

Sumner, Robt.L. KENNEDY FOR PRESIDENT? Wrs. Sword of the Lord Fdn., 1960. A warning not to vote for JFK.

Tillett, Paul ed. INSIDE POLITICS: The National Conventions, 1960. Oceana Publ., 1962.

TIME. "The Campaign" (N.Hampshire). March 21, 1960: 13-14. "The Catholic Issue," Apr.18, 1960:16-20.- "The Kennedy Family" July 11, 1960: 19-23. Family portrait on cover. "The Democrats in Los Angeles" July 18,1960: 9-13. Before the decision- LBJ on cover. "The Campaign: The Power of Negative Thinking," Sept.19, 1960: 21 -22. (The religious issue). "Election Extra," Nov.16, 1960:1-15.

U.S.NEWS AND WORLD REPORT. "Most-talked-about Candidate for 1960" Nov.8, 1957:62-64.+ "Will the Religious Issue Stop Kennedy in'60?" Sept.7, 1959:42-43.- "After New Hampshire - Both Kennedy and Nixon Look Even Stronger." Mar.21, 1960:59-60ff.+ "A Close Look at the Wisconsin Election." Apr.1960:41-50.- "John Kennedy; Who He Is and What He Stands For." May 30, 1960: 75-78. "A Poll of Top Democrats: Kennedy Has Almost Enough Votes, But -" June 27,1960: 52-54ff. -"Union Leaders Size Up Kennedy and Johnson." July 11, 1960: 96-99.+ "Pro and Con of the Issues." Oct.24, 1960:40-44. Also campaign report from Ill., Ind., Mich., Ohio.- "As the Race Ends." Nov.7, 1960:37-53.- "The Kennedy Story..."Nov.21,1960. -

United States Senate Commerce Committee. Subcommittee Report 994 on FREEDOM OF COMMUNICATIONS Covering the Presidential Campaign of 1960. Part I. "The Speeches of John F. Kennedy:" the speeches, remarks, press conferences and statements of Sen.Kennedy Aug.1 through Nov.7, 1960. Part II. "The Speeches of Vice-Pres. Richard M. Nixon," Aug.1 through Nov.7, 1960: the speeches, remarks, press conferences and study papers of V-P Nixon. Part III. "The Joint Appearances of Sen.John F. Kennedy and Richard N. Nixon:" so-called "Great Debates" and other 1960 campaign presentations. Part IV. "The 15-Minute Radio and Television Network Newscasts for the Period Sept.26 through Nov.7, 1960." Part V. "Hearings before the Freedom of Communications Subcomm. Mar.27-29 1961." Part VI. "Recommendations" 1962. Pts.I,III,op.cit. JFK Speeches.   32.

WORKS ABOUT JFK

Election - 1960

Wakin, Edw. and J.F.Scheur. THE DE-ROMANIZATION OF THE AMERICAN
CATHOLIC CHURCH. 1st prtg. Macm. 1966. Chap.11: votes for JFK.

Wandell, Rose M. "Why Shouldn't There Be a Catholic President?"
TORCH, Feb.,1960: 10-11ff.-

Warwick, Loy. "Those Whispers About Jack Kennedy. The '60 Campaign Will Be the Dirtiest in 32 Years." CONFIDENTIAL, Oct.,
1960:10-13ff.

Weisbord, Marvin R. CAMPAIGNING FOR PRESIDENT. A New Look at
the Road to the White House. 1st ed. Public Affairs Pr.,1964.
Chap.12: Nixon and JFK. Rev. and expanded, Wash.Sq.,1966.

White, Theodore. THE MAKING OF THE PRESIDENT: 1960. 1st ed. Ath-
eneum, 1961. Cardinal, wrs. 1962. Signet 1st prtg. 1967.
Review by D.W.Brogan, ENCOUNTER June 1962:66-68. By James Mac-
Gregor Burns, N.Y.T.BK.REV., July 9, 1961:1ff. - Excerpts: LIFE
July 7, 1961: 85-86ff.

Inauguration

AMERICA. "Current Comment: Inauguration Day. Jan.21, 1961:490.-

Frost, Robert. IN THE CLEARING. 1st ed. H.R.&W, 1962. Includes
inaugural poem "The Gift Outright."

Gould, Jean. ROBERT FROST: THE AIM WAS SONG. D-M,(1964). With an
account of "the first inaugural poet:" 1-6.

Legislative Reference Service. INAUGURAL ADDRESSES OF THE PRESI-
DENTS OF THE U.S. FROM GEORGE WASHINGTON, 1789, TO JOHN F. KENNEDY
1961. GPO, 1961.

LIFE. "The Kennedy Inauguration," Jan.27, 1961:16-30. Cover photo.
Life eds. INAUGURAL SPECTACLE. Wrs. Souvenir ed.1961.

Morrison, Kathleen. ROBERT FROST, A PICTORIAL CHRONICLE. 1st ed.
H.R.&W.,1974. Relation between RF and JFK, JBK.

NEW YORKER. "Talk of the Town. JFK's Inaugural Address." Feb.24,
1961:23-24. +

OFFICIAL INAUGURAL PROGRAMS. Jan.20, 1961. Nos.459 and 640,Ltd.ed.

SIGN. "The President's First Words,"by F. Remington.Jan.1961:27-8.

TIME. "The Inauguration of John Fitzgerald Kennedy," Jan.27, 1961:
7-13 - Photo on cover.
U.S.Congress. THE CAPITOL. Wrs. JFK Inaugural Ed. GPO, 1961.Folio

THE KENNEDY FAMILY OF MASSACHUSETTS

Public Opinion Surveys

Carter, Richard. "What Women Really Think of the Kennedys,"
GOOD HOUSEKEEPING. June, 1963: 73-75ff.

Chase, Stuart. AMERICAN CREDOS. What Americans Say They Believe
and What They Really Believe. 1st ed. Harp.,1962. JFK in 5 polls.

Diamondstein, Barbaralee. OPEN SECRETS. Ninety-four Women in
Touch with Our Times. Viking, 1972. Largely media appraisals.

Fenton, John. IN YOUR OPINION... 1st ed. Polls, Politics and
People from 1945 to 1960. L-B, 1960. Autographed. Chap.11: JFK.

Harris, Louis. THE ANGUISH OF CHANGE. 1st ed. Norton, 1973.
Impact on the three Kennedy brothers.

JUBILEE. "Poll: Kennedy, Nixon and Anti-Catholicism." Sept. 1960:
7-11. - JFK on cover.

LOOK. "How The Public Rates JFK." Aug.13, 1963: 34.

McGrory, Mary. "Happy Days Are Here Again!" AMERICA, Feb.3,1962:
582 - Gallup poll re JFK's popularity.

Roper, Elmo. "Who Really Won the Elections of 1962?" SAT.REVIEW,
Dec.15, 1962:13. Influence of JFK's endorsements.

Art and Music

"I see little of more importance to the future of our country and
our civilization than full recognition of the place of the artist.
If art is to nourish the roots of our culture, society must set
the artist free to follow his vision wherever it takes him... Art
is not a form of propaganda, it is a form of truth. Art establishes the basic human truths which must serve as the basic touch-
stones of our judgment." JFK - dedication of a library at Amherst.

Barnes, Clare,Jr. and Croswell. "The Scrimshaw Collector" in AMER-
ICAN HERITAGE, Oct. 1964: 8-13.

Barnes, Clare,Jr. JOHN F. KENNEDY, SCRIMSHAW COLLECTOR. 1st ed.
L-B, 1969. Folio.

Belt, Byron. "JFK Center for the Performing Arts." HIGH FIDELITY
Sept. 1971:52-57. It took an assassination to bring it about.

THE BRANDYWINE HERITAGE. 1st publication of Brandywine Museum:
1971. New and unpublished portraits of JFK by James Wyeth - also
sketches of RFK and EMK.

Burns, Joah Simpson. THE AWKWARD EMBRACE...1st ed. Knopf, 1975.
The Kennedy conception of the federal role in influence on arts.

WORKS ABOUT JFK

Art and Music

Cable, Mary. THE AVENUE OF THE PRESIDENTS. 1st prtg. H-M,1969.
JFK's Commission to turn Pennsylvania Ave. into a place of dignity and beauty. Front DJ photo of JFK's inaugural parade.

CAMELOT Souvenir Book, wrs. National Publ.,n.d. Widely recogni-
zed to be the most admired musical of JFK.

Columbia Masterworks. CAMELOT. Book and Lyrics by Alan Jay
Lerner. Music by Frederick Loewe. Original Broadway cast.
KOS 2031.

Casals, Pablo, as told to Albert E. Kahn. JOYS AND SORROWS. S&S,
1970. JFK and Casals at the White House in 1961.

Cater, Douglas. "The Kennedy Look in the Arts," HORIZON, Sept.,
1961:4-17. Writers, painters, Rhodes Scholars in Kennedy adm.

Coutts-Smith, Kenneth. THE DREAM OF ICARUS. Art and Society in
the Twentieth Century. Brailler, 1970. The "new left" and JFK;
Richard Hamilton portrait of JFK.

Duheme, Jacqueline. JOHN F. KENNEDY: A BOOK OF PAINTINGS (by
Duheme) 1st ed. Atheneum, 1967. A life of JFK for children. JBK
studied with this artist in 1962.

LIFE. "The Painting Pal of the President," (William Walton.)
Mar.17, 1961:149-150.

Lynes, Russell. CONFESSIONS OF A DILETTANTE. 1st ed. H&R,1966.
Role of gov't and arts, Nat'l Arts Council during JFK years.

Mondale, Joan. POLITICS IN ART. Wrs., rev.ed. Lerner, 1972.
Includes 16 Jackies by Andy Warhol, montage with JFK, quote.

von Eckardt, Wolf. "Washington's Chance for Splendor," Harper,
Sept.1963: 54-64. JFK's ambitions for beautification of Wash.

Walker, John. SELF-PORTRAIT WITH DONORS. Confessions of an Art
Collector. 1st ed. L-B, 1974. Reminiscenses include JFK and JBK
and loan of Mona Lisa, refurbishing of White House by JBK, more.

Relations with Economic and Professional Community

Blough, Roger. "My Side of the Steel Price Story." LOOK, Jan.
29, 1963: 19-23. As told to Eleanor Harris.

Brooks, John. THE GO-GO YEARS. W&T, 1973. JFK and Wall Street.

BUSINESS WEEK. "Kennedy-Business Feud Nears Peril Point," July 7
1962: 92-93ff. +

Relations with Economic and Professional Community

COMPUTERS AND PEOPLE. "American Oil Interests, the CIA, and Reversal of JFK's Plans to Get Out of Vietnam," Mar.,1975: 29-32.

Cormier, Frank and Wm.J.Eaton. REUTHER. P-H, 1970. Relations
with three Kennedy brothers.

Dubofsky, Melvyn, ed. AMERICAN LABOR SINCE THE NEW DEAL. Quad-
rangle, 1971.   Text from pages of N.Y.TIMES.

Golden, L.L. ONLY BY PUBLIC CONSENT. American Corporations
Search For Favorable Opinion. 1st. Hawthorn, 1968. JFK and
steel crisis - and as "master of public relations."

Goulden, Jos.C. MEANY. The Unchallenged Strong Man of Ameri-
can Labor. 1st. Atheneum, 1972. Chap.XIII. "Kennedy Years."
THE SUPERLAWYERS: The Small and Powerful World of the Great
Washington Law Firms. W-T, 1972. JFK and Clark Clifford.

Harrington, Michael. THE OTHER AMERICA: Poverty in the U.S.
Macm. 1963.Influenced JFK to national effort to abolish poverty.

Harris, Richard. A SACRED TRUST. NAL, 1966. 1st. Organized
medicine - JFK's fight for medical care for the elderly.

Harris, Seymour E. THE ECONOMICS OF AMERICAN MEDICINE. 1st.
Macm.,1964. JFK and medicare and efforts to improve health care.

Heller, Walter. NEW DIMENSIONS OF POLITICAL ECONOMY. Harvard,
1966. JFK as first modern economist in U.S. presidency.
W.W.Norton, 1967, wrs.

Hunebelle, Danielle. "Jimmy Hoffa, l'Homme le Plus Puissant
des Etats-Unis." REALITES, Oct. 1961:100-107. Re Kennedy.

Hutchinson, John. THE IMPERFECT UNION: A History of Corruption
in American Trade Unions. 1st. Dutton, 1970. RFK and JFK.

Jacobs, Paul. THE STATE OF THE UNIONS. 1st. Atheneum, 1963.
McClelland Committee - RFK and JFK.

JIMMY THE GREEK by Himself. Playboy, 1975. Some anecdotes about
the three Kennedy brothers.

Koenig, Louis W. "The Presidency, Kennedy and Steel: The Great
Price Dispute:" 1-52 in Alan F. Westin ed. THE CENTERS OF POWER.
Harcourt Brace and World, 1964. Wrs.

Lemon, Richard. THE TROUBLED AMERICAN. 1st. S&S, 1969. JFK as
responding to blacks, young and poor with middle class discon-
tent.

Relations with Economic and Professional Community

Levy, Jacques. CESAR CHAVEZ. Autobiography of La Causa. 1st. Norton, 1975. References to association with JFK, RFK, EMK.

LIFE. "Hail and Hurricane to the Chief," April 27, 1962 - "JFK Talks Business at Yale," 38-39 -

Liston, Robt. A. THE AMERICAN POOR. A Report on Poverty in the United States. Wrs. 1st prtg. Dell, 1970. JFK and RFK.

McCLELLAN COMMITTEE HEARINGS - 1957. 1st prtg., wrs. Bureau of Nat'l Affairs, 1958. Day to day report: JFK and RFK.

McClellan, John L. CRIME WITHOUT PUNISHMENT. D.S.& P., 1963. Senate Rackets Committee 1957-1960 - with JFK and RFK.

McConnell, Grant. STEEL AND THE PRESIDENCY - 1962. Wrs. Norton, 1963. The personalities who played key roles.

McDonald, David, J. UNION MAN. 1st ed. Dutton, 1969. McD's relation with Joe Sr., JFK, RFK and EMK; JFK-Blough; tribute.

Matthiessen, Peter. SAL SI PUEDES: Cesar Chavez and the New American Revolution. 1st. Random, 1969. JFK, RFK, EMK.

Mollenhoff, Clark R. TENTACLES OF POWER. The Story of Jimmy Hoffa. 1st. World, 1965. JFK and RFK.

NEWSWEEK. "The Big Steel Story. Blough vs. Kennedy: The Price Wasn't Right," April 23, 1962: 17-21. JFK on cover. "The Stock Market's Wild Week," June 11, 1962: 19-25. "'Myths' and Men and the Economy," June 25, 1962: 17-20. JFK's address at Yale.

REPORTER. "The Economic Education of JFK," Feb.14, 1963: 22-25. Discussed in "Correspondence" in issue of Mar.14, 1963:10-11 + Article by M.J.Rossant. "The Rhetoric of Walter Reuther," by Stanley Levey, Mar. 14, 1963: 26-28. JFK's support of Reuther.

Rukeyser, M.S. THE KENNEDY RECESSION. A Complete Study of the Causes of Our Stagnating Economy and Our Loss of World-Wide Prestige. 1st, wrs. Monarch, 1963.

Sexton,Patricia C. and Brendan. BLUE COLLARS AND HARD HATS. The Working Class and the Future of American Politics. 1st. Random, 1971. MC as victim, courage of JFK, RFK, EMK.

Smith, Richard A. "Behind U.S.Steel's Price Blunder." FORTUNE, Aug. 1962: 75-77ff.

Stein, Herbert. THE FISCAL REVOLUTION IN AMERICA. Univ. of Chicago, (1969). Chaps. 15 and 16 on JFK's economic decisions.

THE KENNEDY FAMILY OF MASSACHUSETTS

Relations with Economic and Professional Community

Shefferman, N.W. with Dale Kramer. THE MAN IN THE MIDDLE. 1st. D'day, 1961. Defense of himself, Dave Beck, Hoffa, McClellan Comm. Hearings, history of management-labor conflicts.

Tabb, Wm.K. THE POLITICAL ECONOMY OF THE GHETTO. 1st, wrs. Norton, 1970. Critique of JFK's and RFK's efforts.

U.S.NEWS AND WORLD REPORT. "Aftermath on the Crackdown on Steel" April 30, 1962: 41-45.

Relations with Entertainers

Allen, Maury. WHERE HAVE YOU GONE, JOE DIMAGGIO? Dutton,(1975). Joe and Marilyn - Norman Rosten's refutation of "rumors about the Kennedys."

Blaik, Earl "Red". THE RED BLAIK STORY. Arlington, (1974). Good relations with JFK and RFK.

Dandridge, Dorothy and Earl Conrad. EVERYTHING AND NOTHING: The Dorothy Dandridge Tragedy. A-S (1970). Brief reference to the Kennedy Foundation for Mental Retardation: 201-202.

Davidson, Bill. "President Kennedy Casts a Movie." SEP, Sept. 8, 1962: 26-27. Role of JFK in PT 109.

Gage, Nicholas, ed. MAFIA U.S.A. Playboy (1972). Chap.19: JFK and Frank Sinatra; RFK's effective fight against organized crime.

Guiles, Fred L. MARION DAVIES. McG-H, (1972). Connection with Kennedy family before and after the death of Hearst.
NORMA JEAN: The Life of Marilyn Monroe. McG-H (1969) Relates the "Happy Birthday" song to JFK at invitation of Peter Lawford.

Lyons, D.L. "Angie Dickenson: JFK and Me." LHJ,June, 1975: 67ff.

LOOK. "The Man JFK Picked to Play His Wartime Role," June 18, 1963: 48-54.

McCALL'S. "The White House Is Still Wondering What To Do With Me," by Peter Lawford as told to Vernon Scott. Jan.1963: 68-69ff.

Mailer, Norman. MARILYN: A Biography. 1st prtg. G&D, 1973. Mailer defends RFK against his critics. Relations with JFK. "Marilyn Monroe: the Men in Her Life...Her Mysterious Death." LADIES H.J. August, 1973. Review of Monroe according to Mailer, MS. Oct., 1973:44-47 by Ingrid Bengis.

Messick, Hank, with Joseph L. Nellis. THE PRIVATE LIVES OF PUBLIC ENEMIES. Wyden (1973). Sinatra and JFK, RFK.

WORKS ABOUT JFK

Relations with Entertainers

Murphy, George, with Victor Lasky. "SAY...DIDN'T YOU USED TO BE GEORGE MURPHY?" 1st. Bartholomew, 1970. Claims his father was friends with "Honeyfitz" Fitzgerald - a relationship which apparently did not extend to JFK, RFK and EMK.

NEWSWEEK. "A Shadow Over Camelot," by Peter Goldman et al. Dec. 29, 1975: 14-16. Linking of Mafia connection Judith Campbell Exner with JFK according to FBI reports. "The Mafia: A Swim In the Bay," Aug.23, 1976. John Rosselli's death, friend of Exner.-

Niven, David. THE MOON'S A BALLOON. Putnam (1972). Friendship with JFK and JBK.

Papich, Stephen. REMEMBERING JOSEPHINE. (Josephine Baker) 1st. B-M, 1976. JFK and RFK assistance with immigration problem.

Sherman, Allan. A GIFT OF LAUGHTER. Autobiography. Atheneum, 1965. Autographed. Admiration for JFK.

Weatherby, W.J. CONVERSATIONS WITH MARILYN. 1st prtg. M/C,1976. Extensive quotes from Marilyn. References to JFK and RFK.

Relations with Ethnic Communities

Bence-Jones, Mark. THE REMARKABLE IRISH. McKay (1966). JFK as personifying the Irish who have emigrated.

Bishop, Jim. THE DAYS OF MARTIN LUTHER KING JR. Putnam (1971). Author's version of relation between JFK and MLK.

Booker, Simeon. BLACK MAN'S AMERICA. P-H (1964). Fight for equality and author's thoughts about JFK and RFK. "JFK Says Nation Not Seriously Divided on Racial Question." JET, Jan.17, 1963: 6-7. "How JFK Surpassed Abraham Lincoln." EBONY, Feb.1964: 25-28ff.- "Pres. Kennedy and the Negroes." CATHOLIC DIGEST, June, 1964: 19-21. Condensed from EBONY, Feb., 1964.- "Robert C. Weaver: Quiet Man Wins Spot in Cabinet." EBONY, April, 1966: 83-84ff.-

Broom, Leonard and N.D.Glenn. TRANSFORMATION OF THE NEGRO AMERICAN. 1st. H&R, 1965. JFK on employment and Negro votes.

Castan, Sam. "A Negro Takes Over Federal Housing." LOOK, April 11, 1961: 33ff. Robert C. Weaver, Federal housing chief.

Chisholm, Shirley. THE GOOD FIGHT. 1st. H&R, 1973. Unique campaign in 1972, with remarks on JFK and RFK.

Considine, Bob. IT'S THE IRISH. Wrs. Avon, 1961. Chap.7: "Politicking Irish," refers to JFK.

THE KENNEDY FAMILY OF MASSACHUSETTS

Relations with Ethnic Communities

Dunbar, Ernest. "A Visit with Martin Luther King." LOOK, Feb. 12, 1963: 92-96. Speaks out on JFK and civil rights.

Egginton, Joyce. "Mississippi Widow: A Visit with Mrs. Medgar Evers." LOOK, June 1, 1965: 62ff. JFK and burial place.

Evers, Myrlie. "He Said He Wouldn't Mind Dying If..." LIFE. June 28, 1963:35-37. With Wm Peters, FOR US THE LIVING. D'day, (1967). Influence of JFK.

Glazer, Nathan and Daniel P. Moynihan. BEYOND THE MELTING POT. Wrs. 1st. MIT, 1964. The Jewish and Irish vote for JFK.

Greeley, Andrew. THAT MOST DISTRESSFUL NATION: THE TAMING OF THE AMERICAN IRISH. 1st. Quad.,1972. Especially JFK, RFK.

Hecht, Jas. BECAUSE IT IS RIGHT; Integration in Housing. 1st. L-B, 1970. Fair housing in Buffalo due to JFK.

Hennessey, Maurice. I'LL COME BACK IN THE SPRINGTIME. Ives W., (1966). JFK's four visits to Ireland.

Isaacs, Harold. THE NEW WORLD OF NEGRO AMERICANS. Day, 1963. Interviews with 107 Negro leaders. Praise and blame for JFK.

Kelleher, John V. "Irishmen in America", Vol.10 MAKERS OF AMER-ICA, Ency.Brit., 1971: 125-129. Reprint from ATLANTIC, 1961.

King, Coretta Scott. MY LIFE WITH MARTIN LUTHER KING JR. H&S, 1970. JFK as MLK's "best friend." "He Had a Dream." LIFE, Sept.12, 1969:54ff.

LIFE. "Hail to the O'Chief" by Dominic Behan. June 21, 1963:12.

Lincoln, C.Eric. THE NEGRO PILGRIMAGE IN AMERICA. 1st. wrs. Bantam, 1967. JFK appt. of first Negro to Federal Dist.Court.

Lomax, Louis E. THE NEGRO REVOLT. 1st. Harp.,1962. Civil rights program tied to rise of the Negro voter. JFK, RFK. "The Kennedys Move In On Dixie." HARPER'S, May, 1962: 27-33. "Why The Negroes Continue To Revolt." LOOK, Sept.10,1963:52ff.

Murray, Albert. THE OMNI-AMERICANS: New Perspectives on Black Experience and American Culture. Dutton (1970). Votes for JFK.

Novak, Michael. THE RISE OF THE UNMELTABLE ETHNICS. 1st. Macm. 1972. Why JFK and RFK had support of ethnic groups.

Shannon, Wm.V. THE AMERICAN IRISH. Macm.(1964). Chap.19. "President John F. Kennedy:" 392-413.

WORKS ABOUT JFK

Relations with Political Community

Allen, Ivan, Jr. with Paul Hemphill. MAYOR: Notes on the Sixties. 1st. S&S, 1971. Support of JFK and civil rights,Atlanta.

Anderson, Clinton. OUTSIDER IN THE SENATE. 1st. World, 1970.
JFK on conservation, health assistance, space programs.

Anson, Robert Sam. McGOVERN: A Biography. HR&W, wrs. (1972).
McGovern's relationship with JFK, RFK and EMK.

Ashman, Chas. CONNALLY. 1st. Morrow, 1974. Sec'y of Navy, JFK.

Baker, Leonard. THE JOHNSON ECLIPSE. 1st. Macm., 1966. As V-P.

Bauer, Fred E., ed. EV: The Man and His Words. Hewitt (1969).
Everett Dirksen, Minority Leader of Senate, cooperation with JFK.

Bingham, June. U THANT: The Search for Peace. 1st. Knopf,1966.
Relations with JFK - the Acting Sec'y Gen. of U.N. in 1961.

Bowles, Chester. PROMISES TO KEEP: My Years in Public Life.
1st. H&R, 1971. In State Dept. under JFK.

Burns, Jas. McGregor. "Political Craftsman in the White House."
N.Y.T.MAG. Jan.15, 1961:5ff.

Carpenter, Liz. RUFFLES AND FLOURISHES. 1st. D'day, 1970. Press
sec'y to Lady Bird Johnson. Loyalty to Johnsons, pique with K's.

Cochran, Bert. ADLAI STEVENSON: Patrician among Politicians.
F&W, (1967). Role as Ambassador to U.N. under JFK.

Coffin, Tristram. SENATOR FULBRIGHT. 1st. Dutton, 1966. Comparison and contrast with JFK.

Collier, Peter and David Horowitz. THE ROCKEFELLERS: An American Dynasty. HR&W,1976. Many situations with JFK and RFK.

Colson, Chas.W. BORN AGAIN. Chosen Bks.(1976). Nixon insider
views attitudes toward JFK, RFK and EMK.

Cormier, Frank. LBJ: THE WAY HE WAS. 1st. D'day, 1977.

Cousins, Norman. THE IMPROBABLE TRIUMVIRATE: Kennedy-Khruschev-
Pope John. Norton, 1972. 1st.

Crass, Philip. THE WALLACE FACTOR. 1st. M/C, 1976. Includes
his relationship with JFK, RFK and EMK.

De Gaulle, Chas. MEMOIRS OF HOPE: RENEWAL AND ENDEAVOR. S&S,
1971. Conversations with JFK, comments on his character.

THE KENNEDY FAMILY OF MASSACHUSETTS

Relations with Political Community

Diederich, Bernard and Al Burt. PAPA DOC: The Truth about Haiti
Today. 1st. McG-H, 1969. JFK refusal to support the dictator.

Douglas-Home, Alec. THE WAY THE WIND BLOWS: an Autobiography.
1st. Quad/N.Y.T., 1976. Includes events with JFK.

Dunbar, Ernest. "The Audacious World of Adam Powell." LOOK, May
7, 1963:3034ff. JFK comments on Powell.

Eisenhower, Dwight D. THE WHITE HOUSE YEARS: Waging Peace...1956-
1961. 1st. D'day, 1965. Much relating to JFK.

Gleason, Bill. DALEY OF CHICAGO. 1st. S&S, 1970. Main focus on
1968 but includes relations with JFK.

Gruening, Ernest. MANY BATTLES. Autobiography. Liveright, 1973.
Describes JFK as accessible and cooperative, a bit conservative.

Harris, Mark. "Fight for a Golden Crown. Nation Stirred by Nixon
vs. Brown." LIFE, Oct.19, 1962:44-53. JFK help for Brown.
MARK THE GLOVE BOY: Autobiography. Or, The Last Days of Richard
Nixon. 1st Macm., 1964. Campaign in California, much about JFK.

Hartke, Vance. INSIDE THE NEW FRONTIER. Wrs. MacFadden, 1962.
Chapter 6: "JFK: a Man to Respect." Mention of EMK and RFK.

Healy, Paul. "'Mr. America' in the Senate." SEP, Dec., 1975: 40-
41ff. John Glenn and his relationship with JFK and RFK.

Herzog, Arthur. McCARTHY FOR PRESIDENT. 1st. Viking, 1969. Eugene McC's animosity and ambivalence toward the Kennedys.

Hodges, Luther H. BUSINESSMAN IN THE STATE HOUSE. U. of N.C.,
1962. Support for LBJ in primary, zealous work for JFK election.

Hughes, Emmet J. THE ORDEAL OF POWER. A Political Memoir of the
Eisenhower Years. Atheneum, 1963. Includes relations with JFK as
senator and president. Also first Dell prtg.,1964. Wrs.

Humphrey, Hubert. THE EDUCATION OF A PUBLIC MAN. 1st. D'day,
1976. Competition with JFK for presidential nomination 1960.
Much about RFK.

Inouye, Daniel K. JOURNEY TO WASHINGTON. P-H, 1967. Support
for LBJ in nomination, JFK for election.

Jennett, Richard P. THAT MAN FROM MINNESOTA. Wrs. Joyce, 1965.
Critique of Humphrey's "alien" ideology. JFK in 1956, 1960-63.

Johnson, Lyndon Baines. THE VANTAGE POINT...1963-1969. 1st.
HR&W, 1971. "This is how I saw it..." ALS 19 lines 1964.

WORKS ABOUT JFK

Relations with Political Community

Review of LBJ's THE VANTAGE POINT by Michael Janeway, ATLANTIC, Feb., 1972: 48-54. Also, by Fawn Brodie in HARPER'S, April, 1977: 61-66ff.

Johnson, Sam Houston. MY BROTHER LYNDON. 1st. Cowles, 1970. The growing disaffection of Lyndon for the Kennedy clan. "My Brother Lyndon" Parts 1 and 2, LOOK, Dec.2, 16, 1969.

Kennedy, Eugene. HIMSELF! The Life and Times of Mayor Richard J. Daley. 1st, Viking, 1978. JFK's 1960 and RFK's 1968 campaigns - EMK in 1968. Acknowledges assistance of Jacqueline Onassis.

Lash, Joseph P. ELEANOR: THE YEARS ALONE. Norton (1972). Re JFK "from friendly cool to friendly warm."

Lewis, Ted. "Kennedy: Profile of a Technician." THE NATION, Feb.2, 1963: 92-94.

LIFE. "Stevenson of Illinois," July 23, 1965:22-29. Much re JFK.

Lincoln, Evelyn. KENNEDY AND JOHNSON. 1st. HR&W, 1968. States JFK's decision to drop LBJ from ticket in 1964.

McCarthy, Abigail. PRIVATE FACES/PUBLIC PLACES. D'day, 1972. The Kennedys as seen in public and private.

McCarthy, Eugene. THE HARD YEARS: A Look at Contemporary America and American Institutions. 1st. Viking, 1975. Praise for JFK.

McGovern, Eleanor, with Mary Finch Hoyt. UPHILL: A PERSONAL STORY. 1st. H-M, 1974. Close relationship with the Kennedys.

McPherson, Harry. A POLITICAL EDUCATION: A Journal of Life with Senators, Generals, Cabinet Members and Presidents. 1st. Atl/L-B 1972. JFK in 1956, 1960, his legislative program; RFK 1968.

Macridis, Roy C., ed. DE GAULLE: IMPLACABLE ALLY. H&R, 1966. The major pronouncements of De Gaulle. Relations with JFK.

Mankiewicz, Frank. PERFECTLY CLEAR: Nixon from Whittier to Watergate. Quad. 1973. Recounts slanders against the Kennedys.

Maxey, David R. "Larry O'Brien: The Pro Takes On the Post Office" LOOK, Feb.8, 1966: 31ff.

Mazo, Earl. RICHARD NIXON: A Political and Personal Portrait. 1st. Harper, 1959. RN in a positive light. Relations with JFK.

Meyer, Karl E. ed. FULBRIGHT OF ARKANSAS: The Public Positions of a Private Thinker. Luce, 1963. Qualified approval of JFK.

THE KENNEDY FAMILY OF MASSACHUSETTS

Relations with Political Community

Miller, Wm.J. HENRY CABOT LODGE. 1st. Heineman, 1967. JFK-Lodge fight for Senate, post in Vietnam. Mutual liking.

Mooney, Booth. THE POLITICIANS 1945-1960. 1st. Lippincott,1970 Different account of LBJ's second place on ticket. LBJ: AN IR-REVERENT CHRONICLE. 1st. Crowell, 1976.

Muller, Herbert J. ADLAI STEVENSON: A Study in Values. H&R,1967 JFK and AS compared and contrasted; the campaign, UN career.

NEWSWEEK. "The Kennedy Rep.ublicans." Jan.29, 1962: 20-22. "The Presidential Bug." Oct.28, 1963:17-20. Nixon vs. JFK.

Nixon, Richard M. SIX CRISES. D'day (1962). Campaign of 1960. 1st Pyramid edition, 1968. New preface and 1968 acceptance. "Great Crises in a Turbulent Political Life." LIFE in three parts Mar.16: 94-106ff; Mar.23: 86-88ff; Mar.30, 1962: 72-80ff.

O'Brien, Lawrence F. NO FINAL VICTORIES. A Life in Politics from John F. Kennedy to Watergate. D'day, 1974. 1st. Incl.RFK.

O'Connor, Len. "REQUIEM: The Decline and Demise of Mayor Daley and His Era. Contemp.1977. Relations with Kennedys.

O'Donnell, Kenneth. "LBJ and the Kennedys." LIFE,Aug.7,1970:44ff

Powell, Adam Clayton, Jr. ADAM BY ADAM. 1st. Dial, 1971. Chap. 17: "Jack Kennedy and LBJ." Also: RFK and EMK.

Prittie, Terence. ADENAUER: A Study in Fortitude. Cowles(1971) Strained relations with JFK: "He is too old and I am too young.."

Riedel, Richard L. HALLS OF THE MIGHTY. My Forty-Seven Years at the Senate. Luce(1969). Portraits of JFK, RFK, EMK.

Roosevelt, Anna Eleanor. "On My Own: of Stevenson, Truman and Kennedy." SEP, Mar.8, 1958: 32-33ff. +

Ross, Walter S. THE LAST HERO: CHARLES A. LINDBERGH. H&R,(1968) Joseph Sr. and JFK.

Schlesinger, Arthur, Jr. THE POLITICS OF HOPE. H-M (1962).

Shadegg, Stephen. CLARE BOOTHE LUCE. 1st S&S, 1970. Biography. Her friendship with JFK and his father.

Sidey, Hugh. A VERY PERSONAL PRESIDENCY: Lyndon Johnson in the White House. 1st. Atheneum, 1968.

Smith, A.Robt. THE TIGER IN THE SENATE...Wayne Morse. 1st. D'day 1962. Chapter 21. "JFK."

WORKS ABOUT JFK

Relations with Political Community

Smith, Margaret Chase. DECLARATION OF CONSCIENCE. 1st. D'day,
1972. Partisanship but growing understanding and respect for JFK

Sorensen, Theodore. THE KENNEDY LEGACY. A Peaceful Revolution
for the Seventies. 1st. Macm. 1969. JFK and RFK.

Swanberg, W.A. NORMAN THOMAS: The Last Idealist. 1st. Scribner
1976. Thomas' relations with JFK as Senator and President.

Szulc, Tad. COMPULSIVE SPY: The Strange Career of E. Howard
Hunt. 1st. Viking, 1974. A hater of JFK, forgery of telegram.

Talbot, Allan R. THE MAYOR'S GAME: Richard Lee of New Haven and
the Politics of Change. 1st H&R, 1967. Supportive of JFK.

Truman, Harry S. "They'll Never Make an Elder Statesman Out of
Me." LOOK, June 21, 1960: 93-.5ff. Adapted from MR. CITIZEN.

Truman, Margaret. HARRY S. TRUMAN. Morrow (1973). Incl. JFK.

U.S.NEWS..."What They Say About JFK: Congressmen Tell What's On
Their Minds:"31-35; "When Kennedy Meets Businessmen:"35,July 30
1962. "Did LBJ Make John Kennedy President? An Untold Story",
Jan.16, 1967: 42-46ff.

Vidal, Gore. AN EVENING WITH RICHARD NIXON. 1st. Random, 1972.
Nixon, Geo.Washington, Eisenhower and JFK.

Wallace, George. STAND UP FOR AMERICA. 1st. D'day, 1976.
Confrontation at the Univ. of Alabama and other events.

Walton, Richard J. THE REMNANTS OF POWER. The Tragic Last Years
of Adlai Stevenson. C-Mc (1968). JFK's foreign policy and AS.
                                    eds.
Watters, Pat and Stephen Gillers/ INVESTIGATING THE FBI: A
Tough, Fair Look at the Powerful Bureau...1st D'day, 1973.

Weinraub, Bernard. "Daniel Moynihan's Passage to India." NYT
MAG. Mar.31, 1974: 16ff. Reminiscences of years with JFK, RFK.

Wheeler, Keith. "Last Big Boss on U.S.Scene." LIFE, Feb.8,
1960: 138-140ff. Richard J. Daley.

White, Theodore H. BREACH OF FAITH. The Fall of Richard Nixon.
1st Atheneum, 1975. Describes the crossing of paths with JFK.

White, William S. THE PROFESSIONAL: LYNDON B. JOHNSON. H-M,1964
Presentation copy - LBJ signature.

Wicker, Tom. "Nixon Starts Over - Alone." NYT MAG.,May 13,1962:
17ff. Examples of bitterness toward JFK. JFK AND LBJ: The Influence of Personality Upon Politics. Morrow, 1968.
                    45.

Relations with Political Community

Review of JFK AND LBJ by Saul Malof in NEWSWEEK,May 27, 1968:96 -

Wighton, Chas. ADENAUER: A Critical Biography. 1st. C-McC,1964
Details of breach with JFK. JFK's triumphal visit to Berlin.

Wills, Gary. NIXON AGONISTES. 1st H-M, 1970. JFK, RFK, EMK.

Witcover, Jules. THE RESURRECTION OF RICHARD NIXON. Putnam(1970)
Relates to JFK and RFK.

Young, Donald. AMERICAN ROULETTE: The History and Dilemma of
the Vice-Presidency. 1st HR&W, 1965.

Young, Stephen M. TALES OUT OF CONGRESS. 1st Lippincott, 1964.
Some comments on JFK and his administration. P.S. on John Glenn.

Zeiger, Henry A. LYNDON B. JOHNSON: Man and President. Wrs.
Popular Library, 1963.

Relations with the Liberals

Bendinger, Robt. "Every President Has His Scapegoat." NYT MAG.,
Nov.4, 1962: 28ff. Claims JFK has Arthur Schlesinger Jr.-

Berle, Adolph. NAVIGATING THE RAPIDS 1918-1971. 1st HBJ, 1973.
Insights into the character and accomplishments of JFK.

Bevington, Helen. ALONG CAME THE WITCH: A Journal of the Sixties.
1st. HBJ, 1976. Includes reflections on JFK, RFK, EMK.

Brower, Brock. OTHER LOYALTIES: A Politics of Personality. 1st
Atheneum, 1968. Related to JFK, JBK, RFK.

Burns, Jas. MacGregor. THE DEAD-LOCK OF DEMOCRACY: Four Party
Politics in America. P-H(1963). JFK as Madisonian-Jeffersonian.

CURRENT. "The Meaning of the Life and Death of John F. Kennedy".
Jan., 1964:1-42. Reactions of 48 intellectuals to JFK.

Feiffer, Jules. "The Interview" (with JFK) HARPER'S, June 1962:
74-75
Feinberg, Barry and Ronald Kasrils eds. DEAR BERTRAND RUSSELL.
A Selection of His Correspondence ...1950-1968. H-M, 1969. 1st.
Some letters: his personal critical opinion of JFK.

Fishwick, Marshall. THE HERO AMERICAN STYLE. Changing Ideas of
Greatness from John Smith to John Kennedy. McKay (1969). Also RFK

Grennan, Jacqueline. WHERE I AM GOING. McG-H 1st, 1968. Contains
unusual anecdotes of JFK.

WORKS ABOUT JFK

Relations with the Liberals

Hemingway, Mary Walsh. HOW IT WAS. Wrs. 1st Ballantine, 1977. Ernest's opinion of JFK. JFK Library recipient of H. papers.

Hofstadter, Richard. ANTI-INTELLECTUALISM IN AMERICAN LIFE. Wrs. Vintage, 1963. JFK: combination of character and intellect.

Kadushin, Chas. THE AMERICAN INTELLECTUAL ELITE. 1st L-B, 1974. Gives climate re Vietnam in Kennedy years.

Kraft, Joseph. "Washington Insight: Kennedy and the Intellectuals." HARPER'S, Nov.1963: 112ff.

Lasch, Christopher. THE NEW RADICALISM IN AMERICA 1889-1963. The Intellectual as a Social Type. 1st Knopf, 1965. JFK's place.

MacLeish, Archibald. A CONTINUING JOURNEY: Essays and Addresses H-M (1967). "Robt.Frost and JFK": 299-306.

Mailer, Norman. THE PRESIDENTIAL PAPERS OF NORMAN MAILER. 1st Bantam, 1964. Wrs. Instructions to JFK as to his role.

Morison, Samuel Eliot. THE OXFORD HISTORY OF THE AMERICAN PEOPLE Oxford U. (1965). From prehistoric man to assassination of JFK.

Morris, Richard B., ed. ENCYCLOPEDIA OF AMERICAN HISTORY, enl. and updated. H&R (1970). Cf. biographical section.

Neill, Thos. "Can a Catholic Be a Liberal?" SIGN,Jan.1961:20ff.-

NEW REPUBLIC. "Kennedy and the Liberals," by Seymour Harris. June 1, 1963: 15-16 - plus editorial on Harris' article.+

Panichas, Geo.A. ed. THE POLITICS OF 20TH CENTURY NOVELISTS. 1st Hawthorn, 1971. Steinbeck and Styron re JFK; Baldwin,RFK.

Pepper, Curtis Bill. "The Truth about Gore Vidal - Right From Gore Vidal." VOGUE, Dec.1974:176ff. Remarks on Kennedys.

Reeve, F.D. "Robert Frost Confronts Khrushchev." ATLANTIC, Sept. 1963: 33-39. The result of JFK's invitation.

"Schlesinger (Arthur, Jr.) at the White House. An Historian's Inside View of Kennedy at Work." A conversation with Henry Brandon. HARPER'S, July, 1964:55-60. -

Shannon, Wm.V. "Washington Report: the President (LBJ) and the Intellectuals." COMMONWEAL, Dec.27, 1963:386-7.- Contrast JFK. "Controversial historian of the Age of Kennedy." (Arthur Schlesinger Jr.) N.Y.T.MAG. Nov.21, 1965:30-31ff.

Relations with the Liberals

Steinbeck, John. A LIFE IN LETTERS, edited by Elaine Steinbeck and Robt. Wallsten. 1st Viking, 1975. Correspondence with JFK,JBK

Truman, Margaret. WOMEN OF COURAGE. 1st Morrow, 1976. Comparison with PROFILES IN COURAGE.

Udall, Stewart L. "...And Miles To Go Before I Sleep." Robert Frost's last adventure. NYT MAG., June 11, 1972: 18-19ff.

Vidal, Gore. ROCKING THE BOAT: A Political, Literary and Theatrical Commentary. 1st L-B, 1962. JFK: 3-14, 281-282. REFLECTIONS UPON A SINKING SHIP. 1st L-B, 1969. "The Holy Family:"160-182; "The Manchester Book:" 183-188.

Relations with the Right

Archer, Jules. THE EXTREMISTS: GADFLYS OF AMERICAN SOCIETY. 1st Hawthorn, 1969. Re JFK, RFK: Chap.16 "Extremism in the Sixties."

Buckley, Wm.,Jr. THE JEWELER'S EYE. Putnam, 1968. JFK and RFK in two essays each. THE GOVERNOR LISTETH: A Book of Inspired Political Revelations. Putnam, 1970. JFK, RFK,EMK, JBK, Ethel. QUOTATIONS FROM CHAIRMAN BILL, compiled by David Franke.Arlington,1970 INVEIGHING WE WILL GO. Putnam, 1972. JFK, RFK, EMK.

Cooke, Alistair. AMERICA: A PERSONAL HISTORY OF THE UNITED STATES. Knopf, 1974. Critical comments on inaugural address.

Epstein, Benjamin R. and Arnold Foster. Report on THE JOHN BIRCH SOCIETY 1966. 1st Random, 1966. All-out drive against civil rights movement. JFK presidency as coinciding with right wing John Birch society rise to national importance.

Evans, M. Stanton. THE FUTURE OF CONSERVATISM. From Taft to Reagan and Beyond. 1st HR&W, 1969. JFK vs. Goldwater.

Foster, Arnold and Benjamin R. Epstein. DANGER ON THE RIGHT. 1st Random, 1964. Cites numerous attacks on JFK.

HUMAN EVENTS. Weekly Washington Newsletter. Jan.-June, 1961. Source book for the conservative position re JFK.+

Lasky, Victor. J.F.K.: THE MAN AND THE MYTH. Macm., 1963. Autograph. This book extensively promoted by HUMAN EVENTS.

LIFE. "The John Birch Society. Patriotic or Irresponsible, It Is a Subject of Controversy." May, 12, 1961:124-128ff. JFK, RFK. Also Editorial: "The Unhelpful Fringes:" 32.

Markman, Chas.L. THE BUCKLEYS: A FAMILY EXAMINED. Morrow, 1973. Comparison with Kennedy family.

WORKS ABOUT JFK

Relations with the Right

Moley, Raymond. THE REPUBLICAN OPPORTUNITY. 1st D.S.& P., 1962.
Advocacy of conservative position. JFK as antithesis of this.

Morrison, Chester. "The Man Behind The John Birch Society" (Robt.
Welch). LOOK, Sept.26, 1961: 23-27.

NEWSWEEK. "Birch View of JFK," Feb.24, 1964: 29-30.-

Novak, Robt.D. THE AGONY OF THE G.O.P. Macm.(1965). The right-
wing take-over of the G.O.P. Chapter 16: "Dallas."

Overstreet, Harry and Bonaro. THE STRANGE TACTICS OF EXTREMISM.
1st Norton, 1964. Includes rightists' criticism of JFK.

Schomp, Gerald. BIRCHISM WAS MY BUSINESS. 1st Macm., 1970.
Details some attacks on JFK and his administration.

Sherwin, Mark. THE EXTREMISTS: Who They Are, What They Are
Fighting, and Where They Are Leading Their Confused Adherents.
St.M's (1963). JFK and his criticism of Far Right in So.Calif.

Turner, Wm.W. POWER ON THE RIGHT. Ramparts (1971). The sixties.

Walker, Brooks R. THE CHRISTIAN FRIGHT PEDDLERS. The Radical
Right and the Churches. 1st D'day, 1964. Re JFK: 257-265.

Westin, Alan, "The John Birch Society: 'Radical Right' and "Ex-
treme Left' in the Political Context of Post World War II":239-
268; and David Riesman, "The Intellectuals and the Discontented
Classes..." 137-159 - both in THE RADICAL RIGHT, edited by Daniel Bell. Wrs. D'day Anchor, 1964. References to JFK.

Relations with the Media

ADLER, Ruth, ed. THE WORKING PRESS. NEW YORK TIMES Reporters
Tell the Story Behind the Story. Putnam,(1966). JFK election,
the debates, press conferences, death. RFK mountain climbing.

Alsop, Stewart. STAY OF EXECUTION: A Sort of Memoir. Lipp.1973
JFK and Peace Corps, the Bay of Pigs, and steroid treaments.

AMERICA. "President Meets the Press." Feb.11, 1961: 613-614.-
"Mr. Salinger 'On Security'," by Wm. Kennedy, Feb.25,1961:687.-
Editorial: "Press Responsibility." May 13, 1961: 270. -

Bagdikian, Ben H. "Television - 'the President's medium'?"
Columbian Jrnlism Rev. Summer, 1962:34-38. "The Morning Line"
(JFK's appetite for newsprint), Fall, 1962: 26-28. "The President Nonspeaks," Spring, 1963: 42-46. "Diggers and Toilers"
('stringers'in general and Sarah McLendon and Mae Craig in particular), Summer, 1963: 36-38. "Journalist meets propagandist."

THE KENNEDY FAMILY OF MASSACHUSETTS

Relations with the Media

Bagdikian, Ben (continued) Fall, 1963: 29-35. THE EFFETE CON-
SPIRACY. 1st H&R, 1972. Experience with JFK's media struggles.

Bingham, Worth and Ward S. Just. "The President and the Press,"
REPORTER, April 12, 1962: 18-23.

Bradlee, Benjamin C. CONVERSATIONS WITH KENNEDY. 1st Norton,
1975. Review by Taylor Branch HARPER'S, Oct. 1975: 36ff.

Broder, David S. THE PARTY'S OVER. The Failure of Politics in
America. 1st H&R, 1972. Chapter 2: JFK.

BUSINESS WEEK. "How Kennedy Sees the Press," June 9, 1962:30-1+

Cassini, Igor. I'D DO IT ALL OVER AGAIN. Putnam's (1977). Con-
tacts with JFK, JBK and RFK.

COLUMBIA JOURNALISM REVIEW. "News Under Kennedy: Reporting in
the First Year," Spring, 1962: 11-20. "To Tell a Columnist II"
Winter, 1963: 20. (JFK, 1961).

Cooke, Alistair. "Too Many Kennedys? The Public Face of JFK."
SHOW, April, 1963: 69-73. -

Cronkite, Walter. EYE ON THE WORLD. 1st Cowles, 1971. "Richard
Nixon is not John Kennedy..." EMK quoted re Nixon also.

Crouse, Timothy. THE BOYS ON THE BUS. Riding with the Campaign
Press Corps. 1st Random, 1973. "..a gung ho Winner's bus."

Dickerson, Nancy. AMONG THOSE PRESENT: A Reporter's View of 25
Years in Washington. 1st Random, 1976. Anecdotes of Kennedys.

Eells, Geo. HEDDA AND LOUELLA. Putnam, 1972. Touches on Hedda
Hopper's opposition to JFK and sponsorship of Richard Nixon.

Elson, Robt.T. TIME INC: The Intimate History of a Publishing
Enterprise 1941-1960. 1st Athen. 1973. JFK and Henry R. Luce.

Friedrich, Otto. DECLINE AND FALL. The Struggle for Power at
the SATURDAY EVENING POST. 1st H&R, 1970. Re JFK articles etc.

Friendly, Fred W. DUE TO CIRCUMSTANCES BEYOND OUR CONTROL. 1st
Random, 1967. Commercial television. JFK and use of TV. THE
GOOD GUYS, THE BAD GUYS AND THE FIRST AMENDMENT. 1st Random1976

Golden, Harry. THE RIGHT TIME. Autobiography. Putnam (1969).
Includes association with JFK and RFK. SO WHAT ELSE IS NEW?
Putnam (1964). JFK: 228-232 and JBK:240.

Graham, Hugh D. CRISIS IN PRINT. Vanderbilt, 1967. Reaction
of Negro press to JFK and civil rights in general.

50.

WORKS ABOUT JFK

Relations with the Media

Jennings, Roger D. THE USE OF TELEVISION AS A POLITICAL TOOL BY THE PRESIDENT: 1952-1968. M.A.thesis U. of N. Carolina, 1972.

John F. Kennedy Library. "The Presidency and the Press - A Bibliography of Books" Unit #5 (draft) Resource Materials VI.

Kendrick, Alexander. PRIME TIME: The Life of Edward R. Murrow. L-B, 1969. Director of USIA under JFK.

Keogh, James. PRESIDENT NIXON AND THE PRESS. 1st F&W, 1972. Contrast with JFK.

Klurfeld, Herman. BEHIND THE LINES: The World of Drew Pearson. P-H (1968). Support for LBJ, critical of JFK.

Krock, Arthur. "Mr. Kennedy's Management of the News." FORTUNE, March, 1963:82ff. IN THE NATION: 1932-1966. 1st McG-H, 1966. Selected columns - many re Kennedy years. MEMOIRS: Sixty Years on the Firing Line. F&W, 1968. Chap.14 on the Kennedys. THE CONSENT OF THE GOVERNED. L-B, 1971. Includes Kennedy family.

Lardine, Robt. "They Loved Him on TV." RADIO TV MIRROR. 3/61:26ff.

Lawrence, Bill. SIX PRESIDENTS: TOO MANY WARS. Sat.Rev.Pr.,1972.

LIFE.   "JFK's Jolly Dodger" (Salinger), July 28, 1961: 15. "Profiles That Cast Long Shadows," Jan.22, 1965.-

LOOK. "Kennedy's Man Salinger," Dec.20, 1960:77-80. "May Craig: TV's Most Unusual Star," April 24, 1962: 109-110ff. By Eleanor Harris. "Kennedy vs. the Press," by Fletcher Knebel, 8/28/62:17ff.

Mayer, Martin. ABOUT TELEVISION. 1st H&R, 1972. JFK and TV.

Minow, Newton. EQUAL TIME: The Private Broadcaster and the Public Interest. L.Laurent ed. 1st Atheneum, 1964. JFK and the Educational TV Act of 1962, free enterprise in space, dedication. Minow with John Bartlow Martin and Lee M. Mitchell. PRESIDENTIAL TELEVISION. 1st Basic Books, 1973.

Montgomery, Ruth. HAIL TO THE CHIEFS. My Life and Times with Six Presidents. C-McC, 1970. Chaps. 21-26: the Kennedy years.

Morgan, Edw.P. CLEARING THE AIR. Luce,1963. Presentation copy. Includes comments on JFK.

Newman, Bernard. MR. KENNEDY'S AMERICA.(Ldn.) Jenkins, 1962.

Newman, Edwin. STRICTLY SPEAKING. Will America Be the Death of English? B-M, 1974. JFK on ongoing vs. adversary dialogue.

THE KENNEDY FAMILY OF MASSACHUSETTS

Relations with the Media

Newman, Larry. "John F. Kennedy" in HEROES FOR OUR TIMES, ed.by Overseas Press Club of America. Stackpole (1968).

New Republic. THE FACES OF FIVE DECADES 1914-1964. S&S, 1964. Decade Five: much about JFK.

N.Y.TIMES MAG. "When the President Goes to the People" by Andrew Hacker, June 10, 1962: 13ff.- "Kennedy as a Public Speakah" by Tom Wicker, Feb.25, 1962: 14ff.-

Pearson, Drew. DIARIES 1949-1959. Tyler Abell ed. HR&W (1974).

Pilat, Oliver. DREW PEARSON: An Unauthorized Biography. Wrs. Pocketbooks 1973. Ambivalent to JFK, strange vendetta re JBK.

Pollard, James E. THE PRESIDENTS AND THE PRESS: Truman to Johnson. 1st Public Affairs Pr. wrs. 1964. Chap.8: "Kennedy Years."

Rienow, Robt. and Leona T. THE LONELY QUEST: The Evolution of Presidential Leadership. 1st Follett, 1966. JFK and TV.

Rovere, Richard H. "Letter from Washington" (managed news.) NEW YORKER, Mar.30, 1963: 164-169.

Salinger, Pierre. WITH KENNEDY. 1st D'day, 1966. Press sec'y to JFK; another portrait of JFK and JBK. Review by Victor Newton, SIGN, Nov.1966: 63ff.- Review NEWSWEEK Sept.12,'66:110-2.-

Saudek, Robt. EIGHT COURAGEOUS AMERICANS- from TV series "Profiles in Courage." Wrs. 1st Bantam, 1965.

Schorr, Daniel. CLEARING THE AIR. 1st H-M, 1977. References to JFK, RFK, EMK. With TLS.

Shepard, Elaine. FORGIVE US OUR PRESS PASSES. P-H (1962). Re JFK in 1956 and 1960. Comments from Nasser et al re JFK.

Smith, Timothy G. ed. MERRIMAN SMITH'S BOOK OF PRESIDENTS: A White House Memoir. Norton (1972).

Stein, M.L. WHEN PRESIDENTS MEET THE PRESS. Messner (1969).

Stein, Robt. MEDIA POWER: Who Is Shaping Your Picture of the World? 1st H-M, 1972. Rich source for Kennedy media connection.

Swanberg, W.A. LUCE AND HIS EMPIRE. Scrib.(1972). 1st Dell, 1973. Wrs. Relation with JFK.

Talese, Gay. THE KINGDOM AND THE POWER. The Story of...THE NEW YORK TIMES. NAL, 1969. Editoral sniping of JFK and more.

WORKS ABOUT JFK

Relations with the Media

Thomas, Helen. DATELINE: WHITE HOUSE. 1st Macm. 1975. From the Kennedys to the Fords.

TIME. "The Press" (reactions to JFK). Jan.20, 1961: 59. "Classic Conflict: The President and the Press," Dec.14, 1962: 45-46. Includes movie magazines' treatment of JBK.-

Trohan, Walter. POLITICAL ANIMALS. 1st D'day, 1975. JFK:316-340

White, Wm.S. "Kennedy's Seven Rules for Handling the Press," HARPER'S, April, 1961: 92-97.+ THE RESPONSIBLES. How Five American Leaders Coped with Crisis:Truman, Taft, Eisenhower, JFK, Johnson. 1st H&R, 1972.

Wyckoff, Gene. THE IMAGE CANDIDATES. American Politics in the Age of Television. 1st Macm., 1968.

Relations with Religious Groups

AMERICA. "Oath of a Catholic President," Jan.19, 1957: 443.- "President at Mass," by Edw. T. Folliard, Dec.24-31, 1960:413.- "The Years Ahead," by Geo.Kelley, Jan.21, 1961:502-504. "Letter to the President," by John LaFarge, Feb.18, 1961: 670-671.- "The Church and the President," Jan.13, 1962: 461-462.- (JFK on cover.) "Mr. President, Sir!" (aid to private education), Jan.27 1962: 554.- Letters to the Editor re "The Church and the President" Mar.3, 1962:717-719.- "Church Leaders Stand Up to Be Counted," by John LaFarge. June 29, 1963: 897.-

Bellah, Robt. "Civil Religion in America" in DAEDALUS: Religion in America. Winter, 1967. JFK inaugural address and death.

Blanchard, Paul. THE IRISH AND CATHOLIC POWER. Beacon, 1953. Chap.11: "The Future of Irish Catholic Power."

Bonnell, John S. PRESIDENTIAL PROFILES: Religion in the Life of American Presidents. Westminster, 1971. JFK: 226-231.

Brogan, D.W. "The Catholic Politician," ATLANTIC, 8/62: 83-89.

Clancy, John G. APOSTLE FOR OUR TIME: Pope Paul VI. Wrs. Avon, 1963. Mention of JFK's visits with John XXIII and Paul VI.

Clark, James A. THE CHURCH AND CRISIS IN THE DOMINICAN REPUBLIC. Newman, 1966. The 1965 revolt and references to JFK.

Cogley, John. "Kennedy the Catholic." COMMONWEAL, 1/10/64:422-4-

Cunningham, Jas.F. AMERICAN PASTOR IN ROME. 1st D'day, 1966. Anecdotes include JFK and Rose.

THE KENNEDY FAMILY OF MASSACHUSETTS

Relations with Religious Groups

Cutler, John H. CARDINAL CUSHING OF BOSTON. Hawthorn, 1970.
Two chapters on relationship with Kennedy family.

Dever, Jos. CUSHING OF BOSTON. A Candid Portrait. Humphries(1965)

Douglas, Jas.W. THE NON-VIOLENT CROSS. Wrs. Macm., 1969. Critical of JFK in Cuban missile crisis.

Dulce, Berton and Edw.J.Richter. RELIGION AND THE PRESIDENCY, A
RECURRING AMERICAN PROBLEM. 1st Macm. 1962. Chaps.9- 13, on JFK.

Fitzgerald, Gordon. A CATHOLIC REBELS. Wrs. (Texas) Dallas,1962.
Re JFK "one of us is wrong."

Fuchs, Lawrence H. "A Catholic as President?" AMERICA, Sept.13
1958: 620-623.- JOHN F. KENNEDY AND AMERICAN CATHOLICISM. 1st
Meredith, 1967. Scholarly work. Review by James O'Gara in COM-
MENTARY, Nov. 1967: 105-108.

Fuller, Edmund and David E. Green. GOD IN THE WHITE HOUSE. The
Faiths of American Presidents. Crown, 1968. JFK: 219-223.

Greeley, Andrew M. THE CATHOLIC EXPERIENCE. 1st D'day, 1967.
JFK: 275-292 plus many additional references.

Hoyt, Robt. "Kennedy, Catholicism and the Presidency." JUBILEE,
Dec.1960: 12-15.-

INTERRACIAL REVIEW. "The President and the Priest" (John LaFarge)
Dec., 1963: 230-231. TLS of 1955.

Jones, Olga. CHURCHES OF THE PRESIDENTS IN WASHINGTON. Exposi-
tion, 1961. Autographed.

Knebel, Fletcher. "The Bishops vs. Kennedy." LOOK, May 23,
1961: 40ff. Letters to editor re this article July 4, 1961.-

Lally, Francis J. THE CATHOLIC CHURCH IN A CHANGING AMERICA.
1st L-B, 1962. Autographed. Contribution of JFK.

Leckie, Robt. AMERICAN AND CATHOLIC: a Narration of Their Role
In American History. 1st D'day, 1970. JFK and prejudice.

Lowell, C. Stanley. EMBATTLED WALL. Americans United (1966).
History of POAU. JFK: 53-80.

Montgomery, J.W. comp. U.S.PRESIDENTS. Their Faces and Their
Faith. Wrs. Bible Study, 1967.

Riemer, Geo. "Kennedy's Priests." GOOD HOUSEKEEPING, July,
1962: 49-51ff. Condensed in CATHOLIC DIGEST Oct.5, 1962: 16ff.

WORKS ABOUT JFK

Relations with Religious Groups

Sheerin, John. "Senator Kennedy Vetoes Aid to Catholic Schools."
CATHOLIC WORLD, April 1959: 4-7. Discussion in letters and editorial comments June, 1959: 178-179. +

SIGN. "The Kennedy I Know, Jan. 1961: 24-26ff.- Cover JFK, JBK
"Kennedy's Dozen," Feb., 1962: 28-35. Both by Paul Healy.

Stedman, Murray S. RELIGION AND POLITICS IN AMERICA. Wrs. H-B,
1964. JFK and Federal aid to education.

Streiker, Lowell D. and Gerald S. Strober. RELIGION AND THE NEW
MAJORITY. Assn., 1972. Billy Graham and relations with JFK.

TIME. "The Unlikely Cardinal" (Cushing). Aug.21, 1964:35-40.

Wicklein, John. "John Kennedy and the Catholic Issue: 1960-
1964:" 215-253 of RELIGION AND CONTEMPORARY SOCIETY ed. by Harold Stahmer, 1st Macm. 1963.

Wills, Gary. BARE RUINED CHOIRS: Doubt, Prophecy and Radical Religion. D'day, 1972. JFK: 79-98; JBK: 118-138.

Yaffe, Jas. THE AMERICAN JEWS: Portrait of a Split Personality.
1st Random, 1968. Catholics gave JFK 81% of vote, Jews, 88%.

Cf. also tape of Houston Ministers' Conference, SPEECHES op.cit.

Relations with Young People

Adler, Bill, ed. JOHN F. KENNEDY AND THE YOUNG PEOPLE OF AMERI-
CA. McKay, 1965. Compiled from letters to JFK and JBK. KIDS'
LETTERS TO PRESIDENT KENNEDY. Morrow, 1961.

Hope, Marjorie. YOUTH AGAINST THE WORLD: Contemporary Portraits
of the New Revolutionaries. 1st L-B, 1970. Mention of JFK.

Lee, Calvin B.T. THE CAMPUS SCENE: 1900-1970. McKay, 1970. Chap.
VI. "The Kennedy Ideal, 1960-1963."

Kinkead, Katherine T. WALK TOGETHER, TALK TOGETHER. The American
Field Service Student Exchange Program. Norton (1962)

TRUE STORY. "JFK Came to Our Prom," n.d. 36ff. - John Burroughs
High School in Burbank Calif., June 7, 1963. -

Cf. also Peace Corps section following under PART TWO. BOOKS
ABOUT THE KENNEDY ADMINISTRATION: FOREIGN AFFAIRS.

Social Activity

Amory, Cleveland. WHO KILLED SOCIETY? Harp.,1960. Warfare of celebrity with aristocracy in America, e.g. Kennedy family.

Baldridge, Letitia. OF DIAMONDS AND DIPLOMATS. 1st H-M, 1968. Autographed. Social secretary in Kennedy Administration.

Birmingham, Stephen. THE RIGHT PEOPLE. L-B (1968). THE RIGHT PLACES (For the Right People). 1st L-B, 1973. Incl. Kennedys.

Gibbs, Margaret. THE D.A.R. 1st HR&W, 1969. JBK and JFK criticism of this organization.

Higgins, Marguerite, and Peter Lisagor. "R.S.V.P. The White House." McCALL'S, Aug. 1962: 110ff.

Hurd, Chas. THE WHITE HOUSE STORY. 1st Hawthorn, 1966. Chaps. 18 and 19 on the Kennedys.

Kahn, E.J. Jr. "Profile: Good Manners and Common Sense - Angier Biddle Duke, Chief of Protocol of the U.S. under JFK." NEW YORKER, Aug.15, 1964: 34-36ff. -

LADIES HOME JOURNAL. "The Kennedys on Vacation, Aug.,1961: 32-37. JBK and Caroline on cover. "Perfect Little Dinners from the White House," May, 1962: 82-83ff. by Elaine Ward-Hanna.

LIFE. "Well-suited for the White House," by John L. Steele, Oct.13, 1961:29ff. JFK and RFK.- "A Brilliant Night to Remember at the White House: Nobel Winners' Party," May 11, 1962:32ff. "Cognoscenti Come to Call," May 19, 1962: 32-41. -

Lincoln, Anne H. THE KENNEDY WHITE HOUSE PARTIES. Viking, 1967.

Mesta, Perle, with Robt. Cahn. PERLE. MY STORY. 1st McG-H,1960. Vignette of JFK - brown loafers with tuxedo.

NEWSWEEK. "He Cooked for the Kennedys," (Rene Verdun) Dec.18, 1967: 17.-

N.Y.TIMES MAG. "Culture Makes a Hit at the White House," Jan.28, 1962: 9-11 ff. by Arthur and Barbara Gelb.- "A Reception at the White House," May, 13, 1962: 12-15.-

TOWN AND COUNTRY. "Who's Afraid of the Social Register?" by Ted Burke:41ff. JFK given entrance visa through marriage; Princess Radziwill deported: 96.

U.S.NEWS... "A Glimpse at Life in Today's White House," Apr.3, 1961: 63-66. -"Glamor Era in the White House," May 14,1962:68ff-

Wright, Wm. THE WASHINGTON GAME: THE SOCIAL ARENA IN THE CAPITOL... 1st Dutton, 1974. JFK and JBK "most dramatic shift."

WORKS ABOUT JFK

Personal Health

L'Etang, Hugh. THE PATHOLOGY OF LEADERSHIP. A History of Disease on 20th Century Leaders. Hawthorn, 1970. JFK: 184-188.

LIFE. "A Lady Doctor in the White House," Feb.17, 1961: 37-38.-
"Presidential Chair Rocks the Country," April 7, 1961:20-27.-
"Backache. The President Is One of 20 Million Americans..."June 23, 1961:51-53.-

Nichols, John. "President Kennedy's Adrenals." Reprint from THE JRNL. OF AMA, July 10, 1967. Re Addison's disease.

Pfister, Herbert R. "Making Your Own Kennedy Rocker." POPULAR SCIENCE, Aug. 1961: 118-122.

STATISTICAL BULLETIN Metropolitan Life. "Presidents and Their Survival," April, 1969:3-4.

Smith, Beverly, Jr. "Doctor in the White House," SEP, Oct.21, 1961:66ff.

Travell, Janet. OFFICE HOURS; Day and Night. 1st World, 1968. JFK's health, his goals for medical education, research and medical care for the aged.

Cartoons and Other Humor

Baker, Russell. NO CAUSE FOR PANIC. Lipp.,1964. 1st. Political atmostphere in Washington 1962-1964.

Birmingham, Frederic A. HOW TO SUCCEED AT TOUCH FOOTBALL. Macm. 1962. "Touch" the symbol of the New Frontier. Also RFK.

Block, Herbert. STRAIGHT HERBLOCK. 1st S&S, 1964. Eight chaps. and 80 cartoons refer to JFK.

Buchwald, Art. I CHOSE CAPITOL PUNISHMENT. 1st World, 1963. Presentation copy. "...AND THEN I TOLD THE PRESIDENT," Putnam, (1965). Also 1st Fawcett Crest wrs., May, 1966.

Hope, Bob. I OWE RUSSIA $1200. 1st D'Day, 1963. Some JFK quips.

Hoppe, Arthur. THE LOVE EVERYBODY* CRUSADE (*Except Antarcticans), 1st D'day, 1963. Humor - mostly about the Kennedys.

Levine, David. NO KNOWN SURVIVORS. 1st Gambit, 1970. Includes JFK, RFK and EMK in political cartoons.

Lewin, Leonard C. Ed. A TREASURY OF AMERICAN POLITICAL HUMOR. Delacorte (1964). Eleven pieces on JFK.

Cartoons and Other Humor

LIFE. "Seeing the Light Side of the Campaign. Famous British cartoonist, Ronald Searl, ribs the two candidates and U.S. policies," Oct.31, 1960: 76-80.- "The Champ Gate-crasher," (Stanley Berman), Mar.2, 1962: 10ff. by Bayard Hooper. "The Kennedy Mimics," Sept. 28, 1962: 129-131ff.

LOOK. Cartoon of TV News announcer: "We begin our newscast with this special bulletin: 'No Kennedy, anywhere, did anything today' - Let me repeat that." May 22, 1962:85

MAD MAGAZINE. Kennedy-Nixon cover congratulations; "The Jack Kennedy Show:" 45-48, Jan. 1961. Cover "This Issue Will Make JFK (MAD)," Oct., 1961. "A Day with JFK:" 43-47; "Famous Test Papers:" 13; "Celebrities Wallets:" 13ff., June, 1962. "Who's in Charge Here?" by Gerald Gardner, Sept. 1962: 22-23. "When Newspaper Editors Go On Vacation:" 23-24ff. Oct., 1962. "Pres. Kennedy and the Washington Crowd...:" Jan. 1963: 14-15. Wm. M. Gaines and Albert B. Feldstein. THE RIDICULOUSLY EXPENSIVE MAD. 1st World, 1969. JFK:6-14, 149; 155-59. Frank Jacobs. THE MAD WORLD OF WILLIAM A. GAINES. Wrs. Bantam, 1974.

Meader, Vaughn. Cadence Record CLP3060/Stereo CLP 25060. FIRST FAMILY. Review: "Entertainment: a Kennedy Spoof Full of 'VIGAH'," by Peter Bunzel. LIFE, Dec.14, 1962: 83-84ff. Also "Of Many Things," by Thurston N. Davis. AMERICA,Jan.19,1963:56.

NATIONAL LAMPOON. Grand Fifth Term Inaugural Issue.Feb.1977:27ff.

N.Y.TIMES MAG. "Introducing JFK To The World," Nov.25,1962:134- "Wits in the White House," by Tom Wicker, May 12,1963:82-83ff.-

Parrish, Joseph. "Off His Rocker" Chicago Tribune, 1962. Framed cartoon- 8½x10½.

West, Dick. THE BACKSIDE OF WASHINGTON. 1st D'day, 1961.

Wortsman, Gene, ed. THE NEW FRONTIER JOKE BOOK. Wrs. McFadden, 1963. Illus. Robt. Weber.

Photographic Collections, Portraits

Asano, Hachiro. FACES NEVER LIE. 1st (Tokyo) 1964. JFK:109-18.

Associated Press. THE WORLD IN 1965, 1966, 1967. 3 vols.Western Prtg. 1966, 1967, 1968. JFK, JBK, RFK, EMK and others.

Collins, Herbert R. PRESIDENTS ON WHEELS. Bonanza, 1971. JFK: 181-189. Includes Lincoln Continental later struck by bullets.

Gardner, Gerald. WHO'S IN CHARGE HERE? Pocketbooks (1962) Wrs.

WORKS ABOUT JFK

Photographic Collections, Portraits

Hoopes, Roy. WHAT THE PRESIDENT DOES ALL DAY. John Day, 1962.
Memorial edition, 1st Dell, 1964. Wrs.

Kurtzman, Harvey. WHO SAID THAT? 1st Fawcett, wrs., 1962.

LIFE. "JFK Picks a Picture for a Great Occasion," Jan.20,1961:
88-89.- "The Official Color Photograph of the President of the
United States," Mar.31, 1961.- "The Closest Look Yet at JFK,"
Apr.28, 1961:35-38ff.- Princess Grace and JFK, June 2, 1961.-
"That Many Kennedys?" July 27, 1962. "JFK and Admirers at Beach
in Santa Monica," Aug.31, 1962:2-3.- "Jackie and Mona Lisa,"
Jan.18, 1963:38-38. "Betancourt and the First Lady," Mar.1,
1963:31.- "Every President Since Lincoln Sat for the Bachrachs",
Aug.9, 1963:30B-30C. "An Image Distilled from 800 Pictures,"
Jan.3, 1964:28-31. "Henry Cabot Lodge and JFK," Mar.20, 1964:
37. "Quest for a Famous Likeness," May 8, 1964 (Commemorative
Stamp). THE BEST OF LIFE, wrs., Avon, 1975. The "best" pic-
tures from the 36 years of this magazine - includes Kennedys.

LOOK. KENNEDY AND HIS FAMILY IN PICTURES by the editors of LOOK
1963. Norman Rockwell, "New Portrait of JFK," July 14, 1964:48.
"Another Wyeth," Apr.2, 1968:56-62. Fold-out in color. Letters
to the editor re this portrait May 14, 1968:16. "The Sixties,"
by Patricia Coffin and Allen Hurlburt, Dec.30, 1969:12-31. RFK
and JBK on cover.

Lowe, Jacques. PORTRAIT: The Emergence of John F. Kennedy.
Bramhall (1961).

MODERN PHOTOGRAPHY. "The Personal Touch," winner of the White
House news photographers' association grand award for 1963,n.d.-

NBC NEWS PICTURE BOOK OF THE YEAR - 1967; 1968; 1969. 3 vols.
Crown, 1967, 1968, 1970. Many pictures of Kennedys.

NATIONAL GEOGRAPHIC. JFK and Jacques Cousteau, July, 1961:147.
JFK and Nasa's Shepard, Sept.1961:444.-

N.Y.TIMES MAG. "The Photos They Like Best," Apr.15, 1962: 48-49-
"White House Winners," Apr.22, 1962:34-35.- "When the President
Goes to the People," Aug.26, 1962:12-13. Cover: JFK with Walter
Schirra, Jr., Sept.,23, 1962. Cover: JFK and DeGaulle, June 30,
1963. "How The President Persuades Congress. A Photo Study,"
Oct.27, 1963:16-17. Cover: JFK with Sen. Dirksen. THE KENNEDY
YEARS, prepared under the direction of Harold Faber. 300 photo-
graphs. Viking, 1966. Text from the N.Y.TIMES.

NOTRE DAME (magazine). "Presentation of Laetare Medal to JFK."
Summer, 1961.

Photographic Collections, Portraits

Photographs: Campaign Poster 23"x30". JFK with Irish top hat. JFK and JBK, color, 22"x17". JFK (color) 11"x14". JFK and JBK box of 24 picture postcards. Cf. also signed photographs op.cit. Portraits: JFK and RFK watercolor print 20"x16" matted, by Alton S. Tobey. JFK original line drawing, framed 11"x14½" unsigned.

PORTRAITS OF AMERICAN PRESIDENTS. Wrs. F&W, 1974.

Saroyan, Wm. with Arthur Rothstein. LOOK AT US ETC. ETC. Cowles, 1967. Five U.S. Presidents including JFK.

Saunders, Doris E. ed. THE KENNEDY YEARS AND THE NEGRO: A Photographic Record. Johnson Publ., 1964.

Schwartz, Urs. JOHN F. KENNEDY 1917-1963. Ldn. Hamlyn, (1964)

Setley, Ruth E. JOHN WE REMEMBER YOU. Wrs. Countryside (1974.)

Shaw, Mark. THE JOHN F. KENNEDYS: A Family Album. F.S. 1964.

Shepard,Tazewell, Jr. JOHN F. KENNEDY, MAN OF THE SEA. Morrow, 1965. More than 100 photographs.

Stoughton, Cecil, Chester V. Clifton, Hugh Sidey. THE MEMORIES 1961 - JFK - 1963. 1st Norton, 1973. Review in PARADE 9/30/73.

THE THOUSAND DAYS; John F. Kennedy as President. Citadel,1964. UPI photos. Edited by Paul Ballot.

TOWN AND COUNTRY (Palm Beach Issue) March, 1974. "1930-1973 A Palm Beach Album" by Bert Morgan. JBK, JFK, EMK, Mr. and Mrs. John F. Fitzgerald, the Joseph P. Kennedys.

United Press Int'l. RETROSPECT: Photographic Review of 1963. Wrs. Ace, 1964. RETROSPECT 1965: Pictorial History of 1964. Ace,1965. THE NEWS THAT MADE THE YEAR 1966. 1st Random, 1966.

U.S.CAMERA, Tom Maloney, ed. U.S.CAMERA'62. 1st DS&P, 1961.Wrs. Presidential highlights and family: 122-129, 132-135. U.S.CAMERA INTERNATIONAL PICTURES, 1963. 1st, wrs. DS&P, 1962: 127,130-139. Ibid. 1964. 1st wrs. U.S.Camera Publ.Co., 1963. Ibid., 1965. 1st wrs., 1964: 93, 176:191. Four vols.

U.S.Capitol Historical Soc. WE THE PEOPLE: The Story of the U.S. Capitol... Wrs. Wash.D.C., 1965.

YEAR. The Picture News Annual 1961, 1961. 1964 Encyclopedic News Annual. Events of Year 1963. Two vols.

JFK's WILL

Collins, H.R. and David B. Weaver. WILLS OF THE PRESIDENTS. Comm. Ch.,1976. Robt. Farmer & Assoc. THE LAST WILL AND TESTAMENT (Of 28 famous...) Arco, 1968. JFK: 55-67.

WORKS ABOUT JFK

Astrology and "Prophetic Voices"

Cooper, Michael and Andrew Weaver. AN ASTROLOGICAL INDEX TO THE
WORLD'S FAMOUS PEOPLE. 1st D'day, 1975.

Dixon, Jeanne, with Rene Noorbergen. MY LIFE AND PROPHECIES.
Morrow (1969).

Gardner, Jeanne, as told to Beatrice Moore. A GRAIN OF MUSTARD
SEED. Trident, 1969. JFK as Senator, as President, RFK also.

Holzer, Hans. THE GHOSTS THAT WALK IN WASHINGTON. 1st D'day,
1971. The Kennedys: 15-43.

Montgomery, Ruth. A GIFT OF PROPHECY. The Phenomenal Jeanne Dixon. Morrow, 1965.

* * * * * * * * * * * * * * * * *

"The main assumption...is that the destinies
of industrial societies depend upon the actions
and ideas of their strategic elites."
                              - Suzanne Keller

"A man operates within the framework of his
times: it is the cardinal rule of biography, and
the hardest to keep."
                              - Catherine Drinker Bowen

PART TWO. WORKS ABOUT THE KENNEDY ADMINISTRATION

"The main lines of his (JFK's) Administration...
a brief and dramatic chapter in the exercise and
defense of Presidential power against the challenges of the states (Mississippi and Alabama),
the challenge of the Communists (Cuba, the Congo
and South Vietnam), the challenge of big business
(the steel crisis), and the constant challenge of
Congress (civil rights and taxes)."
                                        - James Reston

GENERAL WORKS AND BIBLIOGRAPHIES

Agronsky, Martin, et al. LET US BEGIN: the First 100 Days of the
Kennedy Administration. 1st S&S. Includes LP recording of JFK's
inaugural address and facsimile of his first draft of it.

Alsop, Stewart J.O. "White House Insiders," SEP, June 10, 1961:
19-21ff. "How's Kennedy Doing?" SEP, Sept.16, 1961: 44-45ff."Kennedy's Grand Strategy," SEP, Mar.31, 1962:11-15. "The Collapse
of Kennedy's Grand Design," SEP, Apr.6, 1963: 78-81.

Altbach, Philip G. and Robt. Graham. STUDENT POLITICS AND HIGH-
ER EDUCATION IN THE U.S. A Select Bibliography. Wrs. Harvard:
1968. Civil rights: 68-72; Peace Corps: 83.

AMERICA. "Presidential Aides," by Edw.T. Folliard. Dec.10,1960:
365.- "Washington Front: Short Honeymoon," by Folliard. Feb.18,
1961: 657.-"American Intelligence: A Second Look," by Robt. Pell
May 27, 1961: 371-373.- "Learning Process in the White House,"
by Mary McGrory. July 1, 1961:480.- Newspaper headline collage
on press coverage of JFK's first year in office. Feb.10, 1962:
611. - "The President's Serenity Sets a New Tone,"Mary McGrory,
Jan.12, 1963:34.- Editorial "Kennedy Committees." May 25, 1963:
736.-

Anderson, Patrick. THE PRESIDENT'S MEN. FDR to LBJ. 1st D'day,
1968. The Kennedy staff: 195-298.

ATLANTIC MONTHLY. "A Letter to the New President," Jan.1961:37,
by Wm.R. Mathews. "Atlantic Reports - Washington," Feb.1961:6ff
"The President's System for Getting Information, May, 1961:4ff.
"Soviet-American Relationships...the Radical Right," Feb.1962:
25-25ff.

Baltzell, E. Digby. THE PROTESTANT ESTABLISHMENT. Aristocracy
and Caste in America. Random (1964). JFK's awareness.

Barclay, Barbara. OUR PRESIDENTS. Bowmar, 1977. JFK:372-385.

GENERAL WORKS AND BIBLIOGRAPHIES

Berkley, Geo.E. THE ADMINISTRATIVE REVOLUTION. Notes on the Passing of Organization Man. 1st P-H, 1971. Technology and its influence on organizational structures. JFK's claim: problem of the
management of industrial society one of administration.

Bishop, Jim. A DAY IN THE LIFE OF PRESIDENT KENNEDY. 1st Random,
1964. JBK:"There would have to be 48 hours in a day..."

Boorstin, Daniel J. ed. AMERICAN CIVILIZATION. A Portrait from
the Twentieth Century. McG-H, 1972. Includes JFK and family.

Borch, Herbert von. THE UNFINISHED SOCIETY. A Book About America.
1st Hawthorn, 1962. Some words of praise for JFK.

Brogan, D.W. and Douglas Verney. POLITICAL PATTERNS IN TODAY'S
WORLD. Wrs. HB&W, 1963. Contains observations re JFK, respecting
the heterogeneous nature of the U.S.; plan for medical care for
aged.

Brooke, Edw. W. THE CHALLENGE OF CHANGE. 1st L-B, 1966. Crisis
in two party system.

Brooks, John. THE GREAT LEAP. 1st H&R, 1966. Years 1939-1965.
JFK as encouraging "grace and beauty," the young, the moon program.

Burby, John. THE GREAT AMERICAN MOTION SICKNESS. 1st L-B, 1971.
Transportation crisis. JFK's attempts to improve regulations.

Burns, James MacGregor. "A Size-up of Kennedy;"an interview with
his biographer, Jas. MacG. Burns. U.S.NEWS...Nov.28, 1960:72-76.-
"A New Size-up of the President;" an interview. U.S.NEWS... Dec.
4, 1961: 44-46ff. "The Four Kennedys of the First Year," N.Y.TIMES
MAG., Jan. 14, 1962: 9-11ff.- Photographic cover.

BUSINESS WEEK. "Kennedy Moves - Cautiously;" with editorial comment. Feb.4, 1961: 13-16ff.

Coughlan, Robt. "Kennedy's 'Best Men' Move Into Power." LIFE,
Feb.17, 1961: 100-102ff. - "...bright, brisk, tough Cabinet..."

Cramer, Clarence H. AMERICAN ENTERPRISE: Free and Not So Free.
1st L-B, 1972. JFK and Silver Purchase Act of 1963, balance of
payments, civil rights, immigrant quota, Common Market - more.

Crown, James Tracy and Geo. P. Penty. KENNEDY IN POWER. A Critical and Skeptical Analysis. Wrs. Ballantine, 1961.

Davenport, John. "The Priority of Politics Over Economics." FOR-
TUNE, Oct., 1962: 88-91ff.

Donald, Aida DiPace, ed. JOHN F. KENNEDY AND THE NEW FRONTIER.
Wrs. 1st H&W, 1966. Scholarly and valuable collection of essays.

Dorman, Michael. THE SECOND MAN. The Changing Role of the Vice Presidency. Delacorte, 1970. From 1787. Includes JFK-LBJ.

Edelman, Murray. THE SYMBOLIC USES OF POLITICS. U. of Ill. 1964 Brief references to the political leadership of JFK.

Freeman, Orville. WORLD WITHOUT HUNGER. Praeger, 1969. JFK's basic attitude: use of food to bring peace to the world.

Freidel, Frank. OUR COUNTRY'S PRESIDENTS. Nat'l Geog.,1966. JFK: 225-233. THE PRESIDENTS OF THE U.S. OF AMERICA. White House Historical Assn. (1964). Wrs.

Freidin, Seymour and Geo. Bailey. THE EXPERTS. 1st Macm.,1968. Critical of "super-specialists" especially the Kennedys.

Fuller, Helen. YEAR OF TRIAL: KENNEDY'S CRUCIAL DECISIONS. 1st HB&W, 1962. Important background analysis.

Gardner, Wm.E. et al. SELECTED CASE STUDIES IN AMERICAN HISTORY Vol.II. A&B, 1970. Case 14 re gun control.

Gill, Wm. J. THE ORDEAL OF OTTO OTEPKA. Arlington, 1969. JFK and RFK portrayed as his prosecutor under the Espionage Act.

Goodman, Paul. "The Devolution of Democracy," from DRAWING THE LINE, Random, 1962. Reprinted in Herbert Gold ed. FIRST PERSON SINGULAR, Dial, 1963: 101-126.

Green, Jos. Jr. "The Public Image of President Kennedy," CATHOLIC WORLD, May, 1961: 106-112. +

Haines, Aubrey B. "Champion of the New Frontier." TORCH, Feb., 1962:4-7. - JFK on cover.

HARPER'S. "The Cult of Personality Comes to the White House," by Wm. G. Carleton. Dec., 1961: 63-68. "The Kennedy Era, Stage Two: a Forecast," by John Fischer. Feb.1962: 14ff.

Harris, Richard. JUSTICE: The Crisis of Law, Order and Freedom in America. Dutton, 1970. Nixon, Mitchell vs. JFK and RFK.

Heller, Deane and David. THE KENNEDY CABINET. America's Men of Destiny. Wrs. 1st Monarch, 1961.

Hess, Stephen. AMERICA'S POLITICAL DYNASTIES from Adams to Kennedy. D'day, 1966. Kennedy family: 481-528.

Hughes, Emmet John. THE ORDEAL OF POWER. A Political Memoir of the Eisenhower Years. 1st Atheneum, 1963. How Ike and JFK differ.

GENERAL WORKS AND BIBLIOGRAPHIES

Johnson, Richard Tanner. MANAGING THE WHITE HOUSE. An Intimate Study of the Presidency. 1st H&R, 1974. Includes JFK.

Joseph, Peter. GOOD TIMES: An Oral History of America in the Nineteen sixties. Charterhouse, 1973.

Kane, Joseph Nathan. FACTS ABOUT THE PRESIDENTS: from Washington to Johnson. Wrs. Pocket Books, 1964. JFK:391-411.

Kempton, Murray. AMERICA COMES OF MIDDLE AGE. 1st L-B, 1963. Selected columns from N.Y.POST 1950-1962. Some re JFK.

Knebel, Fletcher. "What You Don't Know About Kennedy; the Human Side of Our Next President," LOOK, Jan.17, 1961: 80-82ff. "Kennedy's Decisions; How He Reaches Them," June 20, 1961:27-29.LOOK. "Kennedy and His Pals," LOOK, Apr.25, 1961: 117-118ff.

Knipe, James L. THE FEDERAL RESERVE AND THE AMERICAN DOLLAR. Chap.Hill, 1965. Chapter V. on JFK - other references.

Koenig, Louis W. THE CHIEF EXECUTIVE. HB&W (1964). Describes JFK's administrative methods and role as party leader.

Kraft, Joseph. "The Kennedy Era, State Two," HARPER'S, Feb., 1962: 29-26. "Kennedy's Working Staff," ibid. Dec.1962:29-36. "Treasury's Dillon - the Conservative Power Center in Washington," ibid. June, 1963:51-56. PROFILES IN POWER: a Washington Insight." 1st NAL, 1966. Portraits of JFK and chief advisers.

Lane, Thos.A. THE LEADERSHIP OF PRESIDENT KENNEDY. Wrs. Caxton, 1964. Bypass of the military "even in most important areas."

Lapp, Ralph E. THE NEW PRIESTHOOD. The Scientific Elite and the Uses of Power. 1st H&R, 1965. JFK 1st President to view fully the impact of science on society.

Lear, John. "The White House Summons Science to Apply the Human Equation." SAT. REV., May 5, 1962:35-39.

Lecht, Leonard A. GOALS, PRIORITIES AND DOLLARS. The Next Decade. Free Pr.(1966). JFK's position on eight goals.

Lengyel, Cornel. PRESIDENTS OF THE USA. PROFILES AND PICTURES. Wrs. Bantam, 1961. Chapter on JFK.

LIFE. "The Football Look of Kennedy's Team," Nov.21, 1960:20-21. "The Big Eleven Close Up. On the Intimate Side: Kennedy's Cabinet" Jan.6, 1961:77-84.- "The Grim New Look of Kennedy's Team," May 5, 1961: 32-33. Editorial "Kennedy's Next Three Years," Jan.5,1962: 4. "Uncle Sam's Layaway Gift Plan," Aug.3, 1962:7.- Editorials: "Wheat Controls...The Mail...JFK Deficit...,May, 10, 1963: 4. "JFK's New Garden," May 24, 1963.-

Lincoln, Evelyn. MY TWELVE YEARS WITH JOHN F. KENNEDY. McKay, 1966. ALS 11 lines. Also 1st Bantam, wrs., 1966. "My Twelve Years with Kennedy," SEP, Aug. 14, 1965:23-27ff.; Aug.28, 1965: 36-40ff.

Lippman, Walter. "Kennedy at Mid-Term." NEWSWEEK, Jan.21, 1963: 24-29. JFK on cover.

Liston, Robt.A. PRESIDENTIAL POWER: How Much Is Too Much? McG-H, 1971. Instances re JFK and Congress.

LOOK. "Life on the New Frontier." Twelve articles by Laura Berquist, Fletcher Knebel and LOOK staff on the first year of the Kennedy administration. Jan.2, 1962: 16-19ff. "Another Lincoln in the White House," by Laura Berquist, Oct.9, 1962:36-38ff."Why There's Trouble on the New Frontier," by Sidney Hyman, July 2, 1963:30ff.

McConnell, Grant. THE MODERN PRESIDENCY. Wrs. St.Martin's, 1967. Much on JFK.

Manchester, Wm. PORTRAIT OF A PRESIDENT: John F. Kennedy in Profile. L-B, 1962. 2nd copy rev. ed. L-B, 1967. 3rd, MacF. wrs.1967 "Portrait of a President," HOLIDAY, April, 1962: 76-79ff; May, 1962: 66-67ff.; June, 1962: 64-65ff.

Mann, Dean E. with W. D. Jameson. THE ASSISTANT SECRETARIES, PROBLEMS AND PROCESSES OF APPOINTMENT. 1st Brookings, 1965. 108 appointments during Truman, Eisenhower and JFK administration.

Markmann, Chas.L. and Mark Sherwin. JOHN F. KENNEDY: A SENSE OF PURPOSE. St. Martin's, (1961).

Martin, John Bartlow. ADLAI STEVENSON AND THE WORLD. 1st D'day, 1977. A.D.'s relation to JFK administration.

Maurois, Andre. AN ILLUSTRATED HISTORY OF THE UNITED STATES. Viking (1969). JFK: 273-282.

Merton, Thomas. THOMAS MERTON ON PEACE. McCall, 1971. Missile crisis, Peace Corps, shelter frenzy, MLK, letters from Ethel K.

Meyer, Frank S. THE CONSERVATIVE MAINSTREAM. Arlington, 1969. JFK: 242-254; 376-382, foreign and domestic policy.

Meyer, Karl E. THE NEW AMERICA; Politics and Society in the Age of the Smooth Deal. Basic, 1961. Focus on JFK as new president.

Mollenhoff, Clark R. WASHINGTON COVER-UP. D'day, 1962. Chaps.16, 17, Appendices D and E. 2nd copy 1st Popular Lib.,1963. Wrs.

Morganthau, Hans J. "'Alone with Himself and History,'" N.Y.T. Mag. Nov.13, 1960: 25ff. -

Morgenthau, Hans J. TRUTH AND POWER. Essays of a Decade 1960-1970. Praeger, 1970. The philosophy, the men, the issues.

✓Morris, Richard B. GREAT PRESIDENTIAL DECISIONS. State Papers that Changed the Course of History. Lipp.,1967. JFK and brink of thermonuclear war, detente with Russia, civil rights.

NATION. "Kennedy's First Year," by James MacGregor Burns. Jan.6, 1962: 14-15. Review of five books on Kennedy. Also Indices to vols. 194, 196, 197: Jan.-June, 1962; Jan-June, July-Dec., 1963.

NEW REPUBLIC. "Kennedy's Men," Dec.26, 1960: 3-6. "The Testing of Kennedy," by Sidney Hyman, Oct.2, 1961: 11-14. "Proper Bostonian," by Louis J. Halle, Dec.11, 1961: 9-10. "Criticisms of Kennedy" T.R.B. from Washington, May 18, 1963: 2.

NEWSWEEK. "Kennedy's Washington - a Special Section,"Jan.30, 1961: 15-29. "'New Frontier' Special Section," Jan.23, 1961: 15-32. JFK on cover. "Fast Action on the New Frontier," Feb.1961: 17- 27. "The Big Changes Begin - At Home and Abroad," Feb.13, 1961: 23-26ff. "JFK and His Critics," July 16, 1962: 15-20. "'Voyage, Travel, Change of Place...'" June 17, 1963: 21-22."JFK in the 'Bully Pulpit'," June 24, 1963: 27-28.- "The President: Frosty Philly," Nov.11, 1963: 37ff.

N.Y.TIMES MAG. "Twelve Men Close to Kennedy," by Russell Baker, Jan.22, 1961: 6-7. JFK on cover. "A Day with John F. Kennedy," Feb.19, 1961: 10-13. JFK on cover. "Inside the Kennedy 'Kitchen Cabinet .'" March, 5, 1961: 27ff.- "Washington's No.1 Hostess: Dame Rumor," by Edw. P. Morgan, Feb.11, 1962: 29ff.- "Letters from the People," by Alvin Shuster, April 1, 1962: 96ff.- "JFK Touch in Office Decor," April 8, 1962: 38-39.- "Total Political Animal," by Tom Wicker, April 15, 1962: 26ff.- "Kennedy in '64. The Historic Odds," by Sidney Hyman, July 15, 1962: 9ff.- "President's Pal"(Dave Powers), by Alvin Shuster, Dec.2,1962:47ff.- "Appraisal of Kennedy as World Leader," by Louis J. Halle, June 16, 1963:7ff.- "How Mr. Kennedy Gets the Answers," by Sidney Hyman, Oct.20, 1963:17ff.- "The Politics of the Sixties," by John Emmet Hughes, April 4, 1971:25ff.-

Nieburg, H.L. IN THE NAME OF SCIENCE. Quad.,1966. Re JFK, the problem of the growth of the scientific-milirary-industrial area.

Neustadt, Richard E. PRESIDENTIAL POWER. The Politics of Leadership. Wiley, 1961. JFK's textbook on the subject of leadership. Review by Tom Wicker, N.Y.T.Mag., Dec.18, 1960: 13.- 2nd copy with "Afterword on JFK," wrs. Wiley, 1968. Signet 1st prtg. wrs. 1964. "Size-Up of Kennedy in the White House," U.S.NEWS...July 16 1962: 60-63.+

NEW YORK TIMES Page One: Major Events 1920-1975 as Presented in
N.Y.T. Arno, 1975. Facsimiles of front pages. Kennedy stories in
33 of 42 p. selected for years 1960-1969. N.Y.TIMES INDEX for
years 1961-1964, 1966: Jan.1-Mar.15, Oct.1-Dec.31; 1967: Jan.1-31
Feb.16-Dec.31; 1968: Jan.1-July 31.

O'Neill, Wm. L. COMING APART. An Informal History of America in
the 1960's. 1st Quad.,1971.

Opowtowsky, Stan. THE KENNEDY GOVERNMENT. Wrs. Popular Lib.1961.

Paper, Lewis J. THE PROMISE AND THE PERFORMANCE: The Leadership
of JFK. Crown, 1975.

Peters, Charles and Thomothy J. Adams. INSIDE THE SYSTEM. A
WASHINGTON MONTHLY Reader. Praeger, 1970. Selection of articles
  by Broder, Moyers, Barber, Bell on JFK.

Podhoretz, Norman. MAKING IT. Random, 1967. E.g. JFK and RFK

Price, Don K. THE SCIENTIFIC ESTATE. Belknap (1960). JFK and
oceanography, Office of Science and Tech., support of research.

PROGRESSIVE, Vol.25, 1961. Re JFK, eight articles, 11 editorials

Reston, James. SKETCHES IN THE SAND. Knopf, 1967. Ten portraits
of JFK, one of RFK.

Rose, Richard. PEOPLE AND POLITICS: Observations Across the Atlantic. Basic, 1970. JFK on Cuba, voting rights, F.E.P.C. etc.

Rostow, W.W. THE DIFFUSION OF POWER 1957-1972. 1st Macm, 1972.
Kennedy Administration: 133-302.

Rovere, Richard H. "The Loneliest Place in the World," AMERICAN
HERITAGE, Aug. 1964:28-32. Much about JFK. Special Issue.

Roy, Ralph Lord. "Conflict from the Communist Left and the Radical Right," in RELIGION AND SOCIAL CONFLICT, Robt.Lee and Martin
E. Marty eds. Oxford, 1964: 55-68. JFK and this conflict.

SAT. EVE. POST. "Dear Mr. President," by Robt. Cahn, July 29,
1961: 26-27ff. Report on the President's mail.+ "Help Wanted
in Washington," June 2, 1962:34-38, by Don Oberdorfer. "The Momentous Year of 1962," editorial, Dec.22-29, 1962:76.

Schauinger, J. Herman. PROFILES IN ACTION: ACTION: American
Catholics in Political Life. Bruce (1966). Chap.11 - JFK.

Schwartz, Abba P. THE OPEN SOCIETY. 1st Morrow, 1968. Battle
for JFK's program for the free movement of people and ideas by
the Assistant Sec'y of State in charge of immigration, refugee
and travel control policies.

GENERAL WORKS AND BIBLIOGRAPHIES

Segal, Ronald. THE AMERICANS: A CONFLICT OF CREED AND REALITY. 1st Viking, 1969. Critique of Kennedy-Johnson years. THE RACE War: The World-Wide Clash of White and Non-White. 1st Viking,1967. Re JFK: Cuba, racist judges, violence following assassination.

Shannon, David A. TWENTIETH CENTURY AMERICA. The U.S. Since the 1890's. R.McN, 1963. Continues through first years of JFK.

Sidey, Hugh. "A Notable Kennedy Week..." LIFE, Dec.19, 1960:29ff.

SIGN. "The President's Question: Are the American People Willing To Do What Must Be Done? June, 1961:34.-

Smith, Malcolm E. Jr. KENNEDY'S 13 GREAT MISTAKES IN THE WHITE HOUSE. Nat'l Forum...,1968.

Smith, Merriman. THE GOOD NEW DAYS. B-M, 1963. "Frontiersmen."

Sobel, Lester A. ed. FACTS ON FILE NEWS YEAR 1960. 1st, 1961. JFK presidential campaign, cabinet members, appointments, program.

Sorensen, Theodore C. DECISION-MAKING IN THE WHITE HOUSE. Columbia, 1963. Under "JFK Forewords" op.cit.

Sparks, Will. "WHO TALKED TO THE PRESIDENT LAST?" 1st Norton, 1971. Some allusions to Kennedy years.

Stone, I.F. POLEMICS AND PROPHECIES 1967-1970. 1st Random, 1970. Among 65 articles and essays, several on JFK.

Sundquist, James L. "Politics and Policy in the Kennedy-Johnson Era" in POLITICS AND SOCIETY IN AMERICAN HISTORY ed. by James M. Smith. Wrs. 1st P-H, 1973.

Tanzer, Lester, ed. THE KENNEDY CIRCLE. 1st Van Rees, 1961.

TIME. "The President-Elect," Jan.2, 1961:13-15. - "The Presidency - Seasonal Sum-Up," Apr.14, 1961: 25-27.- "The Presidency: Subtle Changes," Sept.15, 1961: 23-24. "The Presidency," Oct.13, 1961: 23-24.- "The Nation," Nov.3, 1961: 13-19.- "Man of the Year," Jan.5, 1962: 9-16. Cover portrait of JFK.- "The Presidency," Mar.29, 1963: 13-14.

TIME-LIFE BOOKS eds. "This Fabulous Century," Vol.VII. 1960-1970 JFK, JBK, RFK, Ethel.

Truman,Margaret. WHITE HOUSE PETS. McKay, 1969. Chap.15: "More Pets than Kennedys."

U.S.A. 1. "JFK's World" (editorial), April 7, 1962: 22-23. First issue of this national monthly magazine.

THE KENNEDY FAMILY OF MASSACHUSETTS

U.S. NEWS... "Problems the Next President Will Face," "The Idea
Men Around Kennedy," Dec.5, 1960: 44-48, 50-53.+ "As Kennedy
Heads for the Change-Over" Dec.19, 1960:33-34ff. "As Kennedy
Takes Over," Jan.23, 1961: 37-49. "Start of a New Era?" Jan.30,
1961: 27-39. "How Kennedy Works," Mar.6, 1961: 40-49.- "The Kennedy Score After Six Months," July 31, 1961: 26-31. "How Kennedy
Looks to the World Now," Sept.18, 1961: 64-68. "How Kennedy Runs
the White House," Nov.13, 1961: 54-57. "Kennedy's Strategy for Win-
ning Elections," Feb.12, 1962: 74-75. "Kennedy Family's Travels,"
April 2, 1962: 66-67.- "The Kennedy 'Image' - How It's Built,"
Apr.9, 1962: 56-59.- "The Richest President..." June 18, 1962: 82-
84.- "Advisers at the White House," June 25, 1962: 40-42. "Power
of the Kennedy Brothers," July 16, 1962: 56-59. "Kennedy's First
Eighteen Months," July 23, 1962: 39-43. "Promises and Performances
- Two Views of the Kennedy Record," by Charles H.Percy and Chester
Bowles, Oct.29, 1962:112-118.- "The White House at Work," Dec.24,
1962:26-30. "As Kennedy Looks at U.S. and World," Jan.14, 1963:
35-38.+ "Kennedy's Big Week," Jan.28, 1963: 29-34.+ "One Week
With the President," May 13, 1963: 48-52.+ "Is Kennedy in Political Trouble at Home?" July 8, 1963: 38-40.- "Kennedy's Strategy
for the '64 Elections," Aug.19, 1963: 34-36.+

Vinyard, Dale. THE PRESIDENCY. Scrib.,1971. Incl. assessment JFK.

Wallace, Henry A. THE PRICE OF VISION. The Diary of...1942-1946,
John M. Blum ed. 1st H-M, 1973. JFK and RFK ideas presaged by Wallace in 1940's.

Warren, Sidney. "How Powerful is the Presidency?" SAT.REV., July
21, 1962: 12-15.

Weaver, John D. THE GREAT EXPERIMENT. An Intimate View of the Ev-
eryday Workings of the Federal Gov't. 1st L-B, 1965.

Wenk, Edw.Jr. THE POLITICS OF THE OCEAN. U. of Wash.,1972. JFK:
66-85. Proposal for national program on oceanography.

White, Theodore H. "Does He Drive or Is He Driven? Dean Rusk..."
LIFE, June 8, 1962: 72-76ff.-

White, William S. THE RESPONSIBLES: Truman, Taft, Eisenhower,
JFK, Johnson. 1st H&R, 1972. Ambivalent, didactic on JFK.

Whitney, David C. THE AMERICAN PRESIDENTS. D'Day (1967). JFK:
321-332, student, author, war-hero, president.

Weisner, Jerome B. WHERE SCIENCE AND POLITICS MEET. McG-H, 1965.
Author: scientific advisor to JFK. Valuable insights to Kennedy.

Wildavsky,Aaron, ed. THE PRESIDENCY. L-B, 1969. JFK material
included in concepts of role, personality, power.

FOREIGN AFFAIRS IN GENERAL

Wildavsky, Aaron. "The Two Presidencies," in THE POLITICS OF U.S. FOREIGN POLICY MAKING, Douglas M. Fox ed. Goodyear, 1971:175-185. Examples of JFK in domestic vs. foreign policies.

Wittner, Lawrence S. COLD WAR AMERICA. From Hiroshima to Watergate. Praeger, 1974. Wrs. Chap.8: JFK, Chap.10: RFK.

FOREIGN AFFAIRS IN GENERAL

Allen, Steve, Wm. Buckley et al. DIALOGUES ON AMERICANISM. Regnery, 1964. Debate on JFK's foreign policy: 11-63.

Ball, George. THE DISCIPLINE OF POWER: Essentials of a Modern World Structure. L-B, 1968. Kennedy-Johnson period.

Barnet, Richard J. THE ROOTS OF WAR. 1st Atheneum, 1972. The national security managers and JFK and other incidents.

Barraclough, Geoffrey. AN INTRODUCTION TO CONTEMPORARY HISTORY. Basic, 1964. "Contemporary" history begins with JFK presidency.

Bartlett, Ruhl. POLICY AND POWER. Two Centuries of American Foreign Relations. Hill & Wang, 1969. JFK in context of history.

Bowles, Chester. "The Foreign Policy of Senator Kennedy," AMERICA Oct.15, 1960: 69-73.-

Brandon, Donald. "Kennedy's Record in Foreign Affairs," CATHOLIC WORLD, July, 1962: 219-227.+

Brown, Seyom. THE FACES OF POWER. Constancy and Change in U.S. Foreign Policy from Truman to Johnson. Columbia,1968.

Bundy, McGeorge. "The Presidency and Peace," FOREIGN AFFAIRS, Apr.,1964: 353-365. Focus on the years of JFK.

Carleton, Wm. G. THE REVOLUTION IN AMERICAN FOREIGN POLICY: Its Global Range. Random, 1963. Wrs. JFK as promoter of foreign aid, relations with our allies, Russia.

Evans, M. Stanton. THE POLITICS OF SURRENDER. Devin-Adair, 1966. Illustrates how the conservatives viewed JFK.

Fitzsimons, Louise. THE KENNEDY DOCTRINE. 1st Random, 1972. An example of "revisionism" i.e. JFK as never questioning cold war's basic ideology, transforming containment into counterinsurgency.

Freeman, Harrop and Ruth. DEAR MR. PRESIDENT: An Open Letter on Foreign Policy. 1st ltd. 1000c. N.P. 1961. Assesses accomplishments in first six months.

71.

Fulbright, J.Wm. THE CRIPPLED GIANT. American Foreign Policy and Its Domestic Consequences. 1st Random, 1972. Kennedy years contrasted with the Nixon era.

Goldwater, Barry. WHY NOT VICTORY? A Fresh Look at American Foreign Policy. McG-H, 1962. Critical of JFK.

Hilsman, Roger. TO MOVE A NATION: The Politics of Foreign Policy in the Administration of John F. Kennedy. 1st D'day, 1967.
THE CROUCHING FUTURE: International Politics and U.S. Foreign Policy. 1st D'day, 1975. Author: member of State Department under JFK.

Horowitz, David. THE FREE WORLD COLOSSUS. A Critique of American Foreign Policy in the Cold War. H&W, 1965.

LIFE. "America's New President Deals With the Tough Guys of Europe, DeGaulle and Krushchev," by David Snell. June 9, 1961: 42-49. State visit of JFK and JBK to Paris and Vienna. Editorial: "For a Year's Foreign Policy: 'A' for JFK," April 13, 1962: 4.

Lindbergh, Anne Morrow. THE FLOWER AND THE NETTLE. Diaries and Letters 1936-1939. 1st H.B.& J., 1976. Lindberghs meet Kennedys.

Lippman, Walter. CONVERSATIONS WITH WALTER LIPPMAN. 1st L-B,1965. Contains many references to and evaluations of JFK.

Mallory, Walter H. ed. POLITICAL HANDBOOK AND ATLAS OF THE WORLD. H&R (1963). Background for political events in all countries with independent governments - colonies and territories not included.

May, Ernest R. 'LESSONS' OF THE PAST. The Use and Misuse of History in American Foreign Policy. 1st Oxford, 1973.

NBC Overseas News Correspondents. MEMO TO JFK. Putnam's, 1961. Analysis of major world problems with commentary. Cf. Chap.11 by Sander Vanocur for profile of JFK.

NBC News Documentary. American White Paper: UNITED STATES FOREIGN POLICY. 1st Random, 1967. JFK: 28-54; 114-119.

Prescott, Julian K. A HISTORY OF THE MODERN AGE. 1st D'day,1971. Book III. "JFK and the American Epoch:" 247-385.

Pullen, John. PATRIOTISM IN AMERICA: A Study of Changing Devotions 1770-1970. Amer. Heritage, 1971. JFK and moral grounds.

Rainey, Gene E. ed. CONTEMPORARY AMERICAN FOREIGN POLICY: The Official Voice. Wrs. 1st Merrill, 1968. JFK associates.

Rusk, Dean. "The President," FOREIGN AFFAIRS, April, 1960:353-69. Article which influenced JFK to appoint Rusk Secretary of State.

Dean Rusk. THE WINDS OF FREEDOM. Beacon Press, 1963. Selections from speeches and statements, Ernest K. Lindley editor. "The Questions of Peace on Earth, " LADIES H.J., Dec.1962: 14ff. THE MAKING OF FOREIGN POLICY. Wrs. Dept. of State 7658, 1964.

Sheerin, John. "President Kennedy's Foreign Policy," CATHOLIC WORLD, Feb.1961: 260-263.+

Shepherd, Geo.W. ed. RACIAL INFLUENCES ON AMERICAN FOREIGN POLICY. Basic, 1970. JFK: 37, 101, 176.

Stebbins, Richard P. THE UNITED STATES IN WORLD AFFAIRS, 1962. 1st H&R, 1963. Major events, maps, cartoons.

Stebbins, Richard P., ed. with Elaine P. Adams. DOCUMENTS ON AMERICAN FOREIGN RELATIONS 1963. 1st H&R, 1964.

Spanier, John W. AMERICAN FOREIGN POLICY SINCE WORLD WAR II. Wrs. Praeger, 1962. Includes the Kennedy administration.

Steel, Ronald. PAX AMERICANA. 1st Viking, 1967. JFK on Cuba, etc.

U.S. Congress. House of Representatives. FOREIGN APPROPRIATIONS FOR 1962. Hearings...Subcommittee... 87th Congress, 1st sess. Pt. 2. Wrs. G.P.O. 1961.

Waitley, Douglas. THE WAR MAKERS. Luce, 1971. JFK: Chapter 14.

Walton, Richard J. COLD WAR AND COUNTER REVOLUTION: The Foreign Policy of John F. Kennedy. "An anti-Kennedy revisionist judgment" according to Richard J. Whalen. Viking, 1972.

Warren, Sidney. THE PRESIDENT AS WORLD LEADER. 1st Lipp.,1964. JFK: Chapter 22.

Weintal, Edw. and Chas. Bartlett. FACING THE BRINK: An Intimate Study of Crisis Diplomacy. Scrib. (1967). Five international crises since World War II. JFK as seeking out in Southeast Asia.

Wilcox, Francis O. CONGRESS, THE EXECUTIVE AND FOREIGN POLICY. 1st H&R, 1971. JFK and congressional assertiveness.

Yost, Charles W. THE CONDUCT AND MISCONDUCT OF FOREIGN AFFAIRS. Reflections on U.S.Policy Since World War II. 1st Random, 1972. FDR through Nixon administration. Appraisal of JFK - "one with a conscience, a will and a heart;" "military predispositions;" "ambivalent about Vietnam;" "by nature an activist;" "growing fast when he died:" 69-72. Examples of these traits throughout.

FOREIGN AFFAIRS IN PARTICULAR COUNTRIES

Africa

Attwood, William. "A Preview of Kennedy's Foreign Policy." LOOK, Jan.31, 1961: 27-29. THE REDS AND THE BLACKS, 1st H&R, 1967. African policy positions of Kennedy developed.

Mboya, Tom. FREEDOM AND AFTER. 1st L-B, 1963. Autobiography. Includes relations with JFK.

Morrow, John H. FIRST AMERICAN AMBASSADOR TO GUINEA. Rutgers,1968 Describes Guineans'response to JFK - glimpses of RFK and EMK.

Rivkin, Arnold. AFRICA AND THE WEST. Elements of Free World Policy. Wrs. Praeger, 1962. JFK's position as Senator and President.

Arab-Israel

Bar-Zohar, Michael. BEN-GURION: The Armed Prophet. 1st P-H, 1968 Includes correspondence with JFK who sought solution to refugee problem.

Copeland, Miles. THE GAME OF NATIONS: The Amorality of Power Politics. S&S, 1969. Concentration on Middle East, JFK and Nasser.

Greenspun, Hank, with Alex Pelle. WHERE I STAND. The Record of a Reckless Man. McKay, 1966. Gun-runner for Israel, pardoned by JFK.

Heikal, Mohammed H. THE CAIRO DOCUMENTS: The Inside Story of Nasser and His Relationship with World Leaders, Rebels and Statesmen. 1st D'day, 1973. JFK: Chapter VI.

Lilienthal, Alfred. WHAT PRICE ISRAEL. Regnery, 1953. Short reference to JFK: 103-105 re Menachem Begin. THE OTHER SIDE OF THE COIN: An American Perspective of the Arab-Israeli Conflict. Devin-Adair, 1965. JFK: 298-305, 319-322, 306-309 and references.

Polk, William R. THE UNITED STATES AND THE ARAB WORLD. Harvard, 1965. By member of Policy Planning Council of Dept. of State.

Australia

Menzies, Robt. AFTERNOON LIGHT. 1st C-McC, 1968. JFK: 142-148.

Canada

LIFE. "Kennedy's...in Canada," May, 26, 1961: 16-21. JBK on cover.

McLin, Jon B. CANADA'S CHANGING DEFENSE POLICY 1957-1963. The Problems of a Middle Power in Alliance. J.Hopkins, 1967. Mutual distrust between JFK and Canadian Prime Minister Diefenbaker.

FOREIGN AFFAIRS IN GENERAL

Canada

Purdy, Al. THE NEW ROMANS: Candid Canadian Opinions of the U.S. 1st St. Martin's, 1968. To JFK: strong ambivalence, favorable.

Finland

Jakobson, Max. FINNISH NEUTRALITY: A Study of Finnish Foreign Policy Since the Second World War. Praeger, 1969. JFK's respect for Finland's chosen course.

India and Pakistan

Adams, Joey. ON THE ROAD FOR UNCLE SAM. Geis, 1963. Good-will tour in 1962 on JFK's Cultural Exchange Program. Attitudes to U.S.

Galbraith, John K. AMBASSADOR'S JOURNAL: A Personal Account of the Kennedy Years. 1st H-M, 1969. Includes JBK's visit to India. Review by Alex Cambell, NEW REPUBLIC, Oct.25, 1969: 23-24ff.

Hangen, Wells. AFTER NEHRU, WHO? 1st H.B.& W.,1963. Contains JFK's relations with India's leaders.

Hutheesing, Krishna Nehru, with Alden Hatch. WE NEHRUS. H.R.& W. 1967. Describes visit with Sen.JFK and JBK in 1956; JBK in 1962.

Khan, Ayub Mohammad. FRIENDS NOT MASTERS: A Political Autobiography. Oxford, 1967. Events in Pakistan. Detailed account of meetings with JFK and correspondence.

LIFE. "What's So Funny? Ask Nehru." Nov.17, 1961: 4-5.

N.Y.TIMES MAG. Letter to Editor re JFK in India by B.S. Achar, June 6, 1965:94.-

Japan

Reischauer, Edwin O. JAPAN: PAST AND PRESENT. Knopf, 1969. Includes JFK's trade agreement and recognition of sovereignty by Japan over the Ryukyas.

Riesman, David and Evelyn. CONVERSATIONS IN JAPAN: Modernization, Politics and Culture. Has insight into opinion of JFK.

Latin America

Aitken, Thomas,Jr. POET IN THE FORTRESS: Luis Munoz Marin. 1st NAL-W., 1964. JFK and relations with Puerto Rican Governor.

Bosch, Juan. THE UNFINISHED EXPERIMENT. Democracy in the Dominican Republic. Praeger, 1964. Admiration for JFK. PENTAGONISM: A Substitute for Imperialism. 1st Grove, 1968. Relates to JFK.

Latin America

Clark, Gerald. THE COMING EXPLOSION IN LATIN AMERICA. McKay,1963
Explores attitude of JFK in U.S. policy.

Crassweller, Robt. D. THE CARIBBEAN COMMUNITY. Changing Society
and U.S. Policy. Praeger, 1972. JFK and origin of Regional Development Act; EMK and plea not to limit immigration in hemisphere.

Eisenhower, Milton S. THE WINE IS BITTER: U.S. and Latin America.
D'day (1963). Includes policy of JFK administration.

Gerassi, John. THE GREAT FEAR: The Reconquest of Latin America by
Latin Americans. 1st Macm.,1963. Critical of JFK's Alliance for
Progress.

LaFeber, Walter. THE PANAMA CANAL. The Crisis in Historical Perspective. Oxford, 1978. Refers to JFK's Alliance program.

Levinson, Jerome and Juan De Onis. THE ALLIANCE THAT LOST ITS WAY.
Quad.,1970. Includes initial democratic ideals of JFK.

Lieywen, Edwin. GENERALS VS. PRESIDENTS: Neomilitarism in Latin
America. Praeger, 1964. JFK: Chapter 7.

LIFE. "JFK and the Latins Talk and Russians Wonder Why," Sept. 29
1961: 56. "Cheers for the President in Caracas..." Jan.5, 1962:
30-31. "Brim Full of Bienvenido for Kennedy," July 13, 1962:22-
27. JFK and JBK in Mexico. Editorial. Latin America"The Most
Critical Area in the World," Feb.22, 1963: 4B. "JFK Stars in a
New Common Market," Mar.29, 1963: 26-35.- Editorial: "The Senate
Must Save 'Alianza.'" Sept. 27, 1963: 8.

Mander, John. THE UNREVOLUTIONARY SOCIETY: The Power of Latin American Conservatism in a Changing World. 1st Knopf, 1969. JFK's
distaste for military regimes.

Martin, John Bartlow. OVERTAKEN BY EVENTS. 1st D'day, 1966.
Events following assassination of Trujillo in Dominican Republic.
Relationship with JFK and RFK.

Matthews, Herbert L. A WORLD IN REVOLUTION. 1st Scrib., 1971.
Evochs JFK's constructive interest in Latin America.

Morrison, de Lesseps S. LATIN AMERICAN MISSION. 1st S&S, 1965.
By U.S. Ambassador to Organization of American States under JFK.

Petras, James F. and Robt. LaPorte. CULTIVATING REVOLUTION: The
U.S. and Agrarian Reform in Latin America. 1st Random, 1971. Three
case studies in 60's. JFK, the Alliance and agrarian reform.

Pflaum, Irving P. ARENA OF DECISION: Latin America in Crisis.
P-H, 1964. Includes JFK administration and Argentina, Brazil,
Cuba, Dominican Republic, Ecuador, Panama Canal Zone, Latin Am-
erican policy. Presentation copy.

FOREIGN AFFAIRS IN GENERAL

Latin America

Radler, D.H. EL GRINGO. The Yankee Image in Latin America. 1st Chilton, 1962. Critical of JFK and Peace Corps.

Radosh, Ronald. AMERICAN LABOR AND U.S. FOREIGN POLICY. The Cold War in the Unions from Gompers to Lovestone. 1st Random, 1969. JFK and involvement of American labor in Latin America.

Romualdi, Serafino. PRESIDENTS AND PEONS: Recollections of a Labor Ambassador in Latin America. F&W, 1967. The Alliance for Progress and its great potential; JFK and support for labor unions.

Skidmore, Thos. E. POLITICS IN BRAZIL 1930-1964: An Experiment in Democracy. Oxford, 1967. JFK: Chaps. 6-8 and Appendix.

Tannenbaum, Frank. TEN KEYS TO LATIN AMERICA. 1st Knopf, 1962. JFK as bringing scholar and writer back into public and diplomatic life and his support for democracy against dictators.

U.S.Congress, Senate. 91st Congress - 1st Sess. Doc. #91-17. SURVEY OF THE ALLIANCE FOR PROGRESS. Compilation of Studies and Hearings of the Subcommittee on American Republics Affairs of the Committee on Foreign Relations, April 29, 1969. Wrs. N.B. "Columbia - A Case History of U.S.Aid," by Ellen O Schwarz for the first program loan in April, 1962: 659-865.

VENEZUELA UP-TO-DATE, Spring, 1963. Cover photo JFK and Betancourt.

Wagley, Chas. ed. SOCIAL SCIENCE RESEARCH ON LATIN AMERICA. Columbia, 1964. Public interest stimulated by Alliance for Progress.

Wallace, Lucy H. THE INCREDIBLE CITY (Real de Catorce, Mexico). Amigo, 1965. Frontisp. JFK and Lopez Mateos.

Withers, Wm. THE ECONOMIC CRISIS IN LATIN AMERICA. Free Pr.,1964. Critical of JFK's "overemphasis" on social development.

NATO Countries - The Common Market

Archer, Jules. UNEASY FRIENDSHIP: FRANCE AND THE UNITED STATES. Four Winds, 1972. DeGaulle as admiring JFK but not LBJ.

Aron, Raymond. "DeGaulle and Kennedy: the Nuclear Debate," ATLANTIC, Aug., 1962: 33-38.

ATLANTIC. Report on Washington. "JFK and DeGaulle," June'61:4ff.

AVE MARIA. "The Editor's Desk" by John Reedy. Aug.12, 1961:2.- JFK's address to the nation on the Berlin crisis.

BERLINER ILLUSTRIRTE. Special issue "message of friendship and gratitude to the American people and their new President," 1961. Portrait of JFK in color on cover.

77.

THE KENNEDY FAMILY OF MASSACHUSETTS

NATO Countries - The Common Market

BERLIN IM SPIEGEL, 1962. Berlin and the USA, special issue.
JFK and Brandt on front cover. RFK and Ethel, W.Berlin Feb.'62.

Booker, Christopher. THE NEOPHILIACS. 1st Gambit, 1970. Influence
of JFK on British people.

De Vosjoli, P.L.Thyraud. LAMIA. 1st L-B, 1970. Franco-American
relations since W.W.II. and in the Kennedy years.

Ellis, Harry B. THE COMMON MARKET. 1st World, 1965. Numerous
references to JFK and his wish for interdependence with W.Europe.

Finletter, Thos. K. INTERIM REPORT: On the Search for a Substitute for Isolation. 1st Norton,1968. By U.S.Ambassador to NATO.

Hartley, Anthony. GAULLISM: The Rise and Fall of a Political
Movement. 1st O&D, 1971. Incl. DeGaulle's attitude to JFK.

Kleiman, Robt. ATLANTIC CRISIS; American Diplomacy Confronts a
Resurgent Europe. Norton (1964). "Kennedy's Grand Design."

Kraft, Joseph. THE GRAND DESIGN: From Common Market to Atlantic
Partnership. 1st Harp.,1962. N.B. Trade Expansion Act of 1962.

LIFE. "What the President's Speech Means to You," Aug.4, 1961:34ff.
The Berlin crisis. JFK on cover. "Kennedy Enraptures Germany,
Challenges DeGaulle," July 5, 1963:30-31.

Macmillan, Harold. POINTING THE WAY: 1959-1961. 1st H&R, 1972.
Chapter 11. "The New President."

Malraux, Andre. FELLED OAKS: Conversations with DeGaulle. H.R.&W.
1972. Re JFK and JBK: 68-69, 73-79, 124.

Morris, Eric. BLOCKADE: Berlin and the Cold War. 1st S&D, 1973.
JFK and the Berlin Wall.

Nelson, Walter H. THE BERLINERS. Their Saga and Their City.
McKay (1969). JFK and Wall, visit in 1963, reaction of people.

Newhouse, John. DeGAULLE AND THE ANGLO-SAXONS. 1st Viking,1970.
JFK: Chapters 5-7, 9. Relationship of JFK to Macmillan, Adenauer.

NEWSWEEK. "'Ken-ah-dee' Abroad: the 'Common Cause'," July 8,
1963: 31-32ff.- Germany, France, Ireland, England.

N.Y.TIMES MAG. "In Search of the 'Atlantic Community'," May 6,
1962: 17ff. By Sidney Hyman.

Nunnerley, David. PRESIDENT KENNEDY AND BRITAIN. 1st St.Martin's,
1972. Analysis of JFK's impact on British politics.

FOREIGN AFFAIRS IN GENERAL

NATO Countries - The Common Market

Rostow, Eugene. "A New Start for the Alliance," REPORTER, Apr.25, 1963: 23-29. The Atlantic Alliance and DeGaulle.

Rovere, Richard H. "Our Far-Flung Correspondents; Journal of a Pseudo-Event," NEW YORKER, July 13, 1963:76ff. JFK to Europe.

Shanks, Michael and John Lambert. THE COMMON MARKET TODAY - AND TOMORROW. Wrs. Praeger, 1963. JFK's urging for Britain to join.

Smith, Jean Edward. THE DEFENSE OF BERLIN. J.Hopkins, 1963. JFK represented as making concessions to the Russians.

Stikker, Dirk U. MEN OF RESPONSIBILITY. 1st H&R, 1966. By former Sec'y General of NATO (1961-1964).

U.S.NEWS..."U.S.Failing in Europe?" by Joseph Fromm and Frederick Painton. Mar.25, 1963:48-52.+ "Europe After Kennedy: What Changes?" July 8, 1963: 31-35.-

Peace Corps - Third World

Annals of the AAPSS, May, 1966. THE PEACE CORPS, J. Norman Parmer ed. 13 articles including "The Future of the Peace Corps," by Harris Wofford, Associate Director of the Peace Corps.

Ashabranner, Brent. A MOMENT IN HISTORY: the First Ten Years of the Peace Corps. 1st D'day, 1971. The volunteers' dedication to JFK.

Brooks, Rhoda and Earl. THE BARRIOS OF MANTA. A Personal Account of the Peace Corps in Ecuador. 1st NAL, 1965. Presentation copy.

Cowan, Paul. THE MAKING OF AN UN-AMERICAN. 1st Viking, 1970. Influenced by JFK became a Peacecorpsman - then disillusioned.

Ezickson, Aaron J. ed. THE PEACE CORPS: A Pictorial History. H&W, 1965. Sm. folio. Volunteers in training and in the field.

Hapgood, David and Meridan Bennett. AGENTS OF CHANGE. A Close Look at the Peace Corps. 1st L-B, 1968. 17 overseas programs.

Harris, Mark. TWENTYONE TWICE: A Journal. 1st L-B, 1966. Asked by Sargent Shriver to write a report about the Peace Corps.

Haverstock, Nathan A. "Profile of a Peace Corpsman," SAT. EVE. POST, Sept.8, 1962: 77-81.

Hoopes, Roy, ed. THE PEACE CORPS EXPERIENCE. 1st Potter, 1968. THE COMPLETE PEACE CORPS GUIDE. Dial, 1961. Exact account of the origin of the Peace Corps during campaign of JFK. Rev.ed., 1966.

Kittler, Glenn D. THE PEACE CORPS. Wrs. 1st Paperback Lib.1963.

Peace Corps - Third World

LIFE. "Up Front with the Peace Corps," Jan.5, 1962: 18-25. Locale: Columbia. "Shriver of the Peace Corps,"by Richard Stolley, May 1, 1964:40-42ff. "Peace Corps' Re-entry Crisis," by Stolley, Mar.19, 1965: 98-100ff. "Whatever Happened to the Peace Corps?" by Wm.A. McWhirter, Sept.8, 1972: 47ff.

LOOK. "On Trial: Sargent Shriver and the Peace Corps," by Fletcher Knebel, Nov.7, 1961: 34-37. "The Peace Corps: JFK's Bold Legacy" with four paintings in color by Norman Rockwell, June 14, 1966: 34-46.

Luce, Iris, ed. LETTERS FROM THE PEACE CORPS. 1st R.Luce, 1967.

Moyers, Bill. LISTENING TO AMERICA. A Traveler Rediscovers His Country. Harp. Mag.Pr.,1971. Mention of JFK and Peace Corps.

NEWSWEEK. "The Peace Corps' Wartime Problem," Jan.15, 1968: 23.

N.Y.TIMES MAG. "Peace Corps: Alive But Not So Well," by Terence Smith, Dec.25, 1977: 6-9ff.

SAT. REVIEW. "R.I.P. Peace Corps and Vista," Apr.1, 1972: 38-40.

Sclanders, Jan. "The Peace Corps: Nursery for Diplomats," NATION, July 27, 1964: 31-33.

Shriver, Sargent. "Peace Corps Takes Fire in College..." LIFE, Mar. 17, 1961. "Peace Corps: Trial Balance One Year Later," SAT. REVIEW, May 19, 1962: 22-23ff. POINT OF THE LANCE, 1st H&R, 1964. How the Peace Corps evolved and how it was set up. "Ambassadors of Good Will, the Peace Corps," NAT'L GEOGRAPHIC, Sept., 1964: 297-313, with reports from eight volunteers from Bolivia, Tanganyika, Gabon, Turkey, Sarawak, Ecuador: 314-345. "The First Year Was Tough:" 57-67; "Peace Corps Successes:" 99-104; "Some Questions and Answers:" 146-148; "The Peace Corps' Strength:" 156-163 - all four in Madow ed. THE PEACE CORPS op.cit. JFK statements. "Five Years with the Peace Corps," in THE PEACE CORPS READER, Wash.D.C., 1968: 15-24. Wrs. Other authors in this anthology of Peace Corps experience: David Riesman, James Michener, Frank Mankiewicz et al.

SIGN. Editorial: "Kennedy's Peace Corps," Jan. 1961: 10.-

Smith, Ed. WHERE TO, BLACK MAN? Quad.,1967. An American Negro's diary with the Peace Corps in Ghana 1962-1964. Inspired by JFK.

Sullivan, George. THE STORY OF THE PEACE CORPS. 1st Fleet,1964. Intro. by Sargent Shriver. 2nd rev. ed., 1st prtg. Fleet, 1966.

Textor, Robt.B. ed. CULTURAL FRONTIERS OF THE PEACE CORPS. M.I.T. 1966. Presentation. 15 social scientists examine the program.

FOREIGN AFFAIRS IN GENERAL

Peace Corps - Third World

TIME. "The Peace Corps. It Is Almost As Good as Its Intentions,"
July 5, 1963: 18-22.

Unger, Marvin H. PAWPAW, FOOFOO AND JUJU. Recollections of a
Peace Corps volunteer. Liberia, West Africa.

Wingenbach, Chas.E. THE PEACE CORPS. Who, How and Where. Rev.ed.
Day, 1963. Preface by Sargent Shriver. 2nd copy: wrs., Day, 1961.

Zeitlin, Arnold. TO THE PEACE CORPS WITH LOVE. 1st D'day, 1965.
Locale: Ghana, W. Africa.

Russia

Archer, Jules. THE RUSSIANS AND THE AMERICANS. 1st Hawthorn,1975.
Details of the relation between JFK and Khrushchev.

Bohlen, Chas.E. with Charles H. Phelps. WITNESS TO HISTORY 1929-
1969. 1st Norton, 1973. Discusses main foreign policies of JFK.

Brzezinski, Zbigniew and S.P. Huntington. POLITICAL POWER: USA/
USSR. Viking, 1965. Comparative analysis. Case studies of JFK.

De Riencourt, Amaury. THE AMERICAN EMPIRE. 1st Dial, 1968. With
Russia the junior partner. Several decisions of JFK.

Etzioni, Amitai. "JFK's Russian Experiment," PSYCHOLOGY TODAY,
Dec.,1969: 42-45ff.

Kalb, Madeline and Marvin. "How Mr. Kennedy Looks to the Russians"
REPORTER, Dec.8, 1960: 33-34ff.

KHRUSHCHEV REMEMBERS. Trans. and ed. by Strobe Talbott. L-B, 1970.
The drama of the Cuban missile crisis on Iron Curtain side.
Vol.II. 1954-1964. L-B, 1974. Appraisal of JFK, Vienna and Cuba.

LIFE. "What the K's Really Told Each Other," by Hugh Sidey, June
16, 1961: 48-49.- Editorial:"The President Nails a Lie," Dec.8,
1961:4. "Central, Give Me a (Hot) Line," April 26, 1963 by Paul
Mandel.- Editorial: "JFK's Voice Fills a Hush in the Cold War,"
July 12, 1963: 4. "How Harriman 'Earned a Dinner' from Khrushchev"
by Paul Mandel, Aug.9, 1963: 28-30A.

NEWSWEEK. "Personal Diplomacy," June 12, 1961: 21-25. The K's
meet in Vienna. Cover portrait. "Sellout in the Soviet," April 5
1965.- "JFK at the Summit," by Chas. Roberts, Sept.7, 1970: 32-
33.- Based on recollections of 1961 Vienna conference.

N.Y.TIMES MAG. "'Khrushchev is an Open Book'," by Max Frankel,
June 4, 1961:7ff. K's on cover in this and issue of Apr.29,'62.

Russia

Reeve, F.D. ROBERT FROST IN RUSSIA. L-B, 1964. Request of JFK in July, 1962. Proposal for cultural exchange between two poets.

TIME. "The Presidency," March 31, 1961:7-24. US-Soviet relations.-

Wedge, Bryant. "What a Psychiatrist Told JFK about Khrushchev," TRANS-ACTION, Oct.1968:24-28.

Wilcox, Francis O. CONGRESS, THE EXECUTIVE AND FOREIGN POLICY. 1st H&R, 1971. Touches on Cuba, East-West trade.

Russia and Berlin

LIFE. "General K. (Khrushchev) Begins the Berlin Countdown," June 30, 1961: 34-41.

Penkovskiy, Oleg. THE PENKOVSKIY PAPERS. D'day (1965). Re sabotage of Khrushchev's Threatened Berlin showdown in 1961. Victor Marchetti reported to claim this book propaganda distributed by CIA.

Russia and China

Schurmann, Franz and Orville Schell. "Sino-American Relations: the Confrontation of Two Great Powers:" 290-305, in THE CHINESE READER: COMMUNIST CHINA ed. by same. Wrs. Vintage (1967). Change in attitude to China under JFK. The authors acknowledge indebtedness to unpublished ms. of Robert Blum.

Steele, A.T. THE AMERICAN PEOPLE AND CHINA. 1st McG-H, 1966. Based on 200 interviews with Americans in leadership positions. JFK's predisposition to take a more flexible position re China.

Russia and Cuba

Abel, Elie. THE MISSILE CRISIS. 1st Lipp.,1966. Includes RFK.

Alsop, Stewart J.O. "The Cuban Disaster: How It Happened," SEP, June 24, 1961: 26-27ff. With Chas. Bartlett. "In Time of Crisis," SEP, Dec.8, 1962: 15-20.

Alsop, Joseph. "The Most Important Decision in U.S.History and How the President Is Facing It," SAT.REV. Aug.5, 1961: 7-9ff. Editorial by Norman Cousins: "No Extermination Without Represntation:" 20ff.

ATLANTIC. "Report on Washington:" July 1961, 4ff. C.I.A. intelligence failure in Cuba.

Bayard, James. THE REAL STORY ON CUBA. 1st Monarch, 1963. Wrs. Attack on JFK.

FOREIGN AFFAIRS IN GENERAL

Russia and Cuba

Berquist, Laura, (our woman in Havana). "30 Days in Castro's Cuba," LOOK, Nov.8, 1960: 29-55; "Llewellyn Thompson: JFK's Russian Expert," ibid. Feb.12, 1963: 21-25; "My 28 Days in Communist Cuba," Apr.9, 1963: 15-27.

Bethel, Paul D. THE LOSERS...The Communist Conquest of Cuba... Arlington (1969).

Blackstock, Paul W. "THE STRATEGY of SUBVERSION: Manipulating the Politics of Other Nations. 1st Quad. 1964. Bay of Pigs as one case study.

Daniel, James and John G. Hubbell. STRIKE IN THE WEST: The Complete Story of the Cuban Crisis. 1st H.R.& W., 1963.

Daniel, Jean. "When Castro Heard the News," NEW REPUBLIC, Dec.7, 1963:7-9. "Unofficial Envoy: An Historic Report from Two Capitals", ibid. Dec.14, 1963: 15-20. "A Further Clarification: Interviews with Kennedy and Castro," ibid. Dec.21, 1963: 6-7."Boycotting Cuba: Whose Interest Does It Serve?" ibid. Dec.28, 1963: 19-20.

Del Castillo, Michel. "Le Grand Desarroi du Peuple Cubain," REALITIES, Nov.,1962: 58-65.

De Mauny, Erik. RUSSIAN PROSPECT: A Moscow Correspondent ... 1st Atheneum, 1970. Cuban missile crisis: 70-79.

Dewart, Leslie. CHRISTIANITY AND REVOLUTION: The Lesson of Cuba. H&H, 1963. JFK as attempting to prevent Cuba's autonomy.

Donnelly, Desmond. STRUGGLE FOR THE WORLD: The Cold War 1917-1965. St. Martin, 1965. Includes view of JFK and Cuba.

Drummond, Roscoe. "Beyond the Cuban Crisis." SAT.REV. Nov.10,1962 16-18.

Dumont, Rene. CUBA: Socialism and Development. 1st Grove, 1970. Some discussion of Bay of Pigs and Alliance for Progress.

Branch, Taylor and George Crile III. "The Kennedy Vendetta," HARPER, Aug. 1975: 49-53ff. JFK as committing the CIA to a secret war against Cuba.

Hilsman, Roger. "The Cuban Crisis: How Close We Were to War," LOOK, Aug. 25, 1964: 17-21.

Holsti, K.J. INTERNATIONAL POLITICS; A Framework for Analysis. P-H, 1972. Bibliography on materials on the missile crisis.

Hunt, Howard. GIVE US THIS DAY. The Inside Story of the CIA and the Bay of Pigs... Arlington, 1973. Defensive of CIA role. Also Popular Library edition, 1973. Wrs.

Russia and Cuba

Johnson, Haynes, et al. THE BAY OF PIGS. Norton (1964). The leaders' story of Brigade 2506 - a candid history.

Karol, K.S. GUERILLAS IN POWER. The Course of the Cuban Revolution. H&W, 1970. Complex relations between USSR and Cuba. Roles of JFK and RFK - Bay of Pigs, missile crisis, Alliance for Progress.

Knebel, Fletcher. "Washington in Crisis: 154 Hours on the Brink of War. LOOK, Dec.18, 1962: 42-44ff.

Langley, Lester D. THE CUBAN POLICY OF THE U.S.: a Brief History. Wiley, 1968.

Lazo, Mario. DAGGER IN THE HEART. American Policy Failures in Cuba. F&W, 1968.

LIFE. Editorial: "What Should Monroe Doctrine Mean? Blockade." Sept.21, 1962: 4. "Cuba - and the Unfaced Truth," by Clare Boothe Luce, Oct. 5, 1962: 53-56. "The Blockade," by John Dille; "Step by Step In An Historic Week," by Richard Oulahan Nov.2,'62: 34-49."The Historic Letter That Exposed Mr. K's Hand," by John L. Steele: Nov.9, 1962: 36-48. "How Lawyer Donovan Negotiated the Swap," by Warren Young: Jan.4, 1963: 25-26. "We Call on Cuba," Feb.8,1963: 40-40B. "The Men Who Fought Tell the Eyewitness Story..." by John Dille: 20-34ff; "Anatomy of the Snafu," by Tom Flaherty, May 10, 1963: 80-83. "Khrushchev Remembers," Pt.IV. Dec.18, 1970: 16B-25ff.

Lippman, Walter. "Cuba and the Nuclear Risk," ATLANTIC, Feb.,1963: 55-58.

Meneses, Enrique. FIDEL CASTRO. Ldn.,F&F, 1968. Includes relations with JFK, Bay of Pigs and ransom, missile crisis, Cuban exiles.

Miller, Warren, 90 MILES FROM HOME. The Face of Cuba Today. 1st L-B, 1961. Also 1st Crest/Fawcett, wrs., 1961.

Murphy, Chas. J.V. "Cuba: The Record Set Straight," FORTUNE, Sept., 1961: 92-97ff. Professional military view.+

NEWSWEEK. "October 1962 - the Cuba Crisis: Nuclear War Was Hours Away," Oct.28, 1963: 24-26. "JFK, Castro and Controversy,"David Gelman, July 18, 1977: 85. Re Bill Moyer's CBS Report "The CIA's Secret Army," and Arthur Schlesinger's open letter to Moyers in the WALL STREET JOURNAL.

Nixon, Richard M. "Cuba, Castro and John F. Kennedy: Some Reflections on U.S.Foreign Policy." READERS' DIGEST, Nov., 1964: 283-300.-

Pachter, Henry M. COLLISION COURSE: Cuban Missile Crisis and Co-existence. Wrs. Praeger, 1963.

FOREIGN AFFAIRS IN GENERAL

Russia and Cuba

Perkins, Dexter. THE DIPLOMACY OF A NEW AGE. Major Issues in U.S. Policy since 1945. Wrs. Indiana U. 1967. Brief treatment of Cuba.

Pflaum, Irving P. TRAGIC ISLAND. How Communism Came to Cuba. P-H (1961). JFK's "White Paper" on Cuba of April 3, 1961 and more.

Phillips, R.Hart. THE CUBAN DILEMMA. 1st Oblensky, 1962. The Bay of Pigs invasion seen from the inside of Cuba.

Rovere, Richard. "Cuban Crisis," NEW YORKER, Nov.3, 1962: 112-118

Samuels, G. "James Donovan and Castro,"NATION,Apr.13,1963: 299-302

Stevenson, Adlai E. "The Man, the Candidate, the Statesman." Excerpts from speeches incl. U.N. Security Council debate on missile crisis. Recording: Radio Press International, AS101 61447.

Stoessinger, John G. THE MIGHT OF NATIONS. World Politics in Our Time. Random (1967) One of the case studies: Cuban missile crisis.

Szulc, Tad and Karl E. Meyer. THE CUBAN INVASION: The Chronicle of a Di..saster. Wrs. Bal.1962. Ineptness of CIA. THE WINDS OF REVOLUTION, Latin America Today and Tomorrow, by Szulc.Praeg.1963

TIME. "The Cover-Up." (Cuba and the CIA). Mar.8, 1963: 23-25.

Valdes, Nelson P. and Edward Lieuwen. THE CUBAN REVOLUTION: A Research-Study Guide (1959-1969). 1st U. of Mexico, 1971. Bibliography of 3839 items compilers consider most essential. Includes four primary JFK documents and many titles re JFK policy.

Weyl, Nathaniel. RED STAR OVER CUBA...Wrs. Hillman'Mcf., 1961.

Williams, Wm.A. UNITED STATES, CUBA AND CASTRO. Monthly Review, 1962. "The President and His Critics," NATION, Mar.16, 1963:226-8

U.S. NEWS... "As Kennedy Faces the Facts," May 8, 1961: 41-44. "Kennedy's Fateful Decision..." Sept. 17, 1962: 41-42. "What Next for Castro?" and "Real Story of the Bay of Pigs," Jan.7, 1963: 36-41. "We Were Betrayed," by Manuel Penabaz, Jan. 14, 1963: 46-49. "Robert Kennedy Speaks His Mind," (celebrated interview in which the Atty. Gen. denied the U.S. air cover had been withdrawn), Jan. 28, 1963: 54-65. "How President Kennedy Upset the Cuban Invasion of April 1961," and "Cuban Fighters Tell Why They Expected Air Cover," Feb. 4, 1963: 29-36± "The magazine that published the most about the Bay of Pigs is almost the most misleading...articles...some of them appearing to be deliberately written to stir controversy without regard to facts, virtually laid the entire blame on President Kennedy...help explain why the invasion continued to be so controversial an issue in the U.S." - Haynes Johnson.

Vietnam

Acheson, Dean. PRESENT AT THE CREATION. My Years at the State Department.Norton (1969). "The real architect of the American commitment to Vietnam...was Dean Acheson (in the Truman years)" with massive military and economic aid to the French. (Cf. Halberstam)

Ashmore, Harry and Wm.C.Baggs. MISSION TO HANOI: A Chronicle of Double-Dealing in High Places. Berkeley Med. Wrs. 1968.

Cooper, Chester L. THE LOST CRUSADE: America in Vietnam. D-M, 1970. JFK as realistic about Vietnam and pressure of Congress.

Draper, Theodore. ABUSE OF POWER. Viking, 1967. Seven turning points in origin and conduct of Vietnamese war. One of the best.

DuBerrier, Hilaire. BACKGROUND TO BETRAYAL: The Tragedy of Vietnam. West.Isl., 1969. Critical of Vietnam lobby and JFK.

Eagleton, Thos.F. WAR AND PRESIDENTIAL POWER. A Chronicle of Congressional Surrender. Liveright, 1974. Criticism of JFK policy.

Ellsberg, Daniel. PAPERS ON THE WAR. 1st S&S, 1972. Attempt to explain reasons for U.S. policies and intervention in Vietnam.

Fitzgerald, Frances. FIRE IN THE LAKE. The Vietnamese and the Americans in Vietnam. L-B, 1972. Roles of JFK and RFK.

Gallagher, Hugh G. ADVISE AND OBSTRUCT. Role of the U.S.Senate in Foreign Policy Decisions. Delacorte, 1969. Chap.VII. Vietnam.

Gavin, James M. CRISIS NOW. 1st Random, 1968. Reported JFK's unequivocal attitude to Vietnam war.

Glyn, Alan. WITNESS TO VIET NAM: The Containment of Communism in South East Asia. Ldn. 1968. Assessment of American decisions.

Goulding, Phil G. CONFIRM OR DENY: Informing the People on National Security. 1st H&R, 1970. Record of Vietnam decision-making.

Halberstam, David. THE MAKING OF A QUAGMIRE. 1st Random, 1965. "Getting the Story in Vietnam," COMMENTARY, Jan., 1965: 30-34. THE BEST AND THE BRIGHTEST. Random (1972). Narrative of the decision-making process re our position in Vietnam.

Hunt, E. Howard. UNDERCOVER MEMOIRS OF AN AMERICAN SECRET AGENT. Berkeley (1974). His version of the Bay of Pigs, his falsification of Vietnam cables to implicate JFK and subsequent attempts to foist the lie on the media. Investigation of EMK.

Julien, Claude. AMERICA'S EMPIRE. 1st Pantheon, 1971. Thesis: Vietnam the result of a century of imperial expansion. Also case study of CIA and Iran.

FOREIGN AFFAIRS IN GENERAL

Vietnam

Kahin, Geo. and John W. Lewis. THE UNITED STATES IN VIETNAM. Dial, 1967. Limited under JFK, limits removed under LBJ.

Kendrick, Alexander. THE WOUND WITHIN: America in the Vietnam Years 1945-1974. 1st L-B, 1974.

Lodge, Henry Cabot. THE STORM HAS MANY EYES: A Personal Narrative. Norton, 1973. Includes denial that JFK was responsible for the coup against President Diem. AS IT WAS: An Inside View of Politics and Power... 1st Norton, 1976. Relations with JFK.

McCarthy, Mary. THE SEVENTEENTH DEGREE. H.B.J.,1974. On the indochina war. Critique of David Halberstam's theory.

THE PENTAGON PAPERS. The Senator Gravel Edition. The Defense Department History of United States Decision-making on Vietnam. 4 vols. wrs. Beacon Press, 1971. Vol.II: Kennedy years: 1-276. Page 188: JFK's refusal to an unconditional commitment to the war.

Pfeffer, Richard ed. NO MORE VIETNAMS? The War and the Future of American Foreign Policy. 1st H&R, 1968. Kennedy administration.

Rovere, Richard. WAIST DEEP IN THE BIG MUDDY. 1st L-B, 1968. Vietnam, LBJ and JFK.

Schlesinger, Arthur M.,Jr. THE BITTER HERITAGE. Vietnam and American Democracy, 1941-1966. 1st Fawcett Crest, 1967. Wrs.

Schrag, Peter. TEST OF LOYALTY. Daniel Ellsberg and the Rituals of Secret Government. 1st S&S, 1974. Kennedy administration re the Vietnam war.

Schurmann, F., Peter Dale Scott, R. Zelnick. THE POLITICS OF ESCALATION IN VIETNAM. 1st Fawcett, 1966. Wrs. The reversal of policy after JFK assassination.

Scott, Peter Dale. "The Vietnam War and the CIA Financial Establishment," in RE-MAKING ASIA, ed. by Mark Selden: 91-154. 1st Pantheon, 1974. JFK for withdrawal; CIA for escalation.

Taylor, Telford. NUREMBERG AND VIETNAM: an American Tragedy. Wrs. Quad, 1970. References to the three Kennedy brothers and Vietnam.

Thee, Marek. NOTES OF A WITNESS. Laos and the Second Indochina War. 1st Random, 1973. Kennedy administration misconception.

Ungar, Sanford J. THE PAPER AND THE PAPERS. An Account of the Legal and Political Battle Over the Pentagon Papers. 1st Dutton, 1972. JFK administration and Vietnam policy included.

United Presbyterian Church General Assembly. VIETNAM - THE CHRISTIAN - THE GOSPEL - THE CHURCH. 1967. Chapter 5: JFK administration.

Vietnam

Windchy, Eugene. TONKIN GULF. A Documentary of the Incidents...
1st D'day, 1971. Contrast: JFK for limited, LBJ for "total" support for So.Vietnam. JFK as intending a planned withdrawal.

Yugoslavia

NEWSWEEK. "Tito's Date," Oct.28, 1963.- JFK's meeting with, at
White House.

UNITED STATES DEFENSE POLICY

U.S. Defense Policy in General

Barnet, Richard J. THE ECONOMY OF DEATH. Atheneum, 1970. The
basic assumptions behind the defense budget by former member of
U.S. Arms Control and Disarmament Agency under JFK.

Clark, Keith C. and Laurence J. Legere eds. THE PRESIDENT AND THE
MANAGEMENT OF NATIONAL SECURITY. Praeger, 1969. Organizational
structures under last four presidents. JFK and McGeorge Bundy.

Cutler, Robt.B. "Spotlight on McGeorge Bundy and the White House
Situation Room," COMPUTERS AND AUTOMATION, Jan. 1972: 57-58.

Enthoven, Alain C. and Wayne Smith. HOW MUCH IS ENOUGH? Shaping
the Defense Program 1961-1969. 1st H&R, 1971.

Galloway, K.Bruce and Robt.B.Johnson Jr. WEST POINT: America's
Power Fraternity. 1st S&S, 1973. Attacks Roger Hilsman under JFK.

Ginsburgh, Robt.N. U.S. MILITARY STRATEGY IN THE SIXTIES. 1st
Norton, 1965. JFK's address to Congress March 28, 1961, on the
defense budget "the best brief statement of our security policy."

Halberstam, David. "The Very Expensive Education of McGeorge
Bundy," HARPER'S, July, 1969:21-41. "The Programming of Robert
McNamara. Ibid., Feb.1971:37-40ff.

Hyman, Sidney. "When Bundy Says 'The President Wants -'." N.Y.
TIMES MAG. Dec.2, 1962: 30ff.

Kaufman, Richard F. THE WAR PROFITEERS. 1st B-M, 1970. JFK and
purported "missile gap" and decisions re the supersonic SST.

Kaufman, Wm.W. THE McNAMARA STRATEGY. 1st H&R, 1964. The shift
from "massive retaliation" to "balanced defense" and "flexible
response."

Kraar, Louis. "The Two Lives of Robert McNamara," LIFE, Nov.30,
1962: 94-100ff.

FOREIGN AFFAIRS IN GENERAL

U.S. Defense Policy in General

Kolodziej, Edw.A. THE UNCOMMON DEFENSE AND CONGRESS 1945-1963. O.S.U., 1966. Critique of the 87th Congress.

Liberty Lobby. ROBERT STRANGE McNAMARA: The True Story of Dr. Strangebob. 1st, 1967. "...intentionally disarming America..."

Lowe, Geo.E. THE AGE OF DETERRENCE. 1st L-B, 1964. Defense dialogue between the Utopians and the Traditionalists. JFK position.

MacKaye, Milton. "Bundy of the White House," SAT.EVE.POST, Mar. 10, 1962: 82-85.

McNamara, Robt. "Managing the Department of Defense," CIVIL SERVICE JOURNAL, Apr-June, 1964:1-5. THE ESSENCE OF SECURITY: Reflections in Office. 1st H&R, 1968.

Mollenhoff, Clark R. THE PENTAGON. Politics, Profits and Plunder. Putnam, 1967. McNamara and the three Kennedy brothers.

NEWSWEEK. "JFK's McGeorge Bundy," March 4, 1963: 20-24.

Raymond, Jack. POWER AT THE PENTAGON. 1st H&R, 1964. JFK as "active military thinker" who tried to reduce military spending.

Rinehart, Jonathan. "The Man Who Wields the Power," (Robert McNamara). USA 1, May 12, 1962: 13-21.

Swomely, John M. Jr. THE MILITARY ESTABLISHMENT. Beacon, 1964. Growing power of military elite at Pentagon.

Taylor, Maxwell D. RESPONSIBILITY AND RESPONSE. H&R (1967). Argument for immediate response to present Communist threat. SWORDS AND PLOUGHSHARES: a Memoir. 1st Norton, 1972.

TIME. "Defense: the Missile Gap Flop," Feb.17, 1961:12-13. "The Use of Power with a Passion for Peace (Bundy). June 25,'65:26-29.

Trewhitt, Henry L. MCNAMARA: His Ordeal at the Pentagon. 1st H&R 1971. Includes relationship with JFK and RFK.

U.S.NEWS... "Streamlining Defense - What Kennedy Plans." Dec.5, 1960: 80-83.+

Yarmolinsky, Adam. THE MILITARY ESTABLISHMENT. Its Impact on American Society. 1st H&R, 1971. JFK's relations with establishment.

U.S.Defense: Nuclear Test Ban

ATLANTIC. "Arms Control," Mar.1, 1961: 4ff.

LIFE. "Two Views on Bomb Tests," C.J.V.Murphy, Feb.16, 1962:70ff. "President Kennedy Signs Nuclear Test Treaty," Oct.18,'63:44B.

U.S.Defense: Nuclear Test Ban

Newman, James R. "JFK on testing,"+ NEW REPUBLIC, Mar.26,'62:11ff.

Power, Thos.S. DESIGN FOR SURVIVAL. C-McC (1965). Overwhelming nuclear strength as only effective tool of peace. Chap.1: JFK.

Schafly, Phyllis and Chester Ward. THE GRAVEDIGGERS. Pere Marq. 1964. Wrs. Kennedy administration as risking nuclear war.

U.S.Congress. Senate. 88th Congress, 1st sess. "Military Aspects and Implications of Nuclear Test Ban Proposals and Related Matters". Wrs. June and Aug.,1963.

U.S.Defense: Flexible Response

Alsop, Stewart. "McNamara's Strategy. The Alternative to Total War."SEP, Dec.1, 1962: 13-19.

Duncan, Donald. THE NEW LEGIONS. Random (1967). Account of the Special Forces' snow job to impress - successfully - JFK.

Kraft, Joseph. "Hot Weapon in the Cold War," SEP, Apr.28, 1962: 87-91. Special Forces for guerrilla warfare.

Metzger, H. Peter. THE ATOM ESTABLISHMENT. 1st S&S, 1972. 25 years of Atomic Energy Commission. JFK and "flexible response."

Pfaff, Wm. "Confessions of a Green Beret," COMMENTARY, Jan. 1970: 28-34.

Sadler, Barry, with Tom Mahoney. I'M A LUCKY ONE. 1st Macm. 1967. Life before, during and after Green Beret years.

Taylor, Maxwell D. THE UNCERTAIN TRUMPET. Harper (1960). A leader in the doctrine of counterinsurgency.

Wilson, Thos. W. THE GREAT WEAPONS HERESY. The Struggle Behind Our Present Nuclear Dilemma...Tragedy of J. Robert Oppenheimer. 1st H-M, 1970. JFK's position.

Wren, Christopher. "The Facts Behind the Green Beret Myth," LOOK Nov.1, 1966:28-36.

U.S. Defense: Trade Expansion

Baldwin, David A. ECONOMIC DEVELOPMENT AND AMERICAN FOREIGN POL- ICY 1943-1962. U. of Chicago, 1966. Analysis of evolution of soft loan policy, discussion of trade liberalization, investment guarantees, grants and hard loans. JFK: the single most important tool - long-term development loans at low or no rates of interest. An important work.

FOREIGN AFFAIRS IN GENERAL

U.S. Defense: Trade Expansion

Canterbery, E.Ray. ECONOMICS ON A NEW FRONTIER. Wadsw. (1968).
JFK: the first president to utilize fully the economists' skills.

Douglas, Paul. AMERICA IN THE MARKET PLACE. 1st HR&W, 1966. Three
chapters on tariff agreements under JFK.

Feis, Herbert. FOREIGN AID AND FOREIGN POLICY. St.Martin's (1964)
Historical perspective and analytical comments. JFK: foreign aid
is essential to foreign policy. Also 1st Delta, 1966.

Galbraith, John K. ECONOMIC PEACE AND LAUGHTER. 1st H-M, 1971.
Critical of JFK foreign policy; John Steinbeck on JFK.

Hudson, Michael. SUPER IMPERIALISM. The Economic Strategy of
American Empire. 1st HR&W, 1972. Kennedy administration as cen-
tralizing aid program in State Dept. under Agency for International Development.

Kraft, Joseph. "Foreign Aid: Saved by the Bell?" HARPER, Feb.,
1963. Bell: new Director of AID.

Montgomery, John D. THE POLITICS OF FOREIGN AID. American Experience in Southeast Asia. Wrs. Praeger, 1962.

NEWSWEEK. "First Round of the 'Kennedy Round'." May 11, 1964:
80. "To Harness the Free World's Strength," Feb.5, 1962:19-20.

U.S.Congress Joint Economic Committee. Hearings before the Subcommittee on Foreign Economic Policy. FOREIGN ECONOMIC POLICY. Wrs.
Dec.4-14, 1961. GPO, 1962. N.B. Clay Shaw's testimony: 267-280.

U.S. Defense: Espionage

Agee, Philip. INSIDE THE COMPANY: CIA Diary. Stonehill, 1975.
Some passages left blank due to censorship of CIA.

Braden, Tom. "What's Wrong with the CIA?" SAT.REV., April 5, 1975:
14-18. Includes an interview with Allen Dulles.

Colby, William and Peter Forbath. HONORABLE MEN: My Life in the
CIA. 1st S&S, 1978. Career spanned 30 years.

Dulles, Allen. THE CRAFT OF INTELLIGENCE. H&R, 1963. Presentation. Retired under JFK. Brief discussion of Bay of Pigs. Ibid.
HARPER Mag. April, 1963: 127-174.

Kirkpatrick, Lyman B. Jr. THE REAL CIA. 1st Macm. 1968. "...it
leaves much to be said..." - Prouty.

McGarvey, Patrick J. CIA: The Myth and the Madness. Sat.Rev.Pr.,
1972. JFK's attempt to rearrange control over clandestine acts.

U.S. Defense: Espionage

McGeveran, Wm.A. Jr. "Special Report: the Intelligence System,"
1977 YEAR BOOK. Macm/Coll., 1976: 584-585. JFK and CIA. Report
of two congressional committees.

Marchetti, Victor, and John D. Marks. THE CIA AND THE CULT OF
INTELLIGENCE. 1st Knopf, 1974. 168 passages censored by CIA.

Prouty, L. Fletcher. THE SECRET TEAM: the CIA and Its Allies
in Control of the U.S. and the World. P-H, 1973. JFK: Ch. 22.

REPORT TO THE PRESIDENT BY THE COMMISSION ON CIA ACTIVITIES WITH-
IN THE U.S. June, 1975. Nelson A. Rockefeller Chairman. Wrs.
GPO, 1975. Autographed by Rockefeller.

Rovere, Richard H. "The Problem of the CIA," NEW YORKER, Nov.3,
1975: 165-170. JFK's effort to make U.S. ambassadors responsible.

Tully, Andrew. CIA: The Inside Story. Morrow, 1962. JFK's
relationship with this agency.

U.S. Congress, 94th, 1st Sess. Senate Report No. 94-465. AL-
LEGED ASSASSINATION PLOTS INVOLVING FOREIGN LEADERS. An Interim Report of the Select Committee to Study Governmental Operations re Intelligence Activities... Wrs. GPO: 1975. Includes
the questions and arguments raised as to whether JFK and/or RFK
knew of assassination efforts sponsored by intelligence agencies
of U.S. government using Mafia connections. CIA's use of RFK's
name without his knowledge.

U.S. Senate Resolution 21. INTELLIGENCE ACTIVITIES HEARINGS
BEFORE SELECT COMMITTEE TO STUDY GOVERNMENTAL OPERATIONS WITH
RESPECT TO INTELLIGENCE ACTIVITIES. Vol. 7. "Covert Action."
Wrs. 94th Cong. 1st sess. Senate, 1975. Includes Chile 1963-
1970; JFK correspondence re CIA.

Wise, David and Thos. B. Ross. THE INVISIBLE GOVERNMENT. 1st
Random, 1964. A notable early effort to alert nation to dangers
from influence of the CIA. "The Strange Case of the CIA Widows,"
Look, June 30, 1964: 77-78ff. THE ESPIONAGE ESTABLISHMENT. 1st
Random, 1967. Many incidents of JFK years. Also 1st Bantam,1968.

U.S. Defense: The Diplomatic Establishment

Briggs, Ellis. ANATOMY OF DIPLOMACY. The Origin and Execution of
American Foreign Policy. McKay, 1968. Praise and blame for JFK.

Harr, John Ensor. THE PROFESSIONAL DIPLOMAT. Princeton U.,1969.
Kennedy administration as bringing new ferment and energy.

Heller, Deane and David. PATHS OF DIPLOMACY. America's Secretaries of State. 1st Lipp., 1967. Dean Rusk: 165-174.

DOMESTIC AFFAIRS

U.S. Defense: The Diplomatic Establishment

Kennan, George F. MEMOIRS: 1925-1950. L-B, 1967. 25 years of diplomatic history. First meeting with JFK. Pres.JFK on nuclear weapons. MEMOIRS: 1950-1963. 1st L-B, 1972. Includes ambassadorship to Yugoslavia in Kennedy years. Correspondence with JFK.

McCamy, James L. CONDUCT OF THE NEW DIPLOMACY. H&R (1964). American foreign policy in Kennedy years.

Murphy, Robert. DIPLOMAT AMONG WARRIORS. The Unique World of a Foreign Service Expert. D'day (1964). Critical of JFK and Cuban policy.

Tully, Andrew. WHITE TIE AND DAGGER. Inside Embassy Row. Morrow, 1967. JFK and his relation to French, Spanish, English, Indonesians, Cubans and others. References also to JBK and RFK.

U.S. Defense: United Nations

Huss, Pierce John and Geo. Carpozi Jr. RED SPIES IN THE U.N. C-McC, 1965. JFK and spy-swapping, RFK and counter-spy.

LOOK, "Our Man in the Middle," (Adlai Stevenson at the U.N.) Oct. 10, 1961: 37-41.

Steele, John L. "The Adlai Stevenson Affair," LIFE, Dec.14,1962: 44-46.

Stevenson, Adlai. LOOKING OUTWARD: Years of Crisis at the United Nations. H&R (1963) Op.cit. JFK Introductions.

DOMESTIC AFFAIRS

Anti-Poverty Program

Bohn, Dorothy. Chapter 4. "The Areas of Concern," in REPORT ON POVERTY IN MUSKINGUM COUNTY, OHIO. Wrs. Muskingum County Economic Opportunity Action Group Inc., 1965. A part of JFK's Area Redevelopment Program.

Bohn, Dorothy, Mary Beth Koechlin, L.J.Ryan. ECONOMIC DEVELOPMENT AREA SURVEY. Wrs. 1968. Survey of the ghetto areas of Jacksonville, Florida, sponsored by the Jacksonville Urban League for the purpose of obtaining Small Business Administration grants and interesting the Federal government under the Area Redevelopment Act.

Caudill, Harry M. NIGHT COMES TO THE CUMBERLANDS. A Biography of a Depressed Area. LB,1963. Brief account of JFK's reaction to the hunger and depression seen there during his campaign.

THE KENNEDY FAMILY OF MASSACHUSETTS

Anti-Poverty Program

Goodwin, Richard N. THE AMERICAN CONDITION. 1st D'day, 1974. Description of American society and those elements in it which confine human freedom. References to Kennedy years and the difficulties of effecting beneficial social change.

Graham, James. THE ENEMIES OF THE POOR. 1st Random, 1970. The churches, the trade unions and the legal profession as the enemies of the poor. JFK and RFK as vocalizing the grievances of the politically impotent welfare poor.

Hamilton, David. A PRIMER ON THE ECONOMICS OF POVERTY. 1st Random, 1968. Includes JFK and Area Redevelopment Act of 1961.

Harlem Youth Opportunities Unlimited (HARYOU). YOUTH IN THE GHETTO: A Study of the Consequences of Powerlessness and a Blueprint for Change. Wrs. N.Y., 1964. A case study of the work done thru the involvement of the President's Committee on Juvenile Delinquency beginning in 1962 - the work of JFK and RFK. (Cf.Knapp and Polk:4-15 which follows.)

Harrington, Michael. FRAGMENTS OF THE CENTURY. 1st SAT.REV.PR., 1973. Major social and political movements of the 1950's and 60's.

Knapp, Daniel and Kenneth Polk. SCOUTING THE WAR ON POVERTY: Social Reform Politics in the Kennedy Administration. Heath/Lex, 1971. Analysis of forces working for and against the development of new social policy towards the role of the dispossessed. Includes the role of RFK. An important work.

Koechlin, Mary Beth. IDEOLOGY AND INTERACTION IN A COMMUNITY ANTIPOVERTY AGENCY. U. of Fla., 1975. Case study of a Jacksonville community action program under the Office of Economic Opportunity, result of social reform policies in Kennedy administration.

Lampman, Robt. J. THE SHARE OF TOP WEALTH-HOLDERS IN NATIONAL WEALTH 1922-1956. 1st Princeton U., 1962. Useful as part of a scarce literature on the subject of personal wealth and as introduction to Lampman who was influential in program to alleviate poverty at time of Kennedy administration.

Levitan, Sar A. THE DESIGN OF FEDERAL ANTIPOVERTY STRATEGY. U.of Michigan, 1969. Wrs. Origin and intended goals of Economic Opportunity Act. RFK's role in community action programs. FEDERAL AID TO DEPRESSED AREAS. An Evaluation of the Area Redevelopment Administration. The A.R.A. as the first major legislative product of New Frontier. Evaluation of activities of first two years. J. Hopkins Pr., 1964. ECONOMIC OPPORTUNITY IN THE GHETTO. The Partnership of Government and Business. J.Hopkins, 1970. Wrs. Development of A.R.A. into inclusion of Job Corps. Relevance of RFK's tax incentive proposal (S.2088, 90th Cong.).

DOMESTIC AFFAIRS

Anti-Poverty Program

Marris, Peter and Martin Rein. DILEMMAS OF SOCIAL REFORM. Poverty and Community Action in the U.S. Atherton, 1967. Discussion
of specific community action programs, e.g. JFK and RFK in HARYOU.

May, Edgar. THE WASTED AMERICANS. Cost of Our Welfare Dilemma.
H&R 1st, 1964. Autographed. JFK as the first chief executive to
issue a special public welfare message to Congress.

Miller, Herman P. RICH MAN, POOR MAN: The Distribution of Income
in America. Crowell, 1968. The widening of the income gap. How
to adjust employment and distribution of output in an age of abundance tagged by JFK as the No.1 domestic problem in the economic
field.

Ribicoff, Abraham. AMERICA CAN MAKE IT! 1st Atheneum, 1972.
Urges re-ordering of domestic priorities. Illustrations of lessons learned during JFK administration.

Scheibla, Shirley. POVERTY IS WHERE THE MONEY IS. Arlington,1968
Community Action programs as examples of how federal anti-poverty
funds are used to organize militant groups.

Weaver, Robert C. THE URBAN COMPLEX: Human Values in Urban Life.
1st D'day, 1964. JFK and first national moderate-income housing
program; his executive order on Equal Opportunity in Housing;
Federal aid to localities for urban improvement.

The Arts

ART IN AMERICA. Editorial: "The Government's Current Decision to
Ask American Artists to Design U.S. Postage Stamps," April, 1963:
30-32.

Heckscher, August. "Libraries and the Nation's Cultural Life,"
ALA, Sept., 1962: 716-720. By special consultant to JFK.

McDonald, Wm. F. FEDERAL RELIEF ADMINISTRATION AND THE ARTS.
O.S.U., 1969. Includes JFK's creation by executive order on June
12, 1963, of the President's Advisory Council on the Arts.

PUBLISHERS' WEEKLY. "The 1961 Presentation to the Home Library
of the White House," Feb.5, 1962: 40-46. -

Business and Labor

Beirne, Joseph A. CHALLENGE TO LABOR: New Roles for American
Trade Unions. P-H (1969). JFK administion analyzed as part.

Berle, Adolph. THE AMERICAN ECONOMIC REPUBLIC, 1st HB&W, 1963.
Details of the steel crisis in Part I.

Business and Labor

Domhoff, G. Wm. THE HIGHER CIRCLES: The Governing Class in America. 1st Random, 1970. JFK as member of governing class.

Finley, Joseph E. THE CORRUPT KINGDOM. The Rise and Fall of the United Mine Workers. 1st S&S, 1972. Vignette of JFK's efforts to save the "Miners' Hospitals" in Kentucky.

Finn, David. THE CORPORATE OLIGARCH. 1st S&S, 1969. The corporate image and the case of J.M.Shea Jr. of Dallas.

Goldberg, Arthur J. "Meaning of Steel Settlement - A New Era of Labor Peace?" U.S.NEWS... Apr.16, 1962: 64-67. -

Grossman, Jonathan. THE DEPARTMENT OF LABOR. Praeger, 1973. History, congressional relations. Goldberg and Willard Wirtz .

Heath, Jim F. JOHN F. KENNEDY AND THE BUSINESS COMMUNITY. U. of Chicago (1969). Economic history of New Frontier years.

Hodges, Luther H. THE BUSINESS CONSCIENCE. P-H (1963). JFK and the Business Ethics Advisory Council, his 1962 Consumer Protection Message, Big Steel.

Hoffman, Paul. LIONS IN THE STREET. The Inside Story of the Great Wall Street Firms. SAT.REV.Pr. 1973. Relations with JFK.

Krooss, Herman E. EXECUTIVE OPINION: What Business Leaders Said and Thought 1920's-1960's. 1st D'day, 1970. "Their money incomes undoubtedly went up (during JFK years) but they earned no psychic income...they felt like poor relations...invited...to watch the intellectuals, the artists, and the politicians..."

Levitan, Sar and Garth L. Mangun. MAKING SENSE OF FEDERAL MANPOWER POLICY. U. of Mich.,1972. Wrs. After A.R.A. the second of the new programs: "Manpower Development and Training Act" 1962.

McGuiness, Kenneth C. THE NEW FRONTIER NLRB. Labor Policy Assn., 1963. The JFK appointees; the case-by-case approach...

McManus, George. THE INSIDE STORY OF STEEL WAGES AND PRICES 1959-1967. Chilton (1967). Six chapters on the New Frontier.

Miliband, Ralph. THE STATE IN CAPITALIST SOCIETY. An Analysis of the Western System of Power. Basic, 1969. JFK and business community mentioned by Marxist author.

Northrup, Herbert R. COMPULSORY ARBITRATION and Government Intervention in Labor Disputes...Labor Policy, 1966. Intervention by Kennedy administration at behest of or in favor of unions.

Nossiter, Bernard D. THE MYTHMAKERS. Wrs. Beacon, 1967. A "myth" that JFK was anti-business. Two chapters on economics of JFK.

DOMESTIC AFFAIRS

Business and Labor

Okun, Arthur. THE BATTLE AGAINST UNEMPLOYMENT. Wrs. Norton, 1972
Experience with wage-price policies of JFK administration.

Meany, Geo., Roger M. Blough, Neil H. Jacoby. GOVERNMENT WAGE-
PRICE GUIDEPOSTS IN THE AMERICAN ECONOMY. N.Y.U.,1967. Discussion
of JFK's productivity-based wage-price guideposts in Jan. 1962.

Tobin, James. NATIONAL ECONOMIC POLICY. Wrs. Yale U., 1968. The
The unrequited efforts of JFK to win the confidence of business.

U.S.Congress. January 1963 Economic Report of the President. Hearings before the Joint Committee of the U.S. 88th Cong. 1st sess.
Jan.28-Feb.6, 1963. Two parts, wrs.

Uphoff, Walter H. KOHLER ON STRIKE: Thirty Years of Conflict.
Beacon (1966). JFK and RFK and Federal interest in this dispute.

Walsh, Robt.E., ed. SORRY...NO GOVERNMENT TODAY. Unions vs. City
Hall. 1st Beacon, 1969. JFK's promulgation of Executive Order
10988, the Magna Carta of Federal collective bargaining.

Widick, B.J. LABOR TODAY. The Triumphs and Failures of Union-
ism in the U.S. H-M, 1964. JFK administration seen as pro-labor
but not pro-union, as favoring a more active Federal role.

Civil Rights in General

Aptheker, Herbert. THE NEGRO TODAY. M&M, 1962, wrs. Re JFK cf.
"Civil Rights and the Federal Government:" 51-59. SOUL OF THE RE-
PUBLIC. M&M, 1964. Wrs. "...there is a straight historic connection between shooting down the president of the Mississippi NAACP
and shooting down the President of the United States."

Bickel, Alexander M. "The Civil Rights Act Of 1964." COMMENTARY,
Aug. 1964:33-39. Reviews the steps taken by JFK to this end. POL-
ITICS AND THE WARREN COURT. 1st H&R, 1965. Appraisal of civil
rights legislation during JFK administration.

Bohn, Dorothy and L.J.Ryan. THE PRESENT ECONOMIC POSITION OF THE
AMERICAN NEGRO. Unpublished ms. Spring, 1963. Part V. "The
Role of the Government."

Brauer, Carl M. JOHN F. KENNEDY AND THE SECOND RECONSTRUCTION.
1st Columbia U., 1977. Civil rights: roles of JFK, RFK, MLK.

Center for the Study of Democratic Institutions, CIVIL DISOBEDI-
ENCE, H.A.Freeman, Bayard Rustin et al. Wrs. April, 1966.

Clark, Kenneth. DARK GHETTO. Dilemmas of Social Power. 1st
H&R, 1965. Facts of the data gathered by HARYOU. RFK and JFK.

Civil Rights in General

COMMONWEAL. Editorial "A Moral Crisis," June 28, 1963: 363-4.-
"Racial diplomacy," Nov.1, 1963: 155-6. -

EBONY eds. THE NEGRO HANDBOOK. Johnson, 1966. Reference book
of facts, many to JFK, RFK. PICTORIAL HISTORY OF BLACK AMERICA.
Johnson, 1971. Account of JFK years in Vol.III. Three vol. set.

Feiffer, Jules. ON CIVIL RIGHTS. Wrs. 1st Anti-Def., 1966.

Fleming, Harold C. "The Federal Executive and Civil Rights.1961-
1965. DAEDULUS, Fall, 1965: 921-948.

Franklin, John Hope. FROM SLAVERY TO FREEDOM. A History of Negro
Americans. Wrs. Vintage, 1969. JFK years: 623-652.

√ Golden, Harry. MR. KENNEDY AND THE NEGROES. 1st World. Autographed. 1964. Also 1st Crest, wrs., 1964. Review NEWSWEEK, May 11,
1964: 100A.-

Hamilton, Chas.ed. THE BLACK EXPERIENCE IN AMERICAN POLITICS. Putnam, 1973. Student Nonviolent Coordinating Committee: 1960-1967.

√Lewis, Anthony. PORTRAIT OF A DECADE: The Second American Revo-
Χlution. 1st Random, 1964. JFK, RFK, MLK.

Loye, David. THE HEALING OF A NATION. 1st Norton, 1971. Study of
racism with a program for reform, JFK's part in social advances.

Lubell, Samuel. WHITE AND BLACK: Test of a Nation. 1st H&R,1964.
JFK's "fate to be caught in the middle..."

Miller, Elizabeth W., compiler. THE NEGRO IN AMERICA: A Bibliography. Harvard U. 1966. Useful for students of JFK years.

Moellering, Ralph. CHRISTIAN CONSCIENCE AND NEGRO EMANCIPATION.
Fortress, 1965. Praise for JFK and RFK.

NAACP REPORT FOR 1960. Wrs. July, 1961. REPORT FOR 1963. Wrs.

National Advisory Commission on Civil Disorders. REPORT. 1st
Dutton, 1968. Historical sketch includes JFK years.

National Urban League. "Economic and Social Status of the Negro
in the U.S." Wrs., brochure, 1961.

NEWSWEEK. "An End and a Beginning," June 24, 1963: 29-30. -
"Civil Rights: Slack Tide" July 8, 1963: 21-22.- "Negro Goals in
'63," Nov.,1963: 1-8.

Osborne, Wm. THE SEGREGATED COVENANT: Race Relations and American
Catholics. H&H, 1967. Acceleration of civil rights under JFK.

DOMESTIC AFFAIRS

Civil Rights in General

Osofsky, Gilbert. THE BURDEN OF RACE. A Documentary History of
Negro-White Relations in America. 1st Harper Torchbk., 1968 Wrs.

Reitman, Alan ed. THE PULSE OF FREEDOM. American Liberties:
1920-1970's. Norton (1975). JFK years by Milton R. Konvitz.

Rose, Arnold M. ed. ASSURING FREEDOM TO THE FREE. A Century of
Emancipation in the U.S.A. Wayne State U., 1964. Re JFK cf. articles by Myrdal, Robt.C. Weaver, Jas.Q. Wilson, Whitney Young.

Rovere, Richard H. "Determination of the Negroes for Justice,"
NEW YORKER, June 1, 1963: 3-5ff. "Government Is For Complete
Equality for the Negro," ibid. June 22, 1963: 90ff.+ JFK's
civil rights program.

Roche, John P. THE QUEST FOR THE DREAM. 1st Macm. 1963. A social
history of civil rights. JFK and the confrontation of conscience.

SAT.EVE.POST. Editorial: "Mr. Kennedy's Deliberate Speed," Feb.
24, 1962: 98.

√TIME. Civil Rights. "The Awful Roar," Aug.30, 1963: 9-14.

U.S.Commission on Civil Rights. HOUSING. GPO, 1961. Wrs. Ever-
increasing concentration of non-whites in ghettos nationwide.

U.S.Dept. of Commerce. A.R.A. NEGRO-WHITE DIFFERENCES IN GEO-
GRAPHIC MOBILITY by Eva Mueller and Wm.Ladd. Wrs. 1964. Need to
create new employment opportunities for unskilled in depressed
areas.

U.S.Dept. of Labor. THE ECONOMIC SITUATION OF NEGROES IN THE U.S.
From REPORT in 1960. GPO, 1962. Esp. "Employment Policies," Federal Gov't and Gov't-connected work: 11-15.

Wallace, Robt. "Non-whiz Kid with the Quiet Gun. Bruce Marshall,
Center of Racial Hurricane." LIFE, Aug.9, 1963: 75-78ff.

Warren, Robt.Penn. WHO SPEAKS FOR THE NEGRO? 1st Random, 1965.
"The Negro Now," LOOK, Mar.23, 1965: 23-31.

Weyl, Nathaniel and Wm. Marina. AMERICAN STATESMEN ON SLAVERY AND
THE NEGRO. Arlington, 1971. Chap.21: Eisenhower and JFK.

Williams, Edward Bennett. ONE MAN'S FREEDOM. Atheneum, 1962. Defense of some of major precepts of Constitution re rights of the
individual with some of author's experiences at the bar. Praise
for JFK for his stand on equality for Negroes. RFK and the Igor
Melekh case.

√Woodward, C. Vann. THE STRANGE CAREER OF JIM CROW. Wrs. Oxford,
1966. JFK's committment to civil rights.

Civil Rights: Specific Regions

Adelman, Bob and Sue Hall. DOWN HOME. 1st Prairie (McG-H) 1972.
Camden, Ala. photographic portrait. Pictures of JFK, RFK, MLK
prominent in Negro homes. "They was the cause of the few things
we got here now...And they started us off to vote." "They killed
them because they didn't want the Negroes brought out from under
their foots...I don't see nothing else."

American Opinion Reprint. A Report by the General Legislative
Investigating Committee to the Mississippi State Legislature Con-
cerning THE OCCUPATION OF THE CAMPUS OF THE UNIVERSITY OF MISSISS-
IPPI, Sept.30, 1962. Wrs. Description of "Federal take-over."

Ashmore, Harry S. "The Coming Showdown on the Race Crisis," LOOK
July 16, 1963: 62-67. Also "Five Days in Mississippi," by Thos.
Morgan: 86-90.

Boylan, James. "Birmingham: Newspapers in a Crisis. COL.JRNL.REV.
Summer, 1963: 29-33. Examination of the files of the two Birmingham dailies for the first half of May -bombing and riots May 11.

Crawford, Marc. "The Ominous Malcolm X Exits from the Muslims,"
LIFE, Mar.20, 1964: 39A-40A-

Dabbs, Jas. McBRide. THE SOUTHERN HERITAGE. Southern View of Race
Relations. Knopf, 1958. Author: president of Southern Regional
Council during JFK administration. Monitor of registration drive.

Davidson, Bill. "A City in Trouble: The Mess in Washington.
SEP, July 13-20, 1963: 17-23. Segregationists in the House.-

Deming, Barbara. "In the Birmingham Jail," NATION, May 25, 1963:
436-437. The only white person arrested in demonstration.

Dorman, Michael. WE SHALL OVERCOME. A Reporter's Eyewitness Account of the Year of Racial Strife and Triumph (1962). Delacorte,
1964. Roles of JFK and RFK. Important for evoking troubled time.

Farmer, James. FREEDOM - WHEN? 1st Random, 1965. History of
C.O.R.E. with personal experiences.

Forman, James. SAMMY YOUNGE JR. The First Black College Student
to Die in the Black Liberation Movement. 1st Grove, 1968. SNCC.

Hamburger, Robt. and Michael Abramson. OUR PORTION OF HELL: Fay-
ette County, Tennessee, an Oral History of the Struggle for Civil
Rights. 1st Links, 1973. JFK and RFK then LBJ when community action programs passed out of the hands of the poor. Powerful.

Inger, Morton. POLITICS AND REALITY IN AN AMERICAN CITY: The
New Orleans School Crisis of 1960. Wrs. 1st C.U.E., 1969. How it
was when JFK became President.

DOMESTIC AFFAIRS

Civil Rights: Specific Regions

Johnson, Haynes. DUSK AT THE MOUNTAIN: The Negro, The Nation and The Capitol. 1st D'day, 1963. JFK: strong executive action; RFK: harbinger of hope.

Kahn, Thos. "The Political Signifcance of the Freedom Rides," 57-68, in THE NEW STUDENT LEFT, Mitchell Cohen and Dennis Hale, eds. 1st Beacon, wrs., 1967. Reaction of the new left to Kennedy administration emphasis on the objective of winning the ballot.

King, Martin Luther, Jr. STRIDE TOWARD FREEDOM. The Montgomery Story. Harper (1958). "The Case Against 'Tokenism'." N.Y.TIMES MAG. Aug.5, 1962: 11ff."LETTER FROM BIRMINGHAM JAIL," Apr.16,1963 American Friends...May, 1963. STRENGTH TO LOVE H&R, 1963. Autographed. WHY WE CAN'T WAIT. 1st Signet, wrs., 1964. "His (President Kennedy's) last speech on race relations was the most earnest human and profound appeal for understanding and justice that any President has uttered since the first days of the Republic."p.144 "Why the Negro Can't Wait," LIFE, May 15, 1964: 98-102ff. Review: SAT.REV. May 30, 1964: 17-20ff. "Civil Right No.1: The Right to Vote," N.Y.TIMES MAG.,Mar.14, 1965:26-27ff. Untitled article in A GIFT OF LOVE, Priv.pr., 1td. ed. on non-violence and freedom marches. McCall's, 1966. WHERE DO WE GO FROM HERE: Chaos or Community? Autographed. 1st H&R, 1967. Ibid. condensation, No.31 in Sidney Hillman Reprint Series. "I HAVE A DREAM," G&D, n.d. wrs. circa 1968.

Leonard, Geo.B. et al. "How a Secret Deal Prevented a Massacre at Ole Miss," LOOK, Dec.31, 1962: 19-24ff.

Lord, Walter. THE PAST THAT WOULD NOT DIE. 1st H&R, 1965. The climactic "Meredith case."

Mays, Benjamin. BORN TO REBEL: Autobiography. Scrib.(1971) Chapter XVI. "Politicians and President Kennedy."

Meredith, James H. "I'll Know Victory or Defeat. The Mississippi Story," SEP, Nov.10, 1962:14-25. "I Can't Fight Alone," LOOK, Apr.9, 1963: 70-72ff. THREE YEARS IN MISSISSIPPI. Indiana U. 1966 Full report of part the Federal gov't played in struggle.

NEWSWEEK. "'Freedom Riders' Face a Test," June 5, 1961: 18-23. Cover RFK and MLK. "The Lonely Man at 'Ole Miss.'" Jan.21, 1963: 30-31.

Poppy, John. "The South's War Against Negro Votes," LOOK, May 21, 1963: 38ff.

Rowan, Carl. SOUTH OF FREEDOM. Knopf, 1952. JFK's Ambassador to Finland.

Rustin, Bayard. "From Protest to Politics," COMMENTARY, Feb.,1965: 25-31. JFK's "go slow" approach until Birmingham upheaval. TLS.

Civil Rights: Specific Regions

Schoener, Allon ed. HARLEM ON MY MIND 1900-1968. 1st Random,1968.
Pertinent here: 1960-1968 Militancy and Identity: 227-255 for
black New York background.

Sellars, Cleveland with Robt. Terrell. THE RIVER OF NO RETURN.
Morrow (1973). Momentous days of Civil Rights Movement in '60s.

Sherrill, Robt. GOTHIC POLITICS IN THE DEEP SOUTH. 1st Grossman,
1968. JFK and RFK and southern leaders.

Silver, James. MISSISSIPPI: The Closed Society. HB&W (1964). by
a professor of history at the University of Mississippi. Review
by Joseph Epstein, COMMENTARY, Dec.1964: 73-74ff. "Campus Scourge
at Ole Miss" (Dr. James Silver). LIFE, July 17, 1964:74A.-

Smith, Lillian. "'Now the Lonely Decision for Right or Wrong,'"
(Mississippi campus), LIFE, Oct.12, 1962: 32-44.

TIME. "Though the Heavens Fall," Oct.12, 1962: 19-22. Meredith
at University of Mississippi. "Civil Rights. The Central Point,"
Mar.19, 1965:23-28.

Trillin, Calvin. AN EDUCATION IN GEORGIA. The Integration of
Charlayne Hunter and Hamilton Holmes. Viking, 1964.

U.S.NEWS... "Kennedy's Worry: Is the Solid South Lost for '64?"
Oct.28, 1963: 35-37. -

Wainwright, Loudon. "Martyr of the Sit-Ins: Dr. Martin Luther
King, Jr. LIFE, Nov.7, 1960: 123-124ff.

Watters, Pat and Reese Cleghorn. CLIMBING JACOB'S LADDER: The
Arrival of Negroes in Southern Politics. HB&W, 1967. Primarily
about the voter registration in the South. Chapter 8. "Federal
Action and a Crisis in the Courts" 210-243.

Williams, Robt.F. NEGROES WITH GUNS. Wrs. M&M, 1962. A plea for
right to arm in self-defense. The Dept. of Justice "dangerous."

Williamson, S.W. WITH GRIEF ACQUAINTED. Follett, 1964. Negro
American in South Chicago in text and photographs.

Young, Whitney M, Jr. TO BE EQUAL: A Program of Special Effort...
Proposing Practical Alternatives to Continuous Racial Conflict.
1st McG-H, 1964. JFK as reacting intelligently to the demands
of Negro citizens, with summary of his accomplishments. Quotes
his "If peaceful revolution is impossible, then violent revolution is inevitable."

Zinn, Howard. THE SOUTHERN MYSTIQUE. 1st Knopf, 1964. Third
part: case study of Albany, Georgia with response of JFK, RFK.

DOMESTIC AFFAIRS

Civil Rights: Equal Employment Opportunity

PRESIDENT'S COMMITTEE EQUAL EMPLOYMENT OPPORTUNITY. "Report. The
First Nine Months," GPO, 1962. "Equal Employment Opportunity. A
Plan for Progress from North American Aviation," NAA Feb.,1963.
Instructions published by GPO: Notice: Pledge of E.E.O. (Federal
contractors required to post this notice.) Standard forms 40
and 40A Compliance Report. Nondiscrimination provisions of U.S.
Gov't contracts Dec. 1961. Federal Gov't Employment: rules and
regulations effective July 1, 1961, as amended Feb.27, 1962. Questions and answers on the compliance report, Aug. 1962. Gov't contract rules and regulations on employment effective July 22,1961,
as amended Nov.23, 1962. Three LBJ press releases Apr.4, May 19,
1962, Apr.4, 1963. Seven newsletters July-Aug. 1961 - Jan. 1963;
eight press releases May 19, 1962 - May 1, 1963.

Civil Rights: March on Washington

Bohn, Dorothy. A SOCIOLOGICAL STUDY OF SOME NEWSPAPER REPORTING
OF THE MARCH ON WASHINGTON. Dissertation, OSU, 1966. Content an-
alysis of eight metropolitan newspapers to study the effect of the
March as stimulus to change. References to Kennedy administration.

Kempton, Murray. "The Choice, Mr. President..." THE NEW REPUBLIC
(25th Anniversary). 1st S&S, 1964. First published July 6, 1963.
A. Philip Randolph, JFK and the March on Washington.

Leadership Conference on Civil Rights and the March on Washington.
"A Strong Civil Rights Bill by Christmas!" (Flyer)

LIFE. "Marchers' Master Plan. A Nation Uneasily Awaits Its
Greatest Civil Rights Rally," Aug.23, 1963: 63-64ff. by Warren R.
Young and Wm. Lambert. "They Come Marching Up Conscience Road.
Negroes Stir Up Nation in Mighty Washington March," Sept.6, 1963:
20-29. "Letters to the Editor," Sept.27, 1963: 25.

O'Connor, John. "Why a Peace March?" QUEEN'S WORK, Dec. 1963: 4ff.

Recordings. MARCH ON WASHINGTON. The Official Album. WRVR, N.Y.
WE SHALL OVERCOME. Flying Dutchman Production Ltd.

Civil Rights: Women

Group for the Advancement of Psychiatry. THE EDUCATED WOMAN:
Prospects and Problems. Scrib.,1975. Mention of JFK's Commission on the Status of Women in 1963 as a starting point of the
"new" Feminist movement.

U.S. President's Commission on the Status of Women. REPORT: AM-
ERICAN WOMEN 1963. (Op.cit. under JFK Speeches and Public Statements). Eleanor Roosevelt Chairman with Esther Peterson Vice-
Chairman. Referred to as the time things began to change for
women. (Cf.O'Neill, COMING APART: 195-196, op.cit. GENERAL WORKS)

THE KENNEDY FAMILY OF MASSACHUSETTS

Congress

Bailey, Stephen K. THE NEW CONGRESS. St.Martin, 1966. Over-view of mid-60's: presidential influence, party leadership, change by enlargement of Rules Committee under impetus of JFK, necessity of reform of campaign finance laws, e.g. the recommendations of JFK's Commission on Campaign Costs.

Berman, Daniel M. IN CONGRESS ASSEMBLED. 1st Macm., 1964. JFK's relations with Congress.

Burke, Vincent and Frank Eleazer. "How Kennedy Gets What He Wants...Methods to Sway Congress in the Future," NATION'S BUSI-NESS, Sept.,1961: 96-102.+

Cater, Douglas. "What's Happening to the Democratic Party," RE-PORTER, May 10, 1962:23-26. Building a winning coalition.

Clark, Joseph. CONGRESS: THE SAPLESS BRANCH. 1st H&R, 1964. JFK's efforts on major tax reform, delaying tactics of Congress, establishment-oriented Congressional leadership.

CONGRESS AND THE NATION 1945-1964. Review of Government and Poli-tics. CQ, 1965. Summary of all major legislation in historical perspective, biographical index of last ten Congresses, report on all elections and political activities, key votes, review of 216 major Supreme Court cases. Truman, Eisenhower, Kennedy, Johnson.

CONGRESSIONAL DIRECTORY. 87th Cong. 1st Sess. April, 1961.GPO. Shows JFK's appointees to major offices.

Deakin, James. THE LOBBYISTS. Public Affairs Pr., 1966. Re JFK: the Chamber of Commerce, savings and loan assns., Nat'l Riflemen.

Harris, Richard. THE REAL VOICE. Sen. Kefauver's Investigation of the Drug Industry. 1st Macm.1964. JFK's position.

Josephy, Alvin M. Jr. THE AMERICAN HERITAGE HISTORY OF THE CON-GRESS OF THE U.S. Includes profile of JFK's accomplishments with Congress. In slip case with companion volume: AMERICAN TESTAMENT. American Heritage, 1975.

Koenig, Louis W. CONGRESS AND THE PRESIDENT. Wrs. S-F, 1966. Many illustrations of JFK and administration at work.

Lewis, Claude. ADAM CLAYTON POWELL. 1st Goldmark, 1963. His relationship with Kennedy administration: cooperative on whole.

MacNeil, Neil. FORGE OF DEMOCRACY; The House of Representatives. McKay, 1963. Under JFK the Senate as ratifying, the House as chal-lenging his legislative proposals. "The House Confronts Mr. Ken-nedy," FORTUNE, Jan. 1962: 70-73ff.

Meyers, Harold B."Congress Strikes Back at Kennedy," USA1, June 9, 1962: 30-35.

DOMESTIC AFFAIRS

Congress

NEWSWEEK. "'We Might Be Lucky.'" Nov.4, 1963: 27-28. - Threat
to civil rights bill. "JFK and Congress: Counterattack," Nov.25,
1963: 29-30. Also "JFK's Schedule," 30-31.-

N.Y.TIMES MAG. "Why Kennedy Has Trouble on the Hill," by Russell
Baker, April, 16, 1961: 23ff.-"Presidential Popularity Is Not
Enough," by Sidney Hyman, Aug.12, 1962: 10ff.- "Kennedy, Too,
Hits the Election Trail," by Tom Wicker, Oct.14, 1962:24-25. At-
tempt to elect a more sympathetic Congress. "How the President
Persuades Congress," Oct.27, 1963:16-17. Cover photo.

Pearson, Drew, and Jack Anderson. THE CASE AGAINST CONGRESS, S&S
1968. Contains some side lights on JFK.

Polsby, Nelson W. CONGRESS AND THE PRESIDENCY. Wrs. P-H, 1964.
JFK one of the case studies. 2nd ed. rev. P-H, 1971. Wrs.

Ripley, Randall B. MAJORITY PARTY LEADERSHIP IN CONGRESS. 1st
L-B, 1969. Analysis since 1900. JFK's Congress in depth.

SAT. EVE. POST Editorial: "The President and the Congress," Sept.
1, 1962: 86.-

TIME. "Congress: the Case for Subtlety," July 27, 1962: 9-10.
Medicare set-back.

U.S.NEWS... "How Congress Sizes Up President Kennedy," Feb.26,
1962: 50-60. "Why Kennedy's Program Is In Trouble with Congress,"
interview with Sen. Mansfield, Sept.17, 1962: 62-69. "New Help
for Kennedy in Senate," Jan.21, 1963: 34-37.+ "Why Congress Does-
n't Give JFK What He Wants," Mar.18, 1963: 38-42.-

Vinyard, Dale. CONGRESS. Scrib., 1969. Includes JFK in the
electoral arena, legislative environment, contribution to Congressional reform.

White, Wm.S. "The Kennedy Era, Stage Two: The Coming Battle with
Congress, HARPER, Feb.,1963: 96-97ff.

Departments of Agriculture and Interior

Hadwiger, Don F. and Ross B. Talbot. PRESSURES AND PROTESTS: The
Kennedy Farm Program and the Wheat Referendum of 1963. Chandler,
1965. Wrs. Accomplishments with Orville Freeman under JFK.

LIFE. "An Awakening for Orville (Freeman)," July 7, 1961: 48.

McGovern, George, ed. AGRICULTURAL THOUGHT IN THE 20TH CENTURY.
1st B-M, 1967. Wrs. Intro. by McGovern and Freeman on JFK.

Udall, Stewart. "National Parks for the Future," ATLANTIC, June,
1961: 81-84. Cf. also THE QUIET CRISIS op.cit. JFK "Forewords."

Economics of the New Frontier

Brundage, Percival F. THE BUREAU OF THE BUDGET. Praeger, 1970. Complex operations of the Bureau. Description of JFK years.

BUDGET OF THE U.S. GOV'T. Fiscal Year Ending June 30, 1963. Wrs. GPO, 1962. First complete budget of JFK administration.

Flash, Edw.S. Jr. ECONOMIC ADVICE AND PRESIDENTIAL LEADERSHIP. The Council of Economic Advisers. 1st Columbia, 1965. The Council under three of its Chairmen. Chaps. 6, 7: JFK as educable.

Harrington, Michael. TOWARD A DEMOCRATIC LEFT. Macm.,1968. "The Dynamics of Misery," No.32 in Sidney Hillman Reprints. Wrs. SOCIALISM, Sat.Rev.Pr., 1972. JFK as social Keynesian.

Harris, T. Geo. "Walter Heller: 'Mr. Tax Cut'," LOOK, June 18, 1963: 81-82ff.

LIFE. Editorial: "Kennedy Economics, Short Term," Feb.10, 1961: 26. Editorial: "Kennedy's Tax May Not Be One to Grow On," Feb.8, 1963: 4. "Kennedy's Dollar Proposal: Not All Good," Aug.2, 1963.

Mooney, Richard E. "Economic Oracles of the New Frontier," N.Y. TIMES MAG., Aug.4, 1963: 8ff.-

Norton, Hugh S. ECONOMIC POLICY: GOVERNMENT AND BUSINESS. Merrill, 1966. Economic accomplishments of JFK.

Nossiter, Bernard P. "The Day the Taxes Weren't Cut," REPORTER, Sept.13, 1962: 25-28. JFK's decision against a tax cut.

Rostow, Walt W. "Le Credo du President Kennedy," REALITIES, Aug. 1962: 24-27.

Rovere, Richard. "The Kennedy Tax Proposals," NEW YORKER,Aug.25 1962: 101-107.

Seligman, Ben B. "Tariffs, the Kennedy Administration and American Politics," COMMENTARY, March, 1962: 185-196.

TIME. "The Presidency and the Economy," March 16, 1962: 15-16. "The Economy: Tax-Cut Decision," July 20, 1962: 16-17.

U.S.Congress. Joint Economic Committee. JANUARY 1963 ECONOMIC REPORT OF THE PRESIDENT. Hearings, 88th Cong.,1st Sess. 2 Parts. Wrs. GPO, 1963.

Wilkins, B.H. and C.B.Friday eds. THE ECONOMISTS OF THE NEW FRONTIER. 1st Random, 1963.

Winch, Donald. ECONOMICS AND POLICY. A Historical Study. Walker, 1970. JFK as "the first Keynesian President."

DOMESTIC AFFAIRS

Education and Health

Kennedy Program for Health Insurance through Social Security.
EACH FAMILY HAS THREE RESPONSIBILITIES. Brochure, wrs. N.P.,n.d.
Re King-Anderson bill HR4222

NEWSWEEK. "Suddenly- the Crashing Problems" (for Ribicoff), Feb.20
1961: 23-25. "The Great Medicare Debate," June 4, 1962: 28ff.
JFK vs. A.M.A.

O'Neill, James M. "Federal Aid to Religion Is Legal," SIGN,
Nov. 1961: 20-22. -

Price, Hugh Douglas. "The Congress: Race, Religion and the Rules
Committee: the Kennedy Aid-to-Education Bills," in THE USES OF
POWER: Seven Cases in American Politics, HB&W, 1962: 1-71.
"Schools, Scholarships and Congressmen, the Kennedy Aid-to-Educa-
tion Program," in THE CENTERS OF POWER, Three Cases in American
National Government. Wrs. HB&W, 1964: 53-106. Alan F. Westin,
editor of both volumes.

Ribicoff, Abraham. "'To Promote the General Welfare.'" N.Y.TIMES
MAG. July 9, 1961: 9ff.- JFK's proposals for health and education.

Cf. also, Wm.T. O'Hara, ed. JOHN F. KENNEDY ON EDUCATION op.cit.
JFK Writings.

Fallout Shelters

Ephemera: Knox County and City of Mt. Vernon Civil Defense, COM-
MUNITY FALLOUT SHELTER PLAN, Gambier,Ohio:1969. U.S.Dept. of Ag-
riculture in cooperation with the Office of Civil Defense: YOUR
FAMILY SURVIVAL PLAN: FAMILY FOOD STOCKPILE FOR SURVIVAL. U.S.
Dept. of Defense - Office of Civil Defense: WHAT TO KNOW AND DO
ABOUT NUCLEAR ATTACK. GPO, Dec. 1961. Wrs.

Knebel, Fletcher. "The Great Fall-Out Shelter Panic," LOOK, Dec.
5, 1961: 21-25.

Marzani, Carl et al. THE SHELTER HOAX AND FOREIGN POLICY. M&M,
circa 1962, wrs. Author urges universal disarmament.

NEW REPUBLIC. "Shelters and Survival," Jan.15, 1962: 1-40.+

NEWSWEEK. "Shelters: Jitters Ease, Debate Goes On." Jan.15, 1962:
50-51. Re Administration pamphlet on fallout protection.

Rabinowitch, Eugene. "To Build or Not to Build (fall-out shelters). BULL. OF ATOMIC SCIENTISTS, Nov.1961: 354-355.

Reed, Muriel. "Inside a Fallout Shelter," REALITIES, Oct.,
1962: 37.

THE KENNEDY FAMILY OF MASSACHUSETTS

Fallout Shelters

Seton, Cynthia. I THINK ROME IS BURNING. An Embattled Statistic Speaks Her Mind on Issues Ranging From the Cradle to the Fallout Shelter. 1st D'day, 1962.

U.S. Civil Defense FALLOUT SHELTER PROGRAM. Hearings before Sub-committee No. 3 of Armed Services, House of Representatives, 88th Cong.1st sess. June3-July 31, 1963. Part Two: 2 vols. Wrs. GPO.

Young, Warren. "Everybody's Talking About Shelters..." LIFE, Jan.12, 1962: 34-42. Also, editorial: 4.

Federal Bureau of Investigation

Cook, Fred J. THE FBI NOBODY KNOWS. Macm.,1964. A look at Direc-tor J.Edgar Hoover. How he blocked JFK's and RFK's plan for a National Crime Commission. RFK and Valachi, Hiss. "Organized Crime: The Strange Reluctance," 140-166 in INVESTIGATING THE FBI, Pat Watters and Stephen Giller eds. 1st D'day, 1973.

Messick, Hank. JOHN EDGAR HOOVER: A Critical Examination of the Director and of the Continuing Alliance Between Crime, Business and Politics. McKay, 1972. The Kennedy years as "nervous interlude" for Hoover. The assassination of JFK as ending the threat to Hoover's forced retirement.

Phelan, James. "Hoover of the FBI," SAT.EVE.POST, Dec.1975:30-35

Unger, Sanford J. FBI: AN UNCENSORED LOOK BEHIND THE WALLS. 1st L-B, 1975. Includes Hoover's relations with JFK, RFK, EMK.

U.S. Congress, Senate. INTELLIGENCE ACTIVITIES. Hearings before the Select Committee to Study Governmental Operations with Respect to Intelligence Activities. Vol.6. "Federal Bureau of Investiga-tion." Wrs. 94th Cong., 1st sess. GPO, 1975. N.B. Appendix A,"The Performance of the FBI in Investigating Violations of Federal Laws Protecting the Right to Vote - 1960-1967," by John Doar and Dorothy Landsberg: 888:991. INTELLIGENCE ACTIVITIES AND THE RIGHTS OF AMERICANS. Book II. "Final Report of the Select Commit-tee to Study Governmental Operations..." Wrs. 94th Cong., 2d sess. Report 94-755. GPO, 1975. Includes MLK and JFK.

Judicial System

Ashman,Chas. R. THE FINEST JUDGES MONEY CAN BUY, and Other Forms of Judicial Pollution. Nash, 1973. Francis X. Morrissey & Kennedys.

Chase, Harold W. FEDERAL JUDGES: The Appointing Process. U. of Minn.,1972. sCholarly analysis, incl. JFK's administration.

Goldberg, Arthur J. THE DEFENSES OF FREEDOM: Public Papers of... 1st H&R, 1966. Many quotes and references to JFK.

DOMESTIC AFFAIRS

Judicial System

Goulden, Jos.C. THE BENCHWARMERS. The Private World of the Powerful Federal Judges. W&T, 1974. Kennedy appointments, who and why.

Jackson, Donald Dale. JUDGES. 1st Atheneum, 1974. JFK as opening the door to black judges and as criticized, somewhat unfairly
in comparison with Eisenhower, for appointment of Southern segregationists.

Liston, Robt. TIDES OF JUSTICE. The Supreme Court and the Constitution in Our Time. Delacorte, 1969. JFK as political alchemist.

Murphy, Paul L. THE CONSTITUTION IN CRISIS TIMES 1918-1969. 1st
H&R, 1972. Chap.11: "The New Frontier and the Constitution..."

Simon, James F. IN HIS OWN IMAGE. The Supreme Court in Richard
Nixon's America. Recalls JFK's appointments, EMK attacks on Nixon appointees.

Mental Health and Mental Retardation

Loeb, Martin B. "Mental Health: New Frontiers," NATION, May 18,
1963: 418-421. The Kennedy proposal.

President's Panel on Mental Retardation. A NATIONAL PLAN TO COM-
BAT MENTAL RETARDATION... GPO, 1962. REPORT OF THE TASK FORCE ON
LAW. GPO, 1963. Wrs. BIBLIOGRAPHY OF WORLD LITERATURE ON MENTAL
RETARDATION. U.S.Dept. of HEW, 1963. 16,096 entries.

Rogow, Arnold A. THE PSYCHIATRISTS. Putnam, 1970. Includes
community mental health movement under JFK; ethical dilemma of
public analysis of JBK; conflicting psychiatric testimony Sirhan.

Post Office

Cullinan, Gerald. THE POST OFFICE DEPARTMENT. Praeger, 1968. JFK
and his Executive Order 10988 which made management recognition
of postal unions mandatory.

Day, J. Edward. MY APPOINTED ROUND: 929 Days as Postmaster General. 1st HR&W, 1965. Relationships with JFK and RFK.

Presidential Politics

Burns, James MacGregor. THE DEADLOCK OF DEMOCRACY: Four-Party
Politics in America. P-H, 1963. JFK as Senator and President. "Why
We Face a Deadlock in Washington," LOOK, Jan.29, 1963: 52ff. PRES-
IDENTIAL GOVERNMENT. 1st Avon, wrs., 1967. UNCOMMON SENSE, 1st
H&R, 1972. JFK as defeated by present system.

Cater, Douglas. POWER IN WASHINGTON. 1st Random, 1964. Pt.II.JFK.

Presidential Politics

Crane, Philip M. THE DEMOCRAT'S DILEMMA. Regnery, 1964. JFK and the A.D.A.: 178-193.

Dahl, Robt.A. PLURALIST DEMOCRACY IN THE U.S.: Conflict and Consent. McN, 1969. Examples of JFK in presidency, civil rights etc.

Democratic Nat'l Convention Committee. DEMOCRATS IN CONVENTION 1972. Merkle, wrs. JFK: 101-106, place in history; JBK: 144.

Harsch, Jos.C. THE ROLE OF POLITICAL PARTIES IN THE U.S. Wrs. League of Women Voters Education Fund, 1962. Refs. to JFK,cartoon.

Heren, Louis. THE NEW AMERICAN COMMONWEALTH. 1st H&R, 1968. Presidential campaign of JFK: direct appeal to the people.

Hess, Stephen and David S. Broder. THE REPUBLICAN ESTABLISHMENT. H&R (1967). Chaps.5 and 6: JFK and Romney, Nixon.

Hyman, Sidney. THE POLITICS OF CONSENSUS. 1st Random, 1968. JFK as example of prophetic, and LBJ of apocalyptic approaches.

James, Dorothy B. THE CONTEMPORARY PRESIDENCY. 1st Pegasus/B-M, 1979. JFK as example among others.

Michener, James A. PRESIDENTIAL LOTTERY. The Reckless Gamble of Our Electoral System. 1st Random, 1969. JFK's defense of present electoral system: 109.

Peirce, Neil R. THE PEOPLE'S PRESIDENT. THE ELECTORAL COLLEGE... S&S, 1968. How near process has come to back-firing, e.g. JFK's election; his attitude to reform.

Perry, Jas.M. THE NEW POLITICS: The Expanding Technology of Political Manipulation. 1st Potter, 1968. Examines dozens of political campaigns including those of JFK, RFK, EMK.

Phillips, Kevin P. THE EMERGING REPUBLICAN MAJORITY. Arlington, 1969. Study of American voting patterns. JFK: Catholic and ethnic vote.

POLITICAL HANDBOOK AND ATLAS OF THE WORLD. H&R, 1963. U.S. party programs, leaders, Cabinet, newspapers in JFK administration.

Polsby, Nelson W. POLITICAL PROMISES. Oxford, 1974. Essays which include references to JFK, RFK, EMK.

Redford, Emmette S. DEMOCRACY IN THE ADMINISTRATIVE STATE. Oxford 1969. JFK's description of solar system applied to government.

Rousseau, Edw.L. "One President, Two Parties," COMMONWEAL, Nov. 24, 1961: 223-226.-

DOMESTIC AFFAIRS

Presidential Politics

Scott, Hugh. COME TO THE PARTY...Moderate Republicanism. P-H, 1968. Kennedy-Nixon campaign; assessment of JFK.

Tillett, Paul, ed. THE POLITICAL VOCATION. Basic, 1965. Summary recommendations of the Pres. Commission on Campaign Costs, 1962.

Tolchin, Martin and Susan. TO THE VICTOR: Political Patronage from the Clubhouse to the White House. Random (1971). Specifics on how JFK and others "played the game."

Tugwell, Rexford G. HOW THEY BECAME PRESIDENT. Thirty-five Ways to the White House. 1st S&S, 1964. JFK: 456-473.

U.S.News... U.S.POLITICS - Inside and Out. Wrs. (1970) References to Joseph Kennedy Sr., JFK, RFK, EMK.

Regional Political Studies

Costikyan, Edw.N. BEHIND CLOSED DOORS. Politics in the Public Interest. 1st HB&W, 1966. New York, and examples of JFK, RFK.

Hill, Gladwin. DANCING BEAR. An Inside Look at California Politics. 1st World, 1968. JFK, Pat Brown, Jesse Unruh, Sam Yorty.

Knebel, Fletcher. "Washington D.C.: Portrait of a Sick City," LOOK, June 4, 1963: 15-19.

Morris, Willie. "Texas Politics In Turmoil." HARPER, Sept., 1962: 76-77ff.

O'Neill, Edw.A. RAPE OF THE AMERICAN VIRGINS. 1st Praeger, 1972. Critical of Kennedy administration and Stuart Udall in particular.

Price, Willard. AMERICA'S PARADISE LOST: The Strange Story of the Secret Atolls. Day, 1966. JFK as trying to help; more needed.

Secret Service

Baughman, U.E. with L.W.Robinson. "Presidents in Danger," LOOK, Sept.12, 1961: 24-30ff. SECRET SERVICE CHIEF, 1st Harp., 1962. Truman, Eisenhower, Kennedy and their families.

Healy, Paul F. "There Goes the President! An Inside View of the Intricate Planning Which Assures Mr. Kennedy's Safety on His Whirlwind Trips. SAT.EVE.POST, Jan.20, 1962: 80-83.

Shuster, Alan. "The Forty Watchdogs of the President. N.Y.TIMES MAG. Oct.21, 1962: 67ff.- The members of the Secret Service White House detail.

111.

THE KENNEDY FAMILY OF MASSACHUSETTS

Space Program

American Rocket Society. SPACE FLIGHT, ed. by Jerry and Vivian Grey. Basic (1962). JFK and long range planning for moon landing.

Binder, Otto. VICTORY IN SPACE. Walker, 1962. The space race and JFK.

BULL. OF ATOMIC SCIENTISTS. "Space Exploration in the Service of Science," May-June, 1961: 170-240. "Space Developments: Kennedy Action," Sept., 1961: 301.

Caidin, Martin. RENDEZVOUS IN SPACE. 1st Dutton, 1962.

Calder, Nigel. TECHNOPOLIS: Social Control of the Uses of Science. 1st S&S, 1969. JFK's attempt to cooperate with U.S.S.R.

Cox, Donald W. AMERICA'S NEW POLICY MAKERS: The Scientists Rise to Power. 1st Chilton, 1964. JFK as increasing their prestige.

Etzioni, Amitai. THE MOON-DOGGLE. 1st D'day, 1964. Critique of policy. JFK's efforts to interest Russia in space cooperation.

Glenn, John H., Jr. "P.S. I LISTENED TO YOUR HEART BEAT," Letters to Glenn with comments. World Bk., 1964. Presentation copy. ORBITAL FLIGHT OF JOHN H. GLENN JR. Hearing before the Committee on Aeronautical and Space Sciences, U.S.Senate, 87th Cong. 2nd sess. Feb.28, 1962. Wrs. GPO, 1962.

Kennan, Erlend A. and E.H. Harvey. MISSION TO THE MOON. A Critical Examination of NASA and the Space Program. Morrow, 1969. Much about JFK's position.

LIFE. "Emotions of the Nation Ride in Astronout's Capsule, So-" (re Alan Shepherd). May 12, 1961: 18-31. "From the Album of John Glenn..." Feb.2, 1962: 22ff. "He Hit that 'Keyhole in the Sky' - Suspense of a Nation and a Family - the Sweet Pride," Mar.2, 1962: 20-27. Also "For Those Who Cared Most..." by Loudon Wainwright, 28-35.

Mailer, Norman. OF A FIRE ON THE MOON. 1st L-B, 1970. Blend of reportage and reflection on trip to moon initiated by JFK.

Pierce, Philip N. JOHN H. GLENN, ASTRONAUT. 1st F.W., 1962.

"President John F. Kennedy's Last Visit to America's Spaceport, Nov.16, 1963:" 70-71 in CAPE KENNEDY by C.W.Scarboro and Stephen B. Milner. Pioneer, 1966.

> "This is a new ocean and I believe the United States must sail upon it." JFK

> "First I believe that this Nation should commit itself to achieving the goal, before this decade is out, of landing a man on the moon and returning him safely to earth."- JFK

PART THREE. THE ASSASSINATION OF PRESIDENT JOHN F. KENNEDY AND
AFTERMATH

THE ASSASSINATION

Dallas, Texas

Bainbridge, John. "Profiles: The Super-American State," (Texas,
and Dallas). NEW YORKER, May 6, 1961: 49-50ff.+

Elms, Alan C. "Right Wingers in Dallas," PSYCHOLOGY TODAY, Feb.,
1970: 27-31ff.

Leslie, Warren. DALLAS: Public and Private. 1st Grossman, 1964.
Also Avon, 1964, wrs. Review by Lou Tinkle, SAT.REV. Apr.18,1964.-

LIFE. "What Kind of Place Is Dallas?" by Robt. Wallace, Jan.31,
1964: 67-70ff.- "Why Kennedy Went to Texas," by John Connally,
Nov.24, 1967: 86A-86B. Kennedys and Connallys on cover.

LOOK. "Memo From a Dallas Citizen," by J.M.Shea Jr., Mar.24,
1964: 88ff. "Memo About a Dallas Citizen," by George Harris,
Aug.11, 1964: 64ff.

Lyle, Jack. THE NEWS IN MEGALOPOLIS. Chandler, 1967. Study of
two daily newspapers in Dallas during 1960 presidential campaign.

NEWSWEEK. "Texas: What the Casket Cost," Mar.8, 1965: 29.- "The
Assassination: Scene of the Crime," (Dallas) Dec.4, 1967: 31B-32.-
"Dallas: New Questions and Answers," By Peter Goodman and John
Lindsay, Apr.28, 1976: 36-38.

SAT.EVE.POST. "The Shame of Dallas,"Apr.11, 1964: 82. "Dallas:
The Cuban Connection," by George O'Toole and Paul Hoch. Mar,1976:
44-45ff.

Smith, Richard A. "How Business Failed Dallas," FORTUNE, July,
1964: 156-163ff. Leadership failed to condemn hate-mongering.

U.S.NEWS... "A Different Look at Dallas," Feb.3, 1964: 42-46. A
defense. "Dallas: New Questions and Answers," Apr.28, 1975:36-38.
Zerox copy.

Works About the Assassination of President John F. Kennedy

Abrahamsen, David. OUR VIOLENT SOCIETY. F&W, 1970. Chap.6, 7.

Abzug,Bella S. BELLA! Sat.Rev.Pr., 1972. Edited by Mel Ziegler.
Some friendly comments about the Kennedy brothers. Abzug one of
co-sponsors of Gonzalez Resolution re deaths of JFK and others.

Adler, Ruth. A DAY IN THE LIFE OF THE NEW YORK TIMES. 1st Lipp.,
1971. Stories re Clay Shaw and Sirhan. Also EMK.

THE KENNEDY FAMILY OF MASSACHUSETTS

Works About the Assassination of President John F. Kennedy

Allen, Mark, et al. "A Draft for a Brief for Reopening the Investigation Into the Assassination of President John F. Kennedy." CONGRESSIONAL RECORD Apr.16, 1975, sponsor Henry Gonzalez. Reprint

Alpert, Augusta. "A Brief Communication on Children's Reactions to the Assassination of the President," in THE PSYCHOANALYTIC STUDY OF THE CHILD, Vol.19: 313-320. Int'l U.Pr., 1964.

Anson, Robt. S. "The Greatest Cover-Up of All," NEW TIMES, Apr. 18, 1974: 16-26ff. "THEY'VE KILLED THE PRESIDENT!" The Search for the Murderers of JFK. 1st Bantam, 1975, wrs. Review by David C. Anderson N.Y.TIMES BK.REV. Jan.4, 1976: 18-20. "The Man Who Never Was," NEW TIMES, Sept.19, 1975: 14-16. (Two Oswalds).

Apthker, Herbert. "Murders Most Foul!" POLITICAL AFFAIRS, Jan., 1964: 43-50. JFK, Oswald, Tippet.

Ashman, Chas. THE CIA-MAFIA LINK. Wrs. Manor Bks., 1975.

Assassination Information Bureau. CLANDESTINE AMERICA.The Washington Newsletter. Vol.1. July-Aug., 1977 thru Vol.3 No.3, Jan.-Feb., 1980 (last issue). Ltd. to 800 copies of complete sets. Purpose of the newsletter: "to provide critical coverage of events surrounding the House investigation as well as pertinent information related to the general theme of assassination in 'clandestine America.'" ALS Jeff Goldberg, Washington editor, May 29, 1980.

Associated Press. THE TORCH IS PASSED. Western Pr. (1963). Four days in Nov., 1963. Valuable for immediate reports of rumor and facts.

Bagdikan, Ben. "The Assassin," SAT.EVE.POST: 22-26. Also Jimmy Breslin's "A Death in Emergency Room No. One:" 30-31. JFK Memorial issue with Norman Rockwell portrait on cover, Dec.14, 1963.

Bekessy, Jean. DER TOD IN TEXAS; Eine Amerikanische Tragoda. Hans Habe pseud. Wrs. Minchen, K. Desch, 1964. Second copy translated from the German by Evan Butler: THE WOUNDED LAND; Journey Through a Divided America. 1st American ed. C-McC, 1964.

Belin, David W. NOVEMBER 22, 1963: YOU ARE THE JURY. Quad., 1973. Reaffirmation of Warren Commission by attorney on its staff."The Case Against a Conspiracy," N.Y.TIMES MAG., July 15, 1979: 73-75. Published before the House Select Committee on Assassinations released its final report. Reply: "Letters," G. Robt. Blakey, N.Y. TIMES MAG., Aug.19, 1979: 78. By former Committee Counsel.

Belli, Melvin M. with Maurice C. Carroll. DALLAS JUSTICE. The Real Story of Jack Ruby and His Trial. McKay, 1964. Belli alone: THE LAW REVOLUTION. Vol.I. Criminal Law. 1st Sherbourne, 1968. Chapter 16: "The Warren Report and Jack Ruby." MY LIFE ON TRIAL. Morrow, 1976. Chapter 17: Defense of Jack Ruby.

114.

THE ASSASSINATION

Works About the Assassination of President John F. Kennedy

Berkeley, Edmund C., ed. "The Assassination of President John F. Kennedy..." Report No.2. COMPUTERS AND AUTOMATION, July, 1970: 29-36. "Political Assassination in the United States...," Ibid. Mar.,1975: 3. Berkeley author: "Patterns of Political Assassination: How Many Coincidences Make a Plot?" Ibid. Sept. 1970: 39ff.

Bishop, Jim. THE DAY KENNEDY WAS SHOT. F&W, 1968. The book JBK did not want written according to Bishop.

Bloomgarden, Henry S. THE GUN. A "Biography" of the Gun that Killed JFK. 1st Grossman, 1975. Assumes murder gun as 1940 Italian manufacture.

Brashler, Wm. THE DON: The Life and Death of Sam Giancana. Wrs. 1st Ballantine, May, 1978. Associations with Exner, JFK.

Brenier, Milton E. THE GARRISON CASE. A Study in the Abuse of Power. 1st Potter, 1969.

Buchanan, Thos.G. WHO KILLED KENNEDY? 1st Putnam, 1964. Published in France and 18 other countries before American publication. Review by Harrison E. Salisbury, N.Y.TIMES BK.REV. Nov.22,1964:7.

Cameron, James. WHAT A WAY TO RUN THE TRIBE: Selected Articles 1948-1967. 1st McG-H, 1968. Four articles on life and death -JFK.

Canfield, Michael and Alan J. Weberman. COUP D'ETAT IN AMERICA. The CIA and the Assassination of JFK. 1st Third Pr., 1975. Claims JFK killed by elements associated with CIA and Mafia connections.

CBS NEWS. The CBS "Warren Report" Parts I-IV as broadcast over CBS TV network June 25 through June 28, 1967. With correspondents Walter Cronkite, Dan Rather, Eric Sevareid, news director Eddie Barker, executive producer Leslie Midgley. Conclusion: the Warren Report is the best report we are ever likely to have...all objections that go to the heart of the Report...vanish when they are exposed to the light of honest inquiry." Transcript from CBS. 2nd copy Library of Congress, Legislative Reference Service.

Chapman, Gil and Ann. WAS OSWALD ALONE? Wrs. Publ.Exp., 1967.

Colebrook, Joan. INNOCENTS OF THE WEST. Travels Through the Sixties. 1st Basic, 1979. Reflections on after-effects of JFK's death, Warren report controversy, deaths of MLK and RFK.

COLUMBIA JOURNALISM REVIEW. "The Assassination:" 6-36. Op.cit. under JFK "Relations with the Media." Winter, 1963.

COMMITTEE FOR REINVESTIGATING ASSASSINATIONS. "Who Killed Kennedy?" Flyer. ALS Ken A. Cristofani, Chairperson.

THE KENNEDY FAMILY OF MASSACHUSETTS

Works About the Assassination of President John F. Kennedy

COMMENTARY. Editorial: "The Warren Commission," Jan., 1964: 24.
"The Failure of the Warren Report," by Alexander Bickel, Oct.,
1966: 31-39. "Conspiracy Fever," by Jacob Cohen, Oct., 1975: 33-
42. Author accepts and defends the Warren Report.

Committee to Investigate Assassinations - Bernard Fensterwald,Jr.
"Ten Years Later: A Legacy of Suspicion," ESQUIRE, Nov., 1973:
141-143. Doubts about lone assassin in cases of JFK, RFK, MLK,
George Wallace. ASSASSINATION OF JFK BY COINCIDENCE OR CONSPIR-
ACY? Wrs. 1st Zebra, 1977. Directed by Fensterwald, compiled
by Michael Ewing. "...almost endless series of coincidences'..."

COMMONWEAL. "The Prevalence of Violence," by John Cogley, Jan.
24, 1964: 481-483. - Re JFK's death. "Enough Is Enough," by Wm.
V. Shannon, Nov.18, 1966: 191-192. "Almost everything that can
be learned about (JFK's) death is already known."

THE COMPLETE KENNEDY SAGA. Wrs. Spec.Publ., 1963. 4 dark days.

Craig, Barbara. "The President's Pilot," PLAIN DEALDER SUN.MAG.
Nov.18, 1973:6-9. Pilot who flew JFK's body back from Dallas.

CROSS CURRENTS. "Dallas and Beyond," by Joseph E. Cunneen,
Winter, 1964: 1-2.-

Crotty, Wm. ed. ASSASSINATION AND THE POLITICAL ORDER. H&R,1971.
Wrs. Re JFK, RFK, MLK.

Curry, Jesse. JFK ASSASSINATION FILE. Wrs. "Ltd. collectors' edition," presentation. Dallas, 1969. ALS Mrs. Curry 11/2/75.

Cutler, R.B. TWO FLIGHTPATHS: Evidence of Conspiracy. Wrs. Ltd.
to 500 copies. Presentation. Mass., Danvers, 1971. Contains a
summary of the author's THE FLIGHT OF CE399 (priv.pr.). Contra-
dicts the "single bullet theory." CROSSFIRE: Evidence of Conspiracy. Wrs. 1st ltd. 500 c. Presentation. Bett's & Mir.,1975.

DALLAS TIMES HERALD Nov.25, 1963, front page of final edition.
THE HOUSTON CHRONICLE Nov.23, 1963, Sec.1, p.3 "The Day the President Was Shot from Ambush." Facsimile reproductions of combined
pages.

David, Jay (pseud.) THE WEIGHT OF THE EVIDENCE: the Warren Report
and Its Critics. 1st Meredith, 1968. Claims to present the main
theses of attack and defense.

Demaris, Ovid. AMERICA THE VIOLENT. 1st Cowles, 1970. Chap.11.

Dinsmore, Herman. ALL THE NEWS THAT FITS. A Critical Analysis of
the News and Editorial Content of THE NEW YORK TIMES. Arlington,
1969. Chapter 5 on assassination of JFK.

THE ASSASSINATION

Works About the Assassination of President John F. Kennedy

Dirix, Bob. "Why Was JFK Killed?" ATLAS, May, 1967: 10-13.

Donovan, Robt. J. THE ASSASSINS. Wrs. 1st Popular, 1964. Account of the murderous attacks on our presidents.

Dorman, Michael. KING OF THE COURTROOM: Percy Forman for the Defense. Delacorte, 1969. Lawyer for Jack Ruby, Mafia, Gen.Walker.

Eddowes, Michael. THE OSWALD FILE. Potter, 1977. Claims JFK's death the result of Soviet conspiracy.

Epstein, Edw.Jay. INQUEST: The Warren Commission and the Establishment of Truth. Viking (1966). Indictment of findings. Reviews: by Russell W. Gibbons AVE MARIA, Sept.17, 1966: 16-17; by Fletcher Knebel, LOOK, July 12, 1966:66-72-. COUNTERPLOT, Viking, 1966, re Jim Garrison investigation; LEGEND: The Secret World of Lee Harvey Oswald, 1st R.D.Pr./McG-H, 1978

ESQUIRE. "Lee Oswald's Letters to His Mother," May, 1964:67-73ff. "Aftermath of November 22, 1963," Jay Epstein and Sylvia Meagher contributing, Dec.1966: 204ff. "The Avenger..." (Jack Ruby), May 1967:79ff. and June, 1967: 131-135ff. by Ovid Demaris and Garry Wills. "If They've Found Another Assassin..." by John Berendt, Aug. 1967: 80-82ff. SMILING THROUGH THE APOCALYPSE: ESQUIRE'S HISTORY OF THE SIXTIES. McCall, 1969. Includes articles on assassination, e.g. Epstein's "Sixty Versions of the Kennedy Assassination," Dec. 1966 and May, 1967 issues.

Flammonde, Paris. THE KENNEDY CONSPIRACY: An Uncommissioned Report on the Jim Garrison Investigation. 1st Meredith, 1969. Theory: anti-Castro right wing plan to kill Fidel prevented by JFK - who himself became the target.

Ford, Gerald. "Piecing Together the Evidence. Inside Account of the Warren Commission." LIFE, Oct.2, 1964: 42-50A. Other contents: Zapruder film in color, trail to a verdict, blunders. Gerald Ford with John R. Stiles. PORTRAIT OF THE ASSASSIN. S&S, 1965. As Harold Weisberg points out. Ford was the first to quote in print rumor that Oswald was FBI undercover agent. Also, 1st Ballantine, wrs., 1966.

Fox, Sylvan. THE UNANSWERED QUESTIONS ABOUT PRESIDENT KENNEDY'S ASSASSINATION. Wrs. 1st Award, 1965. Inconsistensies in testimony.

FREE PRESS (L.A.) A Larry Flynt Publication. "Special Report Number One: JFK Murder Solved; Killing Coordinated by CIA; Gerald Ford was FBI Spy on Warren Commission; Media Cover-up: TIME -LIFE, N.Y.TIMES Involved." Also $1,000,000 reward for information leading to arrest and conviction of anyone involved offered by Flynt. Wrs. Press West, 1978. (Flynt was shot in the spine March 6, 1978, shortly after this publication.)

THE KENNEDY FAMILY OF MASSACHUSETTS

Works About the Assassination of President John F. Kennedy

Freed, Donald, and Mark Lane. EXECUTIVE ACTION. Assassination of a Head of State. Wrs. Dell, 1974. A "novel of fact." Theory: a maximal conspiracy directed by leaders of American intelligence, big business, organized crime and right-wing military. Filmed as an Edward Lewis production, released by Nat'l General Pictures, starring Burt Lancaster, Robert Ryan and Will Geer.

Friendly, Alfred and Ronald L. Goldfarb. CRIME AND PUBLICITY. 20th C.,1967. Role of the press in JFK assassination.

Frischauer, Willi. WILL YOU WELCOME NOW - DAVID FROST. 1st Hawthorne, 1971. Award-winning documentary on JFK's assassination.

FRONT PAGES RECORDING NOV.22,23,24,25. KMR Publ. n.d. How 91 newspapers recorded JFK's death.

Garrison, Jim. A HERITAGE OF STONE. Putnam, 1970. Inadequacies of Warren Report. Theory: assassination was planned and carried out by extensive domestic intelligence apparatus possibly connected with the CIA. "Jim Garrison and His War with the CIA," interview with Garrison by Allan Frank in WASHINGTON STAR, April 18, 1975. Reprint.

Gay, Donovan L. THE ASSASSINATION OF PRESIDENT JOHN F. KENNEDY: The Warren Commission Report and Subsequent Interest. Wrs. Library of Congress Congressional Research Service, Sept.10, 1975.

Gershenson, Alvin H. KENNEDY AND BIG BUSINESS. Wrs. Bk.Co. 1964 Suggests without documentation that "Big Business' victimized JFK.

Gertz, Elmer. MOMENT OF MADNESS: The People vs. Jack Ruby. 1st Follet, 1968. Gertz: on Ruby defense staff. TO LIFE. McG-H,1974 Autobiography. Material on Jack Ruby and Jim Garrison.

Goldberg, Jeffrey. "Waiting for Justice: The JFK Case is Not Closed," INQUIRY, Jan.7 and 21, 1980: 15-19. Aftermath of the congressional committee investigation findings in 1978. Zerox copy. ALS 14 lines.

Gonzalez, Henry. Copy of H.Res. 204 calling for a select committee to investigate the circumstances surrounding the deaths of JFK, RFK, MLK and attempted assassination of George Wallace (Feb. 19, 1975). Statement of Congressman Gonzalez on introducing H.R. 204. Copy of Congressional Record Feb.19, 1975. Copy of article in WITAN "Assassination and Lingering Doubts," by Gonzalez April, 1975. Three news releases: May 12, July 24, Aug.5, 1975. ALS re H.R. 204, Sept. 21, 1975. Congressional Record reprint: "51 House Members Co-Sponsor Gonzalez Resolution..."Sept.18,1975.

Greenburg, Bradley S. and Edwin B. Parker, eds. THE KENNEDY ASSASSINATION AND THE AMERICAN PUBLIC. 1st Stanford U., 1965. Authors include 38 social scientists and communication media representatives.

THE ASSASSINATION

Works About the Assassination of President John F. Kennedy

Harris, Leon. "Marie Tippit and Marina Oswald: the 'Forgotten' Widows of the Kennedy Tragedy," GOOD HOUSEKEEPING, Apr.1966:94ff.

Harkabi, Yehoshafat. ARAB ATTITUDES TO ISRAEL. Israel U., 1972. Doctoral thesis. Includes accusations of Arab press that the Jews murdered JFK and RFK.

Hempstone, Smith, "A New Investigation of JFK's Assassination," WASHINGTON STAR, Apr.30, 1975: A-15. Reprint.

Henderson, Bruce and Sam Summerlin. 1:33. IN MEMORIAM: John F. Kennedy. 1st Cowles, 1968. World-wide responses to the assassination of JFK. Evolution of more callous attitude to RFK murder.

Hoch, Paul L. and Russell Stetler, "A Legendary Oswald," INQUIRY June 26, 1978:23-24. Off-print. Two TLS April 5 and 21, 1980. Hoch and Jonathan Marshall, "JFK: The Unsolved Murder," INQUIRY, Dec.25, 1978: 10-12. Offprint.

Hunter, Diana and Alice Anderson. JACK RUBY'S GIRLS. 1st Hallux, 1970. Life in Ruby's CAROUSEL in Dallas, his character.

Hurwood, Bernhardt J. SOCIETY AND THE ASSASSIN: A Background Book on Political Murder. Parents (1970). Includes JFK and RFK.

Joesten, Joachim. OSWALD: ASSASSIN OR FALL GUY? Wrs. M&M, 1964. Oswald as scapegoat, a powerful conspiratorial group, Warren Report. Advertising brochure for this title also.

Johnson, Gerald W. HOD CARRIER. Morrow (1964). The issues in 1963 and the assassination of JFK.

Joling, Robt.J. "The JFK Assassination: Still an Unsolved Murder Mystery," SAT.EVE.POST, Dec.1975: 44-45ff.

Jones, Penn, Jr. FORGIVE MY GRIEF. Vols.I-IV. A Critical Review of the Warren Commission Report... 1st prtg., publ. by author, wrs. presentation copies, 1974. THE CONTINUING INQUIRY V.1-II 1976-1978. 24 issues. Penn Jones Jr. ed. Report on developments. Monthly newsletter.

Kaplan, John and Jon R. Waltz. THE TRIAL OF JACK RUBY. Macm. 1966. Atmosphere, legal points at issue, strategies of attys. Review by Martin Mayer: COMMENTARY, Feb.1966: 83-85ff.-

Katcher, Leo. EARL WARREN: A Political Biography. 1st McG-H, 1967. Development as politician and as man; the Commission.

Keats, John. THE NEW ROMANS: An American Experience. 1st Lipp., 1967. The U.S. as schizophrenic. The particular disaster of JFK.

Kirk, John G. ed. AMERICA NOW. 1st Athen.,1968. Cf. articles by Henry Steele Commager, Edmund Stillman, Roger D. Masters.

Works About the Assassination of President John F. Kennedy

Kirkwood, James. AMERICAN GROTESQUE. 1st S&S, 1970. Clay Shaw-Jim Garrison affair in New Orleans.

King, Larry L. CONFESSIONS OF A WHITE RACIST. 1st Viking, 1971. Includes sensitive recounting of reactions to JFK AND RFK murders.

Krieghbaum, Hillier. PRESSURES ON THE PRESS. Crowell (1972). Example of the news coverage of the assassinations of JFK,RFK.

Krupp, George R. "The Day the President Died," REDBOOK, Mar.14, 1964: 49ff. A psychiatrist reports on its meaning to many.

Lane, Mark. RUSH TO JUDGMENT: A Critique of the Warren Commission's Inquiry into the Murders of President John F. Kennedy, Officer J.D.Tippitt and Lee Harvey Oswald. H.R. & W., 1966. Autographed. Persuasive that crucial testimony was excluded and skeptical of theory of single assassin. Also 1st Fawcett,1967, wrs. Reviews: NEWSWEEK, Aug.15, 1966: 30-31ff.; Norman Mailer in EXISTENTIAL ERRANDS, 1st L-B, 1972: 269-283; James J. Graham, COMMONWEAL, Apr.21, 1967: 149-151.- A CITIZEN'S DISSENT: Mark Lane Replies. 1st H.R.& W., 1968. Autographed.

Lattimer, John K. "Similarities in Fatal Woundings of John Wilkes Booth and Lee Harvey Oswald." Reprinted from N.Y. STATE JRNL. OF MEDICINE, July 1, 1966: 1782-4. "The Kennedy-Connally Single Bullet Theory: A Feasibility Study," reprinted from INT'L SURGERY Dec., 1968: 524-532. "Could Oswald Have Shot President Kennedy?" Reprinted from BULL. OF N.Y. ACADEMY OF MEDICINE,Apr., 1972: 513-524. "Observations Based on a Review of the Autopsy Photographs, X-rays, and Related Materials of the Late President John F. Kennedy." Reprint from RESIDENT AND STAFF PHYSICIAN, May, 1972: 34-63. Cf. TLS 11/20/74 re titles defending Warren Commission conclusions. For Lattimer's competence and politics cf. Harold Weisberg's POST MORTEM: 386-402, description to follow.

Lawrence, Lincoln (pseud.) WERE WE CONTROLLED? The Assassination of President Kennedy. Univ.Bks.,1967. Claims manipulation of stock market before and after assassination.

Leonard, John. THIS PEN FOR HIRE. 1st D'day, 1973. Selection of writings, incl. reviews of AMERICAN GROTESQUE by Kirkwood and HERITAGE OF STONE, Garrison, both op.cit. Description of night editor at N.Y.TIMES cutting author's opinion of assassination.

Levin, Bernard. RUN IT DOWN THE FLAGPOLE. Britain in the Sixties 1st Athen.,1971. Includes "the industry" of theories re JFK,RFK.

Lewis, Richard Warren. "A Flashy Lawyer for Oswald's Killer," SAT.EVE.POST, Feb.8, 1964: 28-30. (Melvin Belli) THE SCAVENGERS and Critics of the Warren Report. 1st Dell, 1967, wrs. Review: Wm.Turner in FORGIVE MY GRIEF op.cit. 156-165. "The Scavengers," WORLD JRNL. TRIBUNE MAG. Jan.22, 1967: 3-10.

THE ASSASSINATION

Works About the Assassination of President John F. Kennedy

LIFE. "Murder of the President," selected frames of Zapruder film in b/w, "Theodore White Reports from Washington." Nov.29, 1963: 22-39. JFK on cover. "In Texas a Policeman and an Assassin Are Laid to Rest Too," Dec.6, 1963: 52B-52E; also "End to Nagging Rumors: the Six Critical Seconds:" 52F. "Was Jack Ruby Insane?" by Ernest Haveman, and "Oswald: Evolution of an Assassin," by Donald Jackson:Feb.21, 1964: 26-33; 68A-80. Oswald with rifle on cover. "The Trial of Jack Ruby," by Sybille Bedford, Feb.28, 1964: 36-36B. "Violence, Froth and Sob Stuff: Was Justice Done?" by Sybille Bedford, March 24: 1964: 32-34Aff. "Lee Harvey Oswald's Baby," May 1, 1964: 36B. "Oswald's 'Historic Diary'." July 10, 1964: 26-31. "The Rifle That Killed Kennedy," Aug.27, 1965: 62-65. "That Oswald Acted Alone Is a Matter of Reasonable Doubt," (Gov. Connally) Nov.25, 1966: 38-48B. "Last Seconds of the Motorcade," Nov.24, 1967: 87-97.

Linn, Edw. "The Untold Story of Jack Ruby," SAT.EVE.POST, July 25-Aug.1, 1964: 24-26ff.

LOOK. "We Can Prevent Presidential Assassinations," by John H. Walker, Feb.11: 1964: 124-126. "After the Shots: the Ordeal of LBJ," by Fletcher Knebel, Mar.10, 1964: 26-28ff. "The Persecution of Clay Shaw," by Warren Rogers, Aug.26, 1969: 53-56.

McCALL'S. "Since That Day in Dallas," by Mrs. John Connally, Aug., 1964: 78-79ff.- "...the second bullet hit him..." (her busband.) "Nellie Connally: First Lady in Waiting?" Aug.,1973: 58-59ff. "The Murder of President Kennedy," by Vivian Cadden, Mar.,1977: 119-121ff. Sums up findings of the Church Committee.

McDonald, Hugh C. as told to Geoffrey Bocca. APPOINTMENT IN DALLAS: The Final Solution to the Assassination of JFK. McD.,1975, wrs. "JFK's real assassin and his confession." Review: N.Y. TIMES BK.REV., Jan.4, 1976:18-20, by David C. Anderson.

McMillan, Priscilla J. MARINA AND LEE. H&R (1977). Written with Marina Oswald's permission.

Malcolm X. "I'm Talking to You, White Man." SAT. EVE. POST, Sept. 12, 1964: 30-32ff. Re his statement on the assassination of JFK. AUTOBIOGRAPHY with the assistance of Alex Haley, Grove Pr., 1st, 1965. THE SPEECHES OF... ed. by Archie Epps, wrs. Morrow, 1969. "Chickens coming home to roost" often misused.

Manchester, William. "The Assassination Retold," LIFE, May7, 1965: 46.- THE DEATH OF A PRESIDENT Nov.20-25th, 1963. H&R, 1st, 1967. IBID. LOOK, four parts, Jan.24, Feb.7, Feb.21, Mar.7,1967. "Mort d'un President," PARIS MATCH, 14, 28 Jan. 18 Fev., 1967. JFK and JBK on cover 14 Jan. JFK and John Jr. on cover 28 Jan. Review: by Edward Kosner, NEWSWEEK, Apr.10, 1967: 34-35.- By Joseph Featherstone, NEW REPUBLIC, Apr.22, 1967:20-22. By Paul Cuneo, AMERICA, May 6, 1967: 684-685.

Works About the Assassination of President John F. Kennedy

Marcus, Raymond. THE BASTARD BULLET: A Search for Legitimacy for Commission Exhibit 399. Rendell distr.1966. Presentation. Wrs. "Blow-Up! November 22, 1963," LOS ANGELES FREE PRESS Nov.24-Dec.1 1967."New facts about the Mary Moorman photo."

Meagher, Sylvia. ACCESSORIES AFTER THE FACT: The Warren Commission, the Authorities, and the Report. B-M (1967). A painstaking work of impressive scholarship. Author calls for a new investigation within our lifetime. SUBJECT INDEX TO THE WARREN REPORT AND HEARINGS AND EXHIBITS. Xerox Univ. Microfilms, 1975. Four pages of errata sheets added by request of the author to Univ.Microfilms ed. of 1969. (Original publisher: Scarecrow Press, 1966) Classifies the information in the 26 volumes of HEARINGS AND EXHIBITS as well as that contained in WARREN REPORT. ALS of Feb.19, 1975; TLS of Oct.4, 1975 with enclosed list of 17 of her published magazine articles.

Meeker, Oden. ISRAEL. Ancient Land - Young Nation. 1st Scrib., 1968. Chap.23: "John Fitzgerald Kennedy." Reactions to his death.

Miller, Norman C. THE GREAT SALAD OIL SWINDLE. C-McC, 1965. Swindle depressed stock market on day of JFK's death. Cf. Lawrence, WERE WE CONTROLLED? Op.cit.

Model, F. Peter and Robt. J. Groden. JFK: THE CASE FOR CONSPIRACY. 1st Manor, wrs., 1976. Authors theorize anti-Castro Cubans, CIA operatives, right wing policemen, "hit men" provided by Syndicate were responsible for JFK's murder.

MINDSZENTY REPORT. "Significant Aspects of Pres.Kennedy's Death," (JFK was killed by a Communist) Card. Mind. Fdn., Dec.15, 1963. "Warren Commission and Our Right to Know," (Lee Harvey Oswald was a Communist), Jan.15, 1964.

Morin, Relman. ASSASSINATION. The Death of President John F. Kennedy. 1st Signet, 1968, wrs. Oswald as lone assassin.

Morrow, Robt. D. BETRAYAL. 1st Regnery, 1976. Pictures Cuban exiles conspiring with CIA and FBK.

Moskin, J.Robt. MORALITY IN AMERICA. 1st Random, 1966. JFK's assassination as awakening us to the question of morality in U.S.

Nash, H.C. CITIZEN'S ARREST: THE DISSENT OF PENN JONES JR. IN THE ASSASSINATION OF JFK. 1st Latitudes, 1977. Presentation. TLS July 30, 1977.

NATION. "'Manchurian Candidate' in Dallas," Dec.28, 1963:449ff.+
                                        By Richard Condon.
National Archives of the U.S. INVENTORY OF THE RECORDS OF THE PRESIDENT'S COMMISSION ON THE ASSASSINATION OF PRESIDENT KENNEDY. Record Group 272. Compiled by Marion M. Johnson. Wrs. General Services Administration, 1973.

THE ASSASSINATION

Works About the Assassination of President John F. Kennedy

Newman, Albert H. THE ASSASSINATION OF JOHN F. KENNEDY: The Reasons Why. Potter, 1970. Supports Warren Commission findings. Condensation: ARGOSY, Oct., 1970: 33-40ff.

NEW REPUBLIC. Ten articles on the death of JFK by Jean Daniel, Murray Kempton, James Ridgeway, Gerald W. Johnson, Louis J.Halle others unsigned, Dec.7, 1963: 3-20.- "Seeds of Doubt:" 14-17ff. by Jack Minnis and Staughton Lynd, and "Commentary of an Eyewitness," by Richard Dudman: 18, Dec.21, 1963: 14-17ff.+ "Where the Shots Came From:"17, and Correspondence on "Oswald: Seeds of Doubt," 28-30, Dec.28, 1963.- "Jack Ruby on Trial:'Leave Me a Little Dignity'" by Murray Kempton, Mar.7, 1964: 17-20.- "Oswald: May We Have Some Facts Please?" by Murray Kempton, June 13, 1964: 13-15.- "Warren Report: Case for the Prosecution" by Murray Kempton, Oct.10, 1964: 13-17. "The Last Madness of Jack Ruby," by Ronnie Dugger, Feb.11, 1967: 19-23.

NEWSWEEK. "Assassination Reactions:" 29-34ff.; Letters: 2ff.; "Oswald:" 36ff.; "Ruby:" 44ff.; Dec.9, 1963. "Assassination Reactions. Letters:" 2ff. "A New Life - JBK and Memorials:" 24-25ff. "The Assassination: History's Jury,:" 25-28,Dec.16, 1963.- "How JFK Died," Dec.30, 1963: 55.- "Day in Court," (Jack Ruby) 18-19 and "Awful Interval," 19-20, Jan.6, 1964.- "Dallas: Ruby's 'Fugue State':" 25-26. "Screen Test: Marina Oswald," 48, Feb.10, 1964.- "By Jack Ruby," 79-80, Feb.10, 1964.- "Week in the Sun," (Marguerite Oswald): 29, Feb.24, 1964: 29. - "Trials: War of Nerves: (Ruby): 19, Mar.2, 1964.- "On Camera," (Ruby): 31-32, Mar.16, 1964.- "The Avenger" (Ruby), 28ff. Mar.23, 1964.- "JFK's Murder: Sowers of Doubt," Apr.6, 1964: 22-24.- "Eye on the Window," (Chief Justice Warren's visit to Jack Ruby), June 23, 1964: 32-33.- "When Kennedy Died," Sept.14, 1964: 61.- "The Warren Commission Report," Oct.5, 1964: 32-64. "What They Saw That Dreadful Day in Dallas," (26 vols. of testimony) Dec.7, 1964: 28-30ff.- "Any Number Can Play," Nov.7, 1966: 37-38.- "JFK: The Death and the Doubts," Dec.5, 1966: 25-26.- In same issue: "Eyewitness in Dallas," by Chas. Roberts: 26-29.- "Thickening the Plot," (Jim Garrison trial) Mar.27, 1967:37-38.- "The JFK 'Conspiracy'," by Hugh Aynesworth, May 15, 1967: 36. "Law Unto Himself," (Garrison), Jan.8, 1968: 25-26.

N.Y.TIMES MAG. "The Case of 'Trial by Press'," by Anthony Lewis, Oct.18, 1964: 31ff.- "A New Inquiry Is Needed," by Herbert Mitgang, Dec.25, 1966: 14. "No Conspiracy, But - Two Assassins, Perhaps?" by Henry Fairlie, Sept.11, 1966: 52ff. (Fairlie claims critics of Warren Report "witch hunts.') "The Assassination That Will Not Die," by Jas.R.Phelan, Nov.23, 1974: 28-29ff. (..."irresponsible polemics and absurd theories...")

Nichols, John. "Assassination of President Kennedy," THE PRACTITIONER, Nov. 1973. Reprint. Reasonable doubt re gun firing.

Works About the Assassination of President John F. Kennedy

Noyes, Peter. LEGACY OF DOUBT. 1st Pinnacle, 1973. Wrs. Claims
new evidence about JFK and RFK deaths.

Oglesby Carl. THE YANKEE AND COWBOY WAR. 1st Berk.Med., 1977.
Wrs. Part II. "Dallas" 47-172; Chap.9 "Who Killed JFK?"319-324.

Oswald, Robt.L. with Myrick and Barbara Land. "He Was My Brother," LOOK, Oct.17, 1967: 62-66ff.

O'Toole, George. THE ASSASSINATION TAPES. An Electronic Probe...
Penthouse, 1975. Lee Harvey Oswald as innocent. "The Assassination Probe," SAT.EVE.POST, Nov.1975: 45-48ff. Congress acting.

PARIS MATCH. "Oswald Avec Les Armes Du Crime," 29 Fev., 1964:
40-49. Oswald with gun on cover. "Le Mystere Kennedy. Le Tem-
oiguage Du Gouverneur Connally..."Je n'ai pas ete touche par la
meme balle que le president," 3 Dec., 1966: 64-71.

PEOPLE AND THE PURSUIT OF TRUTH. "The JFK Assassination: Recent
Developments:" 1, and "The Cover-Up of the Cover-Ups," by Richard
E. Sprague: 2-6, Aug. 1975.

Phelan, James. "Rush to Judgment in New Orleans," SAT.EVE.POST,
May 6, 1967: 21-25.-

Podwal, Mark H. THE DECLINE AND FALL OF THE AMERICAN EMPIRE.
Darrien, 1971. Wrs. Folio. Anti-violence drawings, including
Nov.22, 1963, assassination of RFK.

Popkin, Richard H. THE SECOND OSWALD. 1st Avon, 1966. Wrs.
TLS Sept. 8, 1975

PUBLIC OPINION QUARTERLY. "The Assassination of President Kennedy: Public Reactions," by Paul B. Sheatsley and Jacob J. Feld-
man, Summer, 1964: 189-215. Also in this issue: "The Kennedy
Assassination: Early Thoughts and Emotions:" 216-224; and Bradley S. Greenberg, "Diffusion of News of the Kennedy Assassination:" 225-232.

Rajski, Raymond B. ed. A NATION GRIEVED. 1st Tuttle, 1967. 164
editorial cartoons from newspapers in the U.S. and Canada.

RAMPARTS MAGAZINE eds. IN THE SHADOW OF DALLAS: a Primer on the
Assassination of Pres. Kennedy. Wrs. Jan.,1967. David Welsh,
David Lifton, Penn Jones Jr., Jack Ruby represented.

READERS' DIGEST. Statement by the editors: "This Nation, Under
God," Jan. 1964: 37-39. Also "Death in Dallas" condensed from
TIME, Nov.29, 1963.

REPORTER. "The 22nd of November," by Max Ascoli, Dec.5, 1963:19.-
"The Long Vigil" by Marya Mannes, Dec.19, 1963: 15-17.

THE ASSASSINATION

Works About the Assassination of President John F. Kennedy

Rhodes, Richard. THE INLAND GROUND: An Evocation of the American Middle West. 1st Athen.,1970. Contains reactions to JFK's death.

Roberts, Charles. THE TRUTH ABOUT THE ASSASSINATION. The Answer to the Warren Report Critics. G&D, 1967. Wrs. For critique of this book cf. Lane, A CITIZEN'S DISSENT: 172-178, op.cit.

Roffman, Howard. PRESUMED GUILTY: Lee Harvey Oswald in the Assassination of Pres.Kennedy. Fairleigh, 1975.

Russell, Bertrand. AUTOBIOGRAPHY: 1944-1969. 1st S&S, 1969. Re JFK, the Warren Commission, 16 questions, sponsorship of "Who Killed Kennedy Committee," also criticism of Cuban policy.

Russell, G. Darrell,Jr. LINCOLN AND KENNEDY: Looked at Kindly Together. Carlton, 1973. Striking parallels in their lives.

Sahl, Mort. HEARTLAND. 1st H.B.J., 1976. Serious report of results of questioning official accounts of deaths of JFK, RFK.

Salandria, Vincent J. "The Assassination of Pres. JFK: a Model for Explanation." COMPUTERS AND AUTOMATION, Dec. 1971: 32-40.

SAT.EVE.POST. "The Unsolved JFK Murder Mystery," Sept., 1975: 44-50. George O'Toole, Richard Whalen, Mark Lane contributors. "Biographies of Leading Researchers:"50-52; Bibliography for JFK Buffs:52-53ff. Norman Rockwell portrait of JFK on cover. (In November 1975 this magazine offered $250,000 reward to first individual who provides info leading to arrest and conviction of anyone who conspired to murder or assisted in murder of JFK.)

Sauvage, Leo. THE OSWALD AFFAIR: An Examination of the Contradictions and Omissions of the Warren Report. World,1966. 1st. "The Oswald Affair," COMMENTARY, Mar., 1964: 55-65. "Letters to the Editor," ibid. July, 1964: 16-17.-

SAT. REVIEW. Editorial by Norman Cousins, Dec.21, 1963: 14ff. "Congress and the Assassinations. The Curious Politics of the House Inquiry..." by George Lardner, Feb.19, 1977: 14-17.

Schweiker, Richard. "Senate Resolution 243 to Reopen JFK Killing Probe," CONGRESSIONAL RECORD, Sept.8, 1975. Copy of S.Res.243 autographed. (The text of the resolution is supplemented by a number of previously classified documents relating to the Warren Commission investigation.) News release:"Schweiker Asks Reopening of JFK Killing Probe," Sept.8, 1975. "Reopen Inquiry in JFK's Death, Schweiker Urges," WASH.POST, Sept.9, 1975. Reprint. "Behind the News to Reopen JFK Case," interview, U.S.NEWS... Sept.15, 1975. Reprint. "Did Hoover Play Games with Warren Commission on Oswald?" by Norman Kempster, interview with Schweiker Oct.5, 1975. Reprint.

THE KENNEDY FAMILY OF MASSACHUSETTS

<u>Works</u> <u>About</u> <u>the</u> <u>Assassination</u> <u>of</u> <u>President</u> John F. <u>Kennedy</u>

Sevareid, Eric. "A Third Corruption: Publicity," PAGEANT, July, 1964: 152-153.- Oswald as declared guilty before trial.

Schulz, Donald E. "Kennedy and the Cuban Connection." FOREIGN POLICY, Spring, 1977: 121-139. Reprint, presentation copy.

Sherrill, Robt. THE SATURDAY NIGHT SPECIAL...Charter.,1973. Includes JFK and RFK murders and the effect on legislation.

Sparrow, John. AFTER THE ASSASSINATION: A Positive Appraisal of the Warren Report. Chilmark, 1967. Affirms Oswald acted alone.

Sprague, Richard E. "The Assassination of JFK: the Application of Computers to the Photographic Evidence," COMPUTERS AND AUTO-MATION, May, 1970: 30-60. "Computer-Assisted Analysis of Evidence Re the Assassination of JFK," Progress report. Sept.1970: 48. "The American News Media and the Assassination of Pres.JFK: Accessories After the Fact," Part 1. COMPUTERS AND AUTOMATION AND PEOPLE, June, 1973: 36-40. Part 2. July, 1973: 31-38. "The Framing of Lee Harvey Oswald," ibid. Oct., 1973: 21-36. "Governor George Wallace and Gunman Arthur Bremer... COMPUTERS AND PEO-PLE, June, 1974: 26-27ff. "Nixon, Ford and the Political Assass-inations in the U.S., ibid. Jan., 1975: 27-31."The Assassination of Pres.JFK: The Involvement of the CIA in the Plans and Cover-Up," PEOPLE AND THE PURSUIT OF TRUTH, May, 1975: 3. "Another View," by Benjamin Schwarts, COMPUTERS AND AUTOMATION, Mar.1971: 35-39. Attack on application of computers to photographic evidence.

Stafford, Jean. "The Strange World of Marguerite Oswald," McCALL Oct.1965: 112-113ff. A MOTHER IN HISTORY.1st F.S.&G.,1966. Also 1st Bantam, 1966, wrs. Review: by Jean Holzhauer, COMMONWEAL, May, 1966: 233-234.-

Steel, Ronald. IMPERIALISTS AND OTHER HEROES. 1st Random, 1971. JFK's "assassination came almost as a reprieve..." 341.

Stetler, Russell. "Can Congress Crack the Kennedy Assassination?" INQUIRY, Mar.6, 1978: 11-15. Offprint.

Stewart Chas.J. and Bruce Kendall eds. A MAN NAMED JOHN F. KEN-NEDY. Sermons on His Assassination. Paulist, 1964. Wrs.

Sullivan, Wilson. "The Politics of Assassination," MANKIND, Apr.,1969: 8ff.

Taylor, Telford. TWO STUDIES IN CONSTITUTIONAL INTERPRETATION. OSU, 1969. Part II. "Fair Trial and Free Press: First Fruits of the Warren Report." Events immediately following JFK's death.

Thompson, Josiah. SIX SECONDS IN DALLAS. Geis, 1967. Carefully researched. Claims three gunmen murdered the President. "The Cross Fire that Killed President Kennedy," SEP, Dec.2, 1967:27ff. Photo of JFK on cover. Letter NEWSWEEK, Dec.11, 1967: 8.-

THE ASSASSINATION

Works About the Assassination of President John F. Kennedy

Thompson, Josiah, cont'd. Review of SIX SECONDS IN DALLAS and ACCESSORIES AFTER THE FACT by Sylvia Meagher by Alexander Bickel NEW REPUBLIC, Dec.23, 1967: 34

Thomson, George C. THE QUEST FOR TRUTH. A Quizzical Look at the Look at the Warren Report; or, How President Kennedy Really Was Assassinated. Presentation. Thomson, 1964. Wrs.

Thurman, Howard. THE LUMINOUS DARKNESS: A Personal Interpretation of the Anatomy of Segregation... H&R, 1965. JFK: 52-53.

Thurston, Samuel F. "The Central Intelligence Agency and the N.Y. TIMES." COMPUTERS AND AUTOMATION, July, 1971: 51-57.

TIME. "After JFK's Assassination," Dec.20, 1963: 9-14.- "The Warren Commission Investigation," Feb.14, 1964: 16-20.- "Investigations: Jack Ruby; Marguerite Oswald," Feb.21, 1964: 23-24.-

Turner, Wm.W. INVISIBLE WITNESS: The Use and Abuse of the New Technology of Crime Investigation. 1st B-M, 1968. E.g. Oswald. "The Garrison Commission on the Assassination of Pres. Kennedy," RAMPARTS, Jan., 1968: 41-56ff.

TV GUIDE. "America's Long Vigil," Jan.25, 1963: 19-45.

U.P.I. FOUR DAYS; the Historical Record of the Death of President Kennedy. Amer.Her., 1964. Includes Merriman Smith account.

U.S. President's Commission. THE ASSASSINATION OF PRESIDENT JOHN F. KENNEDY. Report. Wrs. GPO, 1964. The final report known as the Warren Report. Bantam ed., wrs. 1964. N.Y.Times ed. publ. MvG-H, 1964. THE WITNESSES. Highlights of the Hearings...McG-H, 1965. N.Y.Times ed. publ. by Bantam, wrs., 1964. THE WARREN REPORT, A.P., 1964. Popular Lib. ed., wrs., 1964. "The Warren Commission Report," TIME, Oct.2, 1964: 45-50ff. "The Book for All to Read," Loudon Wainwright, LIFE, Oct.16, 1964: 35.- "The Warren Report about Pres. Kennedy's Assassination," Natlus. INVESTIGATION OF THE ASSASSINATION OF PRESIDENT JOHN F. KENNEDY. Hearings... pursuant to executive order creating a commission to ascertain, evaluate and report upon the facts relating to the assassination of the late President, John F. Kennedy and the subsequent violent death of the man charged with the assassination. 26 vols. GPO, 1964.

U.S.Commission on CIA Activities Within the U.S. Allegations concerning the assassination of President Kennedy. In its Report to the President. GPO, 1975. Wrs. Autographed by Nelson A. Rockefeller, chairman of the Commission and Vice-President of the U.S.

U.S. Congress, House of Representatives. Hearings...FBI OVERSIGHT. 94th Conf. 1st and 2nd sess. Oct.21, 1975 - Sept.16, 1976. GPO, 1976. TLS from Don Edwards, Chairman, 2/5/76 re destruction of Oswald's note to Special Agent James P. Hosty Jr.

Works About the Assassination of President John F. Kennedy

U.S.Congress. Senate. Select Committee to Study Governmental Operations with Respect to Intelligence Activities. Final report. Book V. THE INVESTIGATION OF THE ASSASSINATION OF PRESIDENT JOHN F. KENNEDY: PERFORMANCE OF THE INTELLIGENCE AGENCIES, GPO, 1976. Report No. 94-755, known as the Church Committee Report. The evidence indicates the investigation by the FBI and CIA of the assasination was deficient and that facts which might have substantially affected the course of the investigation were not provided the Warren Commission. Recommendation: that the Senate Select Committee on Intelligence continue the investigation.

U.S.Congress. House. INVESTIGATION OF THE ASSASSINATION OF PRES. JOHN F. KENNEDY. Hearings before the Select Committee on Assassinations. 95th Congress, 2nd sess. Sept.6-Dec.29, 1978. 5 Vols. Final Report...Summary of Findings and Recommendations, Jan.2, 1979. "Scientific acoustical evidence establishes a high probability that two gunmen fired at President John F. Kennedy...The committee believes...that President John F. Kennedy was probably assassinated as a result of a conspiracy." p.3. Vol.6. Appendix: "Photographic Evidence." Vol.7. Appendix: "Medical and Firearms Evidence." Vol.8. Appendix: "Acoustics, Polygraph, Handwriting, and Fingerprint Evidence." Vol.9. Appendix: "Staff and Consultant's Report on Organized Crime." Vol.10. Appendix: "Anti-Castro Activities and Organizations..." Vol.11.Appendix: "The Warren Commission...The CIA Support to the Warren Commission. The Motorcade. Military Investigation of the Assassination." Vol.12. Appendix: "Conspiring Witnesses in Dealey Plaza. Oswald, Tippit Associates. George de Mohrenschildt. Deposition of Marina Oswald Porter. The Defector Study. Oswald in the Soviet Union." Vols.6-12, March, 1979. Findings and Recommendations, March 29, 1979. 14 items. GPO, 1979. Media response to report: N.Y.TIMES: Jan.7,1979,E6,18.

U.S.NEWS... "The Tragic End of JFK," Dec.2, 1963: 31-35. "In the Kennedy Car - Gov. John Connally's Description," Dec.9, 1963:12. "Strange World of Lee Oswald..." Dec.16, 1963: 60-62. Defense of the Secret Service: 62. "Can You Really Protect the President?" Dec.23, 1963: 38-40.- "In the JFK Murder Case - Chief Investigator Rankin," Dec.30, 1963. "Assassination Inquiry: Slow, Careful," Jan.27, 1964: 49.- "Back of the Secrecy in the Assassination Probe" Feb.24, 1964: 52ff. "Oswald's Own Story as Revealed by His Diary" July 13, 1964: 54-60. "Unraveling the Mystery of the Assassination of JFK," (Warren Report), Oct.5, 1964: 35-42ff. "The Untold Stories," Oct.12, 1964: 58-62. "Assassination - Behind Moves to Re-Open JFK Case," June 2, 1975. Xerox copy.

Vidal, Gore. MATTERS OF FACT AND FICTION. Essays, 1973-1976. Random (1977). One essay on E.Howard Hunt and death of JFK.

Von Faber, Karin. "Marguerite Oswald Talks," COLUMBUS SUNDAY MAGAZINE, Aug.22, 1976: 36-37ff.

Works About the Assassination of President John F. Kennedy

Walker, Edwin A. "The Strange Circumstances of the Murder of Lee Harvey Oswald," AMERICAN MERCURY, Dec., 1963: 35-37.

WANDERER. Advertisement: "Do You Know...the Red Line?" (re JFK's death). Jan.2, 1964.

Warren, Earl. THE MEMOIRS OF... 1st D'day, 1977.

Weaver, John. WARREN: The Man, the Court, the Era. 1st L-B, 1967 On his attitude toward accepting assignment to Commission: 302-03. Chapter 19: on the Kennedy assassination.

Wecht, Cyril H. "The Medical Evidence in the Assassination of President John F. Kennedy," FORENSIC SCIENCE, May, 1964: 105-128. Reprint. "Pathologists View of JFK Autopsy: An Unsolved Case," MODERN MEDICINE, Nov.27, 1972: 28-32. Reprint. "JFK Assassination: 'A Prolonged and Willful Cover-Up," MODERN MEDICINE, Oct. 28, 1974. Reprint. "Why Is the Rockefeller Commission So Single-minded About a Lone Assassin in the Kennedy Case?" JRNL. OF LEGAL MEDICINE, July/Aug., 1975: 22-25.

Weisberg, Harold. WHITEWASH: The Report on the Warren Report. 1st Dell, 1966. Wrs. The first critical close analysis of the 26 volumes of the Hearings of the Warren Commission. Indicates the offical theory does not hold up. Review: by Edw. Jay Epstein, NEW REPORTER, June 25, 1966: 23-25. WHITEWASH II: the FBI-Secret Service Coverup. Weisberg, 1966. Wrs. Represents the doctoring and destroying of evidence on the part of the Warren Commission staff; the FBI as creating chaos and confusion; the too secret Secret Service. Presentation. OSWALD IN NEW ORLEANS. Case of Conspiracy with the CIA. Canyon, 1967. Wrs. FRAME-UP. The Martin Luther King - James Earl Ray Case...1st O&D, 1971. Presentation. Explores RFK - MLK - J.Edgar Hoover relationship; similarity of FBI's handling with that of JFK and other circumstances. PHOTOGRAPHIC WHITEWASH - Suppressed Kennedy Assassination Pictures. Weisberg, 1966. Wrs. Presentation. WHITEWASH IV: Top Secret JFK Assassination Transcript. With a Legal Analysis by Jim Lesar. Weisberg, 1974. Wrs. Presentation. This session dealt with rumor that Oswald was an FBI undercover agent. Gerald Ford's statements.Excerpts of Executive Session of Jan.21, 1964 and transcript of Jan.27, 1964, annotated. TLS 11/13/74. POST MORTEM. JFK Assassination Cover-Up Smashed! Weisberg, 1975. Wrs. Presentation. Suppressed offical evidence and photos. No Attempt to solve the crime but the story of how the crime was left unsolved. Documentary appendix. TLS, April 3, 1980: 30 lines explaining the numbering system of FBI files of JFK assassination. Numbered list of FBI files. ALS Mar.21, 1980 re HSCA.

Whalen, Richard. "The Kennedy Assassination," SAT. EVE. POST, Jan. 14, 1967: 19-25ff.

Works About the Assassination of President John F. Kennedy

White, Stephen. SHOULD WE NOW BELIEVE THE WARREN REPORT? 1st Macm., 1968. Relies heavily on CBS News Reports of 1966, 1967, and publications of Warren Commission.

Whitney, David C. THE AMERICAN LEGACY...Ferguson, 1975. Merriman Smith and Wendell Berry on the assassination of JFK: 337-340.

Wilson, H.H. THE MOOD OF A NATION (November 22-29, 1963). M&M. Wrs. Cross section of the national mood of the press and readers.

Wise, David. "Secret Evidence on the Kennedy Assassination," SAT.EVE.POST, April 6, 1968:70-73.

Wolfenstein, Martha and Gilbert Kliman, eds. CHILDREN AND THE DEATH OF A PRESIDENT. 1st D'day, 1965. Multidisciplinary studies.

Youngblood, Rufus W. 20 YEARS IN THE SECRET SERVICE: My Life With Five Presidents. S&S (1973). Six chapters on JFK, Dallas and the Warren Report. Claims Oswald acted alone.

Zaiden, Abe. "Community Conscience," COMMENTATOR, Dec.10, 1963: 1ff. Other JFK material: 4-10.

Zoppi, "Tony" "JFK And Jack Ruby," CORONET, Nov.1973: 9-21. JFK cover painting. Author: Dallas newspaperman and friend of Ruby.

(Recording) THE ASSASSINATION OF A PRESIDENT. Documentary recording reconstructing the period event by event from Nov.22 to Nov.25, 1963. Written and recorded by Richard Levitan. American Society of Recorded Drama. LH10.

(Recording) FOUR DAYS THAT SHOOK THE WORLD. Colpix Records with U.P.I. CP-2500.

(Recording) THAT WAS THE WEEK THAT WAS. The British Broadcasting Corporation's Tribute to John Fitzgerald Kennedy telecast Nov.23, 1963. Decca DL 9116.

(Recording) SIX WHITE HORSES. Tommy Cash. Epic Records CBS. 5-10540

Bibliographies of Assassination Material

Committee to Investigate Assassinations. AMERICAN POLITICAL ASS-ASSINATIONS: A Bibliography of Works Published 1963-1970 Related to the Assassinations of John F. Kennedy, Martin Luther King, Robert F. Kennedy. Wrs. Washington D.C., 1973.

COMPUTERS AND PEOPLE. "Political Assassinations in the United States: Inventory of Articles. May, 1975: 29-30.

THE ASSASSINATION

Bibliographies of Assassination Material

Guth, DeLoyd and Wrone, David R. comp. THE ASSASSINATION OF JOHN F. KENNEDY. A Comprehensive Historical and Legal Bibliography, 1963-1979. Maps. Greenwood, 1980. An invaluable guide and reference.

Thompson, W.C. A BIBLIOGRAPHY OF LITERATURE RELATING TO THE ASSASSINATION OF PRESIDENT JOHN F. KENNEDY with 1971 supplement. Thompson, 1972. Wrs. Autographed.

U.S. Library of Congress Information Bulletin. Appendix II. "The Assassination of President John F. Kennedy: Moves to Reopen the Investigation." A Selected List of References compiled by Donald A. Baskerville, Dec.3, 1976. Zerox copy.

Wrone, David R. "The Assassination of John Fitzgerald Kennedy: An Annotated Bibliography," wrs. Reprint from WISCONSIN MAGAZINE OF HISTORY, Autumn, 1972: 21-36.

Cf. also THE KENNEDY LITERATURE by James Tracy Crown: Chapter 8; A BIO-BIBLIOGRAPHY OF THE KENNEDY FAMILY by Martin H. Sable: 155-183, op.cit. p.11.

Tributes, Memorials and Assessments

Ambassade De France (N.Y.) "France's Tribute to the Late President Kennedy." French Affairs No. 164. November, 1963. Wrs.

AMERICA. "May He Rest in Peace," Dec. 7, 1963: 728-729. "A Fitting Memorial," Feb.8, 1964: 186-188.-

Barber, James David. THE PRESIDENTIAL CHARACTER. Predicting Performance in the White House. P-H, 1972. JFK as "active positive."

Bradlee, Benjamin. THAT SPECIAL GRACE. 1st Lipp., 1964.

Broder, David S. THE PARTY'S OVER: the Failure of Politics in America. 1st H&R, 1972. JFK - "what might have been."

Brooks, John. THE GREAT LEAP: The Past 25 Years in America. 1st H&R, 1966. Kennedy years in this perspective.

Califano, Joseph A. Jr. A PRESIDENTIAL NATION. 1st Norton, 1975. Includes the personality of JFK, his program and methods.

Childs, Marquis. WITNESS TO POWER. McG-H, 1975. Chapter IX. Triumph and Tragedy: the Kennedys.

COMMONWEAL. "Death of the President," Dec.6, 1963: 299-201ff.- "The Kennedy Legacy, the People's Task," Dec.13, 1963: 335-336ff. "Cynics, Critics and Presidents," by Wm.V.Shannon, Jan.24, 1964: 473-474. JFK and LBJ. "JFK - a Final Word," May 8, 1964: 190-1.-

THE KENNEDY FAMILY OF MASSACHUSETTS

Tributes, Memorials and Assessments

Crown, James Tracy. "President Kennedy - As the World Knew Him," CORONET, Jan.1964: 18-25. -

Cushing, Richard Cardinal. "Eulogy," Nov.24, 1963, wrs. "Sermon," at Civic-Religious Memorial honoring JFK, Jan.19, 1964, wrs.

Dector, Midge. "Kennedyism," COMMENTARY, Jan. 1970: 19-27.

DEMOCRAT. "In Memoriam JFK" Dec.9, 1963: 1-8.

Donovan, John C. THE POLICY MAKERS. Pegasus, 1970. American policies in the 1960's. JFK's struggle for manpower training, his impressive record in the field of economic policy and more.

ESQUIRE. "When JFK Was Rich, Young and Happy,"by Harry Muheim, Aug.1966: 64-66ff. "The Kennedy Dynasty: an Appraisal," Nov., 1969: 162-163ff. by Denis Brogan. "Is It Still O.K. to Admire JFK? Yes," by Tom Wicker, June, 1977: 65-69. JFK on cover.

Fairlie, Henry. THE KENNEDY PROMISE. The Politics of Expectations. 1st D'day, 1973. Revisionist speculation of JFK,RFK. Review: by Tom Wicker, N.Y.TIMES BK.REV. Jan.21, 1973: 1ff.

Fine, Wm.M. ed. THAT DAY WITH GOD November 24, 1963. 1st McG-H, 1965. The religious expression of all faiths. Includes three sermons from Dallas with historical significance.

GOOD HOUSEKEEPING. "A Last Loving Remembrance of John F. Kennedy" by Jim Bishop, Mar. 1964:71-74ff.- "The Lonely Days of JFK's Best Friend," (Dave Powers) by Douglas Kiker, Aug.1964: 64-65ff. "Yours Is a Kind and Noble Spirit" (JFK and Elmer Paul Brock) by Chas. U. Daly, Sept., 1964: 36ff. "The Day JFK Died: What People Remember Now," by Alan Levy, Nov.1965: 84-87ff. "Remembering John F. Kennedy," Nov., 1973: 90-97ff.

Greeley, Andrew. "John Fitzgerald Kennedy: Doctor of the Church?" CRITIC, Oct.-Nov., 1967: 40-44ff.

HARVARD ALUMNI BULLETIN (Special JFK Issue) Dec.7, 1963. JFK on cover. Editorial comment and memorial addresses. Op.cit. p.2.

Heren, Louis. NO HAIL, NO FAREWELL...Events of the Johnson Years ..." 1st H&R, 1970. JFK, RFK, LBJ - more sympathy for latter.

Hinkel, John V. ARLINGTON: Monument to Heroes. P-H, 1970. JFK's "Eternal Flame," and RFK's adjoining gravesite.

JOHN F. KENNEDY, CHAMPION OF FREEDOM. Worden & Childs, 1964.

John F. Kennedy International Airport. Folder of 14 postcards in color. Dexter Press, 1964.

THE ASSASSINATION

Tributes, Memorials and Assessments

JOHN FITZGERALD KENNEDY. A Pictorial Tribute. A.A.Wyn, 1964.

Jurasko, J.J. PRESIDENT JOHN F. KENNEDY, A Spiritual Biography.
(Miami,Fla.) Brower Press n.d. Wrs.

Kavanaugh, James J. "A Visit to the Grave," CATHOLIC DIGEST,
July, 1964: 8-11. Condensed from MICHIGAN CATHOLIC 3/26/64. -

Kraft, Joseph. "John F. Kennedy, Portrait of a President,"
HARPER'S Jan. 1964: 96ff.

Kupferberg, Herbert. "A New Teaching Approach. The Kennedy Library Goes to School," PARADE, Nov.18, 1963: 8-11.

LADIES HOME COMPANION. "President Kennedy's Last Day in the White
House. Feb., 1964: 88-99.- "The Kennedy's One Year Later. A
Special Memorial Section." Nov.1964: 18-31. JFK and JBK on cover.

LIFE. "John F. Kennedy Memorial Edition," Dec., 1963. Made up
largely of articles and photos from Nov.26 and Dec.6 issues.
"President Kennedy Is Laid to Rest," Dec.6, 1963: 38-49, 117-126,
ff. JBK and children on front cover. Photograph: "President Says
Goodbye to John Kennedy," Jan.3, 1964:22. Also Eulogy by LBJ at
Lincoln Memorial. "Kennedy Art Center. A Memorial to Kennedy,"
Feb.7, 1964: 47-48ff. "A Visit to the Grave," by Loudon Wain-
wright, Feb.14, 1965: 15. Photograph: "The Kennedys Gather at
the Future Library," April 24, 1964: 42B.- "Over-rated JFK Movie"
(YEARS OF LIGHTNING, DAY OF DREAMS) Jan.22, 1965: 34D. "England
Builds a Monument to JFK," tribute at Runnymede. May 28, 1965:
75-78ff. "The 60's, Decade of Tumult and Change," Dec.26, 1969.

Lincoln, Evelyn. "Memo from a Secretary about Her Boss: John
Fitzgerald Kennedy," McCALL'S, July, 1964: 66ff.-

Logan, Andy. "JFK: The Stained Glass Image," AMERICAN HERITAGE,
August, 1967: 4-7ff.

LOOK. "The JFK Memorial Issue:" Nov.17, 1964. 13 articles on JFK
and his family. JBK and son John on cover. "In Memory of John F.
Kennedy," by Wm. Attwood, Dec.31, 1963: 11-13. "The Kennedy
Legend," by Jack Star, June 30, 1964: 19-21. "JFK Memorial Book,"
1964. "Letters to editor" Dec.29, 1964: 11-12ff. re JFK memorial issue.-

N.Y. HERALD TRIBUME. 1964 PRESIDENTIAL ELECTION GUIDE. Whitney,
1964. 1st. Re JFK, Allan Nevins, Rowland Evans and Robt.Novak,
Gerald Gardner et al. Profiles of RFK and Sargent Shriver.

Roberts, Edwin A. Jr. ELECTIONS 1964. NATIONAL OBSERVER, 1964.
JFK and intra-party warfare, campaign techniques, RFK,Shriver.

THE KENNEDY FAMILY OF MASSACHUSETTS

Tributes, Memorials and Assessments

Macfadden-Bartell. FIRST FAMILY ALBUM, 1963. A JOHN F. KENNEDY MEMORIAL ALBUM, 1964. Wrs.

McGrory, Mary. "In Memoriam: John F. Kennedy," WASHINGTON STAR, 1963. Compilation of articles appearing Nov.23-26, 1963. Zerox.

Manchester, William. THE GLORY AND THE DREAM. A Narrative History of America 1932-1972. 2 Vols. L-B, 1974.

MATADOR MAG. "In Memoriam One Year Later," n.d.

Merton, Thomas. "The Black Revolution," ALBERTUS MAGNUS ALUMNA. Spring: 1964: 8-13. JFK on cover.

Miscellaneous Tributes: ALUMNAE JRNL. OF TRINITY COLLEGE (Wash.) "In Memory of JFK," Autumn, 1963: 1. AVE MARIA, "From Death... Life," Dec.7, 1963: 16-17. "President Kennedy's Death - Why?" by Joseph Breig. EBONY, Feb., 1964: 13-14ff. FAMILY WEEKLY, "A Letter to Young John Kennedy," by Francis A. Quinn, Nov.22, 1964: 6.- I.U.D. BULL. Photo of JFK with quote on front page.- JOHN HANCOCK INSURANCE CO. statement on the death of JFK with portrait n.d. MACO, "The Trial of Love," by Fulton J. Sheen, 1964: 6-7. Malania, Fae, A SEARCH FOR JOY, Hallmark, 1969: 24-27. Mauldin's cartoon "Lincoln Weeping," c.1963. NATION, "JFK: A Most Unstuffy Man," by H. Stuart Hughes, Dec.14, 1963: 408-409. NOTRE DAME ALUMNUS. photographs of JFK front and back covers, dedication,1963. PHOTOPLAY "Tribute to John F. Kennedy," by Gerald R. Bartell, Feb. 1964. WASHINGTON D.C. photos of JFK and his gravesite. Also JBK's memorial gown. Wrs.

MINDZENTY REPORT. Dec.15, 1963; Jan.15, 1964.

Morison, Samuel Eliot. "Confidence in Our Country, Even in Ourselves:" 366-371 in NATION UNDER GOD Francis Brentano ed. 1st enlarged Channel Pr., 1964. A eulogy in tribute to JFK which first appeared in ATLANTIC MONTHLY Feb., 1964.

Mossman, B.C. and M.W. Stark. THE LAST SALUTE: Civil and Military Funerals 1921-1969. 1st Dept. of Army, 1971. JFK:188-215,401. RFK: 324-337, 428.

NATIONAL GEOGRAPHIC. "The Last Full Measure," by Melville Bell Grosvenor and staff. March, 1967: 307-355.

Neustadt, Richard. "Kennedy in the Presidency: a Premature Appraisal," POLITICAL SCIENCE QUARTERLY, Sept.1964: 321-334.

NEW REPUBLIC. "Let Us Continue," Dec.7, 1963. Contributors:T.R.B. Jean Daniels, Murray Kempton, James Ridgeway, Gerald W. Johnson, Louis J. Halle.+ "The Kennedy Tragedy Is That He Tried to Modernize America and Congress Defeated Him, by T.R.B. Dec.14, 1963:2.

THE ASSASSINATION

Tributes, Memorials and Assessments

NEWSWEEK. "John Fitzgerald Kennedy 1917-1963," Dec.2, 1963: 15ff.
"Enterprise: Memorial Boom," Dec.30, 1963: 49-50. "JFK's Last Campaign," Mar.9, 1964: 25ff.- "Anniversaries: a JFK Legacy," June 8
1964: 46-48.- "Lesson of History," Feb. 15, 1965: 58.- "JFK Censored?" Oct.3, 1966: 65-66.- "The In-and-Outers," Oct.31, 1966:
96.- "Kennedy Center Slowdown," Mar.10, 1969: 109.- "Closets of
Camelot," by David Gelman and Stephan Lesher, Jan.19, 1976: 31.
"JFK Revised - Letters," Feb.23, 1976: 5.

NEW YORKER. "The Death of the President," by Richard Rovere,
Nov.30, 1963: 49-50. "Funeral of JFK," Dec.7, 1963: 45. "JFK's
Memorial Service in N.Y.C.," Dec.14, 1963: 45-46. "West Berlin
and Death of the President," Jan. 18, 1964: 41-42.

N.Y.TIMES MAG. "The Legacy of the 1000 Days," by James MacGregor
Burns, Dec.1, 1963: 27ff. "What Was Killed Was Not Only the Pres-
ident but the Promise," Nov.15, 1964: 24-25ff.by James Reston.
"He Was a Man of Only One Season," by Henry Fairlee, Nov.21, 1965
28-29ff. Two last items have JFK on front cover. "Where Are They
Now - the Camelotians?" by Donald Smith, Nov.4, 1973: 38-39ff.

N.R.REVIEW OF BOOKS. "Reflections on the Fate of the Union: Kennedy and After," by David Riesman, Richard H. Rovere and 15 others.
Dec. 26, 1963: 3-11.

THE PRESIDENT NOBODY KNEW. P.S.L. Publ., n.d. wrs.

REDBOOK. "In Memory of John F. Kennedy: a Special 14 Page Section,
Nov. 1964: 68-81.- JFK on cover. Seven poems included.

Reynolds, Quentin. "On the Occasion of JFK's Birthday," FAMILY
WEEKLY, May 24, 1964: 4-6.- JFK on cover.

Roche, John P. "Will the Kennedy Legacy Prevail?" CURRENT, Oct.
1964: 11-13.-

Royster, Vermont. A PRIDE OF PREJUDICES. 1st Knopf, 1967. "Re-
quiescat in Pace: JFK," 99-102. Many other references to JFK.

Salinger, Pierre and Vanocur, Sander eds. A TRIBUTE TO JOHN F.
KENNEDY. Ency. Brit., 1964. Tributes from newspapers and magazines, broadcasts, distinguished U.S. citizens and foreign leaders and from letters written to the Kennedy family. Includes a
never-before-published watercolor by JBK, poem by John Masefield.
Also 1st Dell, 1965, wrs.

SAT.EVE.POST. "A Eulogy: John Fitzgerald Kennedy," by Arthur M.
Schlesinger Jr. Dec.14, 1963: 32ff. "The Legacy of JFK," by
Stewart Alsop, Nov.21, 1964: 15-21. "Was JFK a Great Man?"
by Stewart Alsop, Dec.3, 1966:16.-

THE KENNEDY FAMILY OF MASSACHUSETTS

Tributes, Memorials and Assessments

SATURDAY REVIEW. "Countdown for Kennedy," by Irving Kolodin,
July 31, 1971: 37-39ff. The Kennedy Center. "The Improbable
Triumvirate: Khrushchev, Kennedy, Pope John."Oct.30, 1971:24- 35

Schlesinger, Arthur. "Kennedy Ten Years After," ILLUS. LONDON
NEWS, Nov. 1973: 43ff.

SEPIA. "Special Kennedy Section. Good-by Mr. President," Feb.,
1964: 7-26.- JFK on cover.

Seymour, Peter ed. COURAGE. Hallmark (1969). JFK: 58-61.

SIGN. Editorial: "JFK" by Ralph Gorman, Jan. 1964:2.- "JFK:
a Personal Memoir," by Jacques Lowe, Feb., 1964: 11-19. JFK on
cover. "The Sound of a Voice That Is Still," by Theodore Sorenson, July, 1964: 10-12.-

Sorenson, Theodore. THE KENNEDY LEGACY. 1st Macm., 1969. Concepts
and philosophy of JFK and RFK and application to present issues.
Review: by David Halberstam, HARPER'S, Nov. 1969:90-92.

Sullivan, Edw.J. "A Living Library for JFK," SIGN, July, 1964:
7-10.- The Kennedy Memorial Library. TLS Dave Powers, Museum
Curator, John F. Kennedy Library, Sept.22, 1975.

TIME. "Publishing," (JFK memorial issues produced by newspapers
and magazines), Dec.20, 1963: 31-32.

Tugwell, Rexford G. OFF COURSE From Truman to Nixon. Praeger,
1971. JFK's "curiously small achievement;" Nixon as first true
national political professional since Roosevelt.

U.S.88th Cong. 1st sess. Senate Document 46. JOHN FITZGERALD KEN-
NEDY. Eulogies to the Late President Delivered in the Rotunda of
the U.S.Capitol, Nov.24, 1963. GPO, 1963. Wrs. 2nd sess.,1964.
Senate Document 59. MEMORIAL ADDRESSES IN THE CONGRESS OF THE
U.S. and tributes in eulogy of John Fitzgerald Kennedy...GPO,
1964.

U.S.NEWS..."It's One Year After JFK - the Changes:" 60-63; "Pres.
Kennedy's Place in History - a New Size-up," by James Macgregor
Burns: 64-66. Nov.23, 1964.

Wallace, Irving. THE SUNDAY GENTLEMAN. 1st S&S, 1965. "The
Chair in the Oval Office," - last chapter.

WAY. "John F. Kennedy," by Clayton C. Barbeau, Jan-Feb., 1964:
2-10." Also Arthur Hoppe: 11-12.

Whalen, Richard. TAKING SIDES. A Personal View of America from
Kennedy to Nixon to Kennedy. 1st H-M, 1974. The core of the Kennedy legacy to which we must return.

THE ASSASSINATION

Tributes, Memorials and Assessments

Whittbourne, John ed. RUNNYMEDE MEMORIAL. Excel, n.d., wrs.
One acre of British soil with marker. JBK's personal message.

Wills, Garry. "Ten Years After - Opinion," PLAYBOY, Nov.1973:
169ff.

Wright, Emmett Jr. POLITICAL LEADERSHIP IN AMERICA. S-F, 1966.
Wrs. JFK: 153-160, "reliance on general excellence."

(Recording) MEDITATION IN ARLINGTON. A Tribute to John Fitzgerald
Kennedy. Conference-a-Month Club (N.J.) CMC-401

(Recording) THE LAMENT OF JOHN F. KENNEDY and IN REMEMBRANCE OF
PRESIDENT KENNEDY. Shamrock Souvenir Records SSR314, SSR312.

Fiction

Note: Each of the following selection of novels is related
by inference or statement to the life and/or death of JFK.

Bourjaily, Vance. THE MAN WHO KNEW KENNEDY. Dial (1967)

Briskin, Jacqueline. CALIFORNIA GENERATION. 1st Lipp. 1970.

Burdick, Eugene and Harvey Wheeler. FAIL-SAFE. McG-H (1962)

Caldwell, Taymor. CAPTAINS AND THE KINGS: a Novel About an American Dynasty. 1st D'day, 1972.

Condon, Richard. THE MANCHURIAN CANDIDATE. 1st McG-H, 1959. (Cf.
NATION op.cit. p. 122). Also 1st Dell, 1974, wrs. WINTER KILLS.
Dial, 1974, wrs.

Crosby, John. CONTRACT ON THE PRESIDENT. 1st Dell, 1973.

DiMona, Joseph. LAST MAN AT ARLINGTON. Fields (1973).

Galbraith, John Kenneth. THE TRIUMPH. 1st H-M, 1968

Gallagher, Louis J. EPISODE ON BEACON HILL. 1st Benziger, 1950.
Autographed.

Garrison, Jim. THE STAR SPANGLED CONTRACT. 1st McG-H, 1976.
1st Warner, 1977, wrs.

Garson, Barbara. MacBIRD. Grassy Knoll Press, 1966. Also 1st
Grove Press, Evergreen Black Cat ed., 1967. Both wrs.

Grady, James. SIX DAYS OF THE CONDOR. Norton, 1974.

Horan, James D. THE RIGHT IMAGE. Crown (1967).

Fiction

Kennedy, Adam. THE DOMINO PRINCIPLE. 1st Viking, 1975.

Knebel, Fletcher and Chas. W. Bailey. SEVEN DAYS IN MAY. H&R (1962) "It could happen in this country...but not on my watch:" JFK. Knebel. THE ZINZIN ROAD. D'Day (1966).

Lewis, Norman. THE SICILIAN SPECIALIST. 1st Random, 1974.

McCarry, Charles. THE TEARS OF AUTUMN. Sat.Rev.Pr. (1975).

Moore, Robin. THE GREEN BERETS. Crown (1965).

Oates, Joyce Carol. THE ASSASSINS. Vanguard, 1975.

Reichley, James. HAIL TO THE CHIEF. 1st H-M, 1960.

Rennert, Maggie. A MOMENT IN CAMELOT. 1st Geis, 1968.

Rogers, Edward A. FACE TO FACE. Morrow, 1962.

Rogers, Thomas. THE PURSUIT OF HAPPINESS. NAL, 1968.

Roth, Philip. OUR GANG. Random (1971).

Salinger, Pierre. ON INSTRUCTIONS OF MY GOVERNMENT. 1st D'day, 1971. 2nd copy publ. in England under title FOR THE EYES OF THE PRESIDENT ONLY. Fontana, 1972, wrs.

Serling, Robt. J. THE PRESIDENT'S PLANE IS MISSING. Dell (1970) wrs.
Sheed, Wilfred. PEOPLE WILL ALWAYS BE KIND. FS&G, 1973.

Stone, Chuck. KING STREET, 1st B-M, 1970.

Thurston, Wesley S. THE TRUMPETS OF NOVEMBER. 1st Geis, 1966.

West, Morris L. THE SHOES OF THE FISHERMAN. Morrow, 1963.

Wylie, Philip. THE SPY WHO SPOKE PORPOISE. 1st D'day, 1969.

Juvenile Literature

Algieri, Shirley. EVENTS THAT SHOOK THE WORLD. Xerox Corp. 1974. Chapter 6. "The Day the World Wept." Wrs.

Allen, Harold C. TWO TRAGIC DEATHS: JFK and RFK. Young Readers 1970, wrs.

Beard, Chas., with Wm. Beard. THE PRESIDENTS IN AMERICAN HISTORY Messner, 1965.

THE ASSASSINATION

Juvenile Literature

Davidson, Bill. PRESIDENT KENNEDY SELECTS SIX BRAVE PRESIDENTS. H&R, 1962. Op.cit. p.11. Also Popular Lib.ed. 1963. 1st, wrs.

Frolich, S.J. ONCE THERE WAS A PRESIDENT: For Children to Remember. Kanrom, 1964.

Graves, Charles P. JOHN F. KENNEDY: New Frontiersman. Wrs. Dell, 1966. 1st, wrs.

HEADLINE STORIES OF THE '60's. Scholastic, 1969. Wrs.

Hirsch, Phil ed. ThrillingCombat Exploits of THE KENNEDY WAR HEROES. 1st Pyramid, 1962. Wrs.

Hoopes, Roy. WHAT THE PRESIDENT DOES ALL DAY. Day, 1962. Also Memorial ed. 1st Dell, 1964, wrs.

Knight, David C. ed. AMERICAN ASTRONAUTS AND SPACECRAFT. Watts, updated 1975.

Lee, Bruce. JFK: BOYHOOD TO WHITE HOUSE. 1st Crest, 1963. Wrs.

Mehlinger, Howard and John J. Patrick. AMERICAN POLITICAL BEHAVIOR. Ginn, 1972. Also mention of RFK.

Miers, Earl Schenk. THE STORY OF JOHN F. KENNEDY. G&D, 1964.

THE MODERN REVOLUTION 1950-1970. Field, 1971. Wrs.

PEOPLE WHO MADE AMERICA. Vol.9: 647-717, U.S.History Soc.,1973. JBK, JFK, RFK, EMK, Joe,Sr.

Reidy, John P. and Norman Richards. People of Destiny Series: Vol.1. JOHN F. KENNEDY. Children's Pr., 1967.

Sammis, Edw.R. JOHN FITZGERALD KENNEDY: YOUNGEST PRESIDENT. Scholastic (1961). Wrs.

Schoor, Gene. YOUNG JOHN KENNEDY. HB&W (1963). Also McF-B, 1963.

Shapp, Martha and Chas. LET'S FIND OUT ABOUT JOHN FITZGERALD KENNEDY. Watts (1965).

Strousse, Flora. JOHN FITZGERALD KENNEDY: Man of Courage. 1st Signet Key, 1965. Wrs.

Tregaskis, Richard. JOHN F. KENNEDY AND PT-109. Landmark,1962.

Waters, Barbara. Unit No.3 (draft) SEVEN ROLES OF THE PRESIDENT. Students' Guide, Teacher's Guide. JFK Lib.n.d. Includes cassette.

Webb, Robt.N. THE LIVING JFK. G&D (1964).

THE KENNEDY FAMILY OF MASSACHUSETTS

Juvenile Literature

Weingast, David E. WE ELECT A PRESIDENT. Messner, 1966.

White, Nancy Beane. MEET JOHN F. KENNEDY. Random (1965).

Wood, James P. and Editors of Country Beautiful. THE LIFE AND WORDS OF JOHN F. KENNEDY. Country Beautiful, 1964. Also Scholastic, 1967, wrs.

Poetry

Bishop, Jim, "Kennedy's Favorite Poem," PAGEANT, July, 1964:137-

Berry, Wendell. "November 26, 1963," NATION, Dec.21, 1963:437.+ NOVEMBER TWENTY-SIX NINETEEN HUNDRED SIXTY THREE. 1st Braziller, 1964.

Butler, William. "November 25, 1963," HARPER'S Feb.,1964: 72.

Flood, Paul T. "John Fitzgerald Kennedy," in A TREASURY OF DELAWARE POETRY, 1st Dover, 1967.

Geer, Candy. SIX WHITE HORSES. Quill, 1964.

Glikes, Erwin A. and Paul Schwaber, eds. OF POETRY AND POWER; Poems Occasioned by the Presidency and by the Death of John F. Kennedy. Basic, 1964. Includes Auden, Berryman, Gwendolyn Brooks, Frost, Ginsberg, Zukofsky and 72 others.Rauschenberg's portrait. Review: by Lloyd Frankenberg, N.Y.TIMES BK.REV. Nov.22, 1964:6.-

Hague, Richard (poem), John Shanley (illus.) "The Will Be Done," THE CRUSADER, Steubenville, O., 1964: 5.

Jones, Barbara. "Special Delivery from Heaven," SIGN, Dec.,1963: 1, with story of how the poem came to be written.

Lampee, A.C. "Smilin' Jack on PT109," GENERATION, Christmas, 1964: 28.

Mannes, Marya. "The Pampered," in BUT WILL IT SELL? 1st Lipp., 1964: 150-151.

Margeson, June A. "Bulletin from Dallas," in OUR BEST TO YOU, Verse Writers of Ohio, 1968. Wrs. Presentation copy.

Nachant, Frances G. SONG OF PEACE. Golden Quill, 1969.

Spicer, Jack. LANGUAGE, White Rabbit Pr., 1970: 8, 57-66.

Stanislaus, Sister M. "A Poet's Memories of John Kennedy," (13 poems). SIGN, Nov.1964: 16-21.

THE ASSASSINATION

Memorabilia

BOOK OF THE MONTH CLUB NEWS, April, 1967. For May THE DEATH OF
THE PRESIDENT, Manchester. Wrs.

Certificate of Appreciation from the Trustees of the John Fitzgerald Kennedy Library No. A7056.

Czesany, Gerhard and Jack H. Green. JOHN F. KENNEDY STAMPS OF
THE WORLD. American Topical Assn, 1965. Wrs.

Gannon, Thos.M. "The Kennedy Memorabilia," AMERICA, Sept. 19,
1964: 304-306.-

Gemming, Elizabeth and Klaus. PORTRAITS OF GREATNESS: "Learning
Through Stamps," Vol.3. JFK U.S.1964 stamp with biography: 63.
Barre, 1969.

Goldman, Alex J. JOHN FITZGERALD KENNEDY: THE WORLD REMEMBERS.
Fleet, 1968. Collection of memorials from 28 countries. Also
homage on stamps, medals and metal.

Hamilton, Charles. COLLECTING AUTOGRAPHS AND MANUSCRIPTS. 1st
U. of Okla.Pr., 1961. Includes variant signatures of JFK.

"The John F. Kennedy Library Exhibit," Program produced as a
public service by NAT'L GEOGRAPHIC, 1964. Wrs.

John F. Kennedy Library Materials: Historical Materials plus
supplement, 1975, wrs. Historical Resources. JFK Reading List
July, 1974. The Kennedys - A Reading List for Young People, Nov.
1974. Guide to the Use of Oral History Interviews, Nov., 1974.
The JFK Library Oral History Program. The JFK Library Audio-
visual Collection. Eric/Chess: Profiles of Promise. Bringing
the JFK Library into the Classroom. Kennedy subject headings
from cataloguer's working file. Unit No.4 (Draft) prepared by
John F. Stuart: Educational Resources of the JFK Library.
Memoranda for the President: Collection of Documents prepared
for JFK by members of the White House Staff 1961-1963. Facsimiles of memoranda from the files of Evelyn Lincoln. Discussion
questions, activities. Mimeo., wrs.

JFK Stamps - miscellaneous articles. "The New Kennedy Stamp,"
by Jerry Klein, LOOK, June 16, 1964: 32.- "Memorial in Stamps,"
CINCINNATI PICTORIAL ENQUIRER, Nov.15, 1964: 34-35.- "The Big
Boom in JFK Stampts," by Ernest Dunbar, LOOK, Nov.29, 1966: 52-
54. -"The Design That Didn't Make It...and the One that Did,"
MINKUS STAMP JRNL. V.1,n.4:28-29. -

Mayhew, Aubrey. THE WORLD'S TRIBUTE TO JFK IN MEDALLIC ART.
Morrow, 1966. Comprehensive reference to this date.

Memorabilia

Memorabilia: 150 pieces of memorial and historic places brochures and postcards; photographs and memorial cards; Kennedy
museum, stamp news, flyers, 1960 campaign buttons, bumper stickers, flyers; press clippings and others.

Minkus. JOHN F. KENNEDY WORLD WIDE MEMORIAL STAMP ALBUM, 1964,
with early supplements. Includes all U.S. stamps; early releases and souvenir sheets from Grenada, Dominica, Columbia, Mexico,
Paraguay, Guatemala, Dominican Republic, Brazil, El Salvador,
Honduras, Nicaragua, Costa Rica, Panama, Bolivia, Venezuela,
Ecuador, Paraguay, Uruguay, San Marino, Argentina, Chile, Baham-
as, Germany, Berlin, Nigeria, Monaco, Cyprus, Malta, Philip-
pines, Maldive Islands,Mali Republic, Guinea (first country af-
ter U.S. to issue a stamp honoring JFK), Sierra Leone, Liberia,
Central Africa Republic, Niger, Ivory Coast, Senegal, Upper
Volta, Ghana, Togo, Cameroons, Chad, Gabon, Mauretania, Dahomey,
Rwanda, Burundi, Congo, Ajman, Dubai, Fujeira, Jordan, Khor Fak-
kan, Ras al Khaima, Sharjah, South Arabia, Kathiri, South Arabia,
Mahra State, Um-Al-Qiwain, Yemen, Davaar Island. Also first
day of issue: JFK, May 29, 1964, envelope and 5x7 photograph;
JBK Nov.22, 1966 3rd anniversary.

Montgomery, Herb and Mary. "The Kennedy Half Dollar," CATHOLIC
DICEST, July, 1964: 79-81.-

Notlep, Robert. THE AUTOGRAPH COLLECTOR. Crown, 1968. Includes
JFK and RFK and how obtained.

NOTRE DAME. (Qtly.) Summer - 1961. JFK Laetare Medalist - 1961.

Printed card: "The President and Mrs. Kennedy deeply appreciate
your thoughtfulness and expression of sympathy at this time."
Addressed to Mrs. Lucy Ryan. Envelope dated 5,Sep.,1963 from "The
White House."

Taylor, John M. FROM THE WHITE HOUSE INKWELL. American Presidential Autographs. 1st Tuttle, 1968. Chap.18: Kennedy and Johnson.

U.S.NEWS... "A Kennedy Coin, a Kennedy Stamp," Dec.23, 1963:11.-

Wenger, Kenneth. JOHN F. KENNEDY: MEMORIAL STAMP ISSUES OF THE
WORLD. Ft.Lee, 1970. 1st, wrs.

THE ELECTION OF 1964 AND AFTER

Alexander, Herbert E. FINANCING THE 1964 ELECTION. Citizens' Research n.d. Wrs. Useful as comparison with 1960 elections.

Alsop. Stewart. THE CENTER. People and Power in Political Washington. 1st H&R, 1968. LBJ, but many anecdotes of JFK.

THE ELECTION OF 1964 AND AFTER

Amrine, Michael. THIS AWESOME CHALLENGE. The Hundred Days of Lyndon Johnson. Putnam, 1964. Discussion of JFK's programs. Also 1st Popular Lib.ed., 1967.

Bayh, Birch. ONE HEARTBEAT AWAY. 1st B-M, 1968. From the death of JFK to final ratification of 25th Amendment in Feb.,1967, to adopt effective succession procedures to the presidency.

Bell, Jack. THE JOHNSON TREATMENT. 1st H&R, 1965. Effect of his method on the passage of bills originated by JFK.

CBS News Election Unit, Stanford Mirkin ed. 1964 GUIDE TO CON- VENTIONS AND ELECTIONS. 1st Dell, 1964. Wrs. JFK and RFK incl.

Cummings, Milton C. Jr. ed. THE NATIONAL ELECTION OF 1964. 1st Brookings, 1966. Re JFK: S. Kelley, H.E.Alexander, Paul Tillett, N. Polsby, A.Campbell.

Demaris, Ovid. DIRTY BUSINESS. The Corporate-Political Money- Power Game. 1st HARPER'S, 1974. Praise and blame:JFK,RFK,EMK.

DEMOCRATIC NATIONAL CONVENTION 1964. Program Comm., 1964. Ded- icated to JFK with essays by Schlesinger, Martin, Means.

Donovan, John C. THE POLITICS OF POVERTY. Pagasus, 1970. Wrs. LBJ as failing to carry out JFK's plan for domestic reform.

Evans, Rowland and Robt. Novak. LYNDON B. JOHNSON: The Exercise of Power. 1st NAL, 1966. Public lives of LBJ, JFK, RFK.

Faber, Harold ed. THE ROAD TO THE WHITE HOUSE: The Story of the 1964 Election by Staff of N.Y.TIMES. McG-H, 1965. 1st. LBJ, JFK and RFK.

Gallois, Pierre. "America's Getting Tough - and It's All to Our Good." REALITIES Nov.1965:33-37. LBJ as greater than JFK.

Getlein, Frank. THE POLITICS OF PARANOIA. F&W, 1969. Mostly about the Johnson years with reference to the three Kennedys.

Geyelin, Philip. LYNDON B. JOHNSON AND THE WORLD. Praeger, 1966. LBJ vs. JFK on foreign policy.

Goldman, Eric F. THE TRAGEDY OF LYNDON JOHNSON. 1st Dell, Wrs. 1969. Much material on Kennedy administration and family.

Greene, Felix. THE ENEMY: What Every American Should Know About Imperialism. 1st Random, 1970. Refs. to JFK and RFK.

Hebers, John. THE LOST PRIORITY: What Happened to the Civil Rights Movement in America? F&W, 1970. Impetus of JFK,RFK.

Howar, Barbara. LAUGHING ALL THE WAY. Fawcett, 1964, wrs. Outsider in the Kennedy years - discusses them from that viewpoint.

INAUGURAL 1965. Threshold of Tomorrow: The Great Society. Program and Book Comm.,1965. Paul Horgan re JFK: 94-95.

Johnson, Lyndon B. et al. THE NEGRO AS AN AMERICAN. Center for Study of Democratic Institutions, 1965, wrs. LBJ edited by James MacGregor Burns, TO HEAL AND TO BUILD, The Programs of LBJ. 1st McG-H, 1968. 47 presidential speeches, with discussion of JFK by S.Udall,Ralph Ellison, Heller, Bundy, LBJ.,Burns.

Kearns, Doris. LYNDON JOHNSON AND THE AMERICAN DREAM. 1st H&R, 1976.

Kluckhohn, Frank L. LYNDON'S LEGACY: A Candid Look at the President's Policymakers. Devin,Adair, 1964. Kennedy's inner circle.

LOOK. "The Campaign and the Candidates," by Fletcher Knebel, Nov.3, 1964: 23-25. "Conspiracy USA: a Plot that Failed," by Patricia Swank. Jan.26, 1965. (Birch society)."The Texanization of Washington," April 6, 1965: 30-34. "How Goes the War on Poverty?" by Sargent Shriver, July 27, 1965:30-31ff.

Mollenhoff, Clark E. DESPOILERS OF DEMOCRACY. 1st D'day, 1965. "...many of the administrations political sore spots seemed to be linked with the Lone Star State and LBJ men."

Ogden, Daniel M., Jr. ELECTING THE PRESIDENT: 1964. Chandler,1964. Wrs. The two major parties in 1960 and expectations for 1964.

Reedy, George. THE TWILIGHT OF THE PRESIDENCY. An Examination of Power and Isolation in the White House. World, 1970. JFK and Cuba, his cabinet and Congress, the executive order; RFK 1968.

SAT.EVE.POST. "Letters" Jan. 18, 1964:4-5.- Nixon: 6,10. "Why John Glenn Is Entering Politics," by H.Martin and D.Oberdorfer, Feb.22, 1964: 21-25. The death of JFK as catalyst.

Schlafly, Phyllis. A CHOICE NOT AN ECHO. Marquette, 1964. Wrs. "...the inside story of how American Presidents are chosen..."

Schlesinger, Arthur M. Jr. THE IMPERIAL PRESIDENCY. H-M (1973). White House as a court not one's experience in the Kennedy years.

Shadegg, Stephen. WHAT HAPPENED TO GOLDWATER? The Inside Story of the 1964 Republican Campaign. 1st HR&W, 1965. Political biography paralleling the lives of Barry Goldwater and JFK.

Sherrill, Robt. ACCIDENTAL PRESIDENT. 1st Grossman, 1967. Review of LBJ's career, contrast to JFK.

Sidey, Hugh. "Departure of a 'Deputy President'. Ted Sorenson: JFK's All-Purpose Man," LIFE, Mar.6, 1964: 105-106ff.

Sutherland, Elizabeth ed. LETTERS FROM MISSISSIPPI. 1st McG-H, 1965. Summer of 1964, "Freedom Schools," registration of Negroes.

Thimmesch, Nick. THE CONDITION OF REPUBLICANISM. 1st Norton,1968. Includes Nixon vs. Kennedy in 1960, JFK as president, his death.

Udall, Stewart. 1976: AGENDA FOR TOMORROW. 1st HB&W, 1968. Reflections of public service under LBJ, JFK. Also RFK.

White, F. Clifton with Wm. J.Gill. SUITE 3505: The Story of the Draft Goldwater Movement. Arlington, 1967. The conservative view of the 1960 election, Bay of Pigs, JFK death and 1964 election.

White, Theodore H. THE MAKING OF THE PRESIDENT 1964. 1st Athen. 1965. The part played by JFK's vision. Review: NEWSWEEK, Dec. 27, 1965: 72.-

Wicker, Tom. "The President," in NEW YORK TIMES ELECTION HANDBOOK, McG-H, 1964. On JFK re the limits and opportunity of power.

Wise, David. THE POLITICS OF LYING. Government Deception, Secrecy and Power. Random (1973) Official deception from 1964. Also LBJ and his plan to undermine RFK's presidential bid.

145.

PART FOUR.   JACQUELINE BOUVIER KENNEDY ONASSIS

JACQUELINE BOUVIER

Writings of Jacqueline Bouvier

"People I Wish I Knew," THE WORLD IN VOGUE, op.cit. page 2. The
winning essay written for VOGUE'S Prix de Paris, 1951.

With Lee Bouvier. ONE SPECIAL SUMMER. Delacorte, 1974. Autographed edition limited to 500 c. Trip to Europe in 1951 "with not a
word or pen stroke changed." Also 1st trade edition. Ibid.
LADIES' HOME JRNL. Nov.,1974: 107-111. Lee and JB on cover.

Writings About Jacqueline Bouvier

Burton, Katherine. "A Famous American Family," (Bouvier), SIGN,
June, 1961: 56. -

Cassini, Igor. "Panorama" in TOWN AND COUNTRY, June, 1962:78-79ff.
The Debutante Issue. JB in Debutante Hall of Fame; photograph
taken in 1947.

Davis, John H. THE BOUVIERS: Portrait of an American Family.
FS&G (1969). Also 1st Avon prtg. 1970. Wrs.

Rhea, Mini, with Frances Spatz Leighton. I WAS JACQUELINE KENNE-
DY'S DRESSMAKER. Fleet, 1962. Presentation copy. Jacqueline as a
young girl and as inquiring photographer. "The Young Jacqueline
Kennedy As I Knew Her," L.H.JRNL., Jan., 1962:36-37ff.

Congdon, Thos.B.Jr. "Ann Lowe: Society's Best Kept Secret," SEP,
Dec.12, 1964. The great-granddaughter of a slave and dressmaker
for Jacqueline Bouvier.

JACQUELINE KENNEDY

Writings of Jacqueline Kennedy

"Your Child's World," AMERICAN WEEKLY, Dec.11, 1960: 4-5. -

Foreword to THE WHITE HOUSE. An Historic Guide. 2nd ed. Wash.,1962.
Wrs. First publication of the White House Historical Assn. con-
ceived by the then First Lady as a means of paying for the renov-
ation and re-decoration of the White House. Second copy, 4th ed.,
includes the JFK tree in the Presidents' Park: Magnolia Soulang-
eana. "Your Society's President Reports a Year of Widening Hor-
izons, by Melville B. Grosvenor, NAT'L GEOGRAPHIC, Dec., 1962:
888-893. Explains the planning and execution of WHITE HOUSE book.

"A Christmas Message," LOOK, Dec.31, 1963: 14. Written before the
death of JFK.

JACQUELINE KENNEDY

Writings of Jacqueline Kennedy

"'These Are the Things I Hope Will Show How He Really Was,'"
LIFE, May 29, 1964: 32-34A. With additional comment by Richard
B. Stolley: 34B. Cover photo of JBK. Re JFK Library Exhibit.

"'How I Hope He'll Be Remembered,'" GOOD HOUSEKEEPING, 1964:79.
Plans for the JFK library with additional comment by Robt. G.
Deindorfer: 79ff. -

Foreword to THE JOHN F. KENNEDY LIBRARY EXHIBIT. N.P., n.d. wrs.
Catalog of the memorabilia, books and documents of exhibit.

"A Memoir," LOOK (Memorial Issue) Nov.17, 1964: 36. Op.cit. 133.
JBK on cover.

Writings About Jacqueline Kennedy

Armstrong, Nancy. "Jackie," USA 1, April 7, 1962:34-35. First
issue of this national monthly magazine.

Associated Press. WORLD IN 1966... 1968...1975. Op.cit. 58.

Bair, Marjorie ed. JACQUELINE KENNEDY IN THE WHITE HOUSE. 1st
Paperback Lib., 1963. Wrs. Many and unusual photographs.

Barzman, Sol. THE FIRST LADIES. Martha Washington to Pat Nixon.
1st Cowles, 1970. JBK: 328-337.

Bender, Marylin. THE BEAUTIFUL PEOPLE. C-McC (1967). JBK, Caroline and John Jr. included.

Bennett, Arnold. JACKIE, BOBBY & MANCHESTER. The Story Behind
the Headlines. Bee-Line, 1967. wrs.

Buck, Pearl. THE KENNEDY WOMEN: A Personal Appraisal. 1st
Cowles, 1970.

Carr, Wm. H.A. THOSE FABULOUS KENNEDY WOMEN. Wisdom, 1961. Wrs.

Chaffin, Lillie and Miriam Butwin. AMERICA'S FIRST LADIES. (Juv.)
Lerner, 1970.

Christy, George. "Heaven or Hell...the Best-Dressed List," TOWN
AND COUNTRY, Oct., 1967: 105ff. Lee Radziwill and JBK on list.

Corry, John. THE MANCHESTER AFFAIR. Putnam (1967). Claims to
describe the attempted suppression of THE DEATH OF A PRESIDENT.
"The Manchester Papers," ESQUIRE, June, 1967: 83-91ff. Also
additional comment by Gay Talese: 92-94ff. JBK on cover.

Curran, Robt. THE KENNEDY WOMEN: Their Triumphs and Tragedies.
Lancer, 1964. Wrs.

Writings About Jacqueline Kennedy

Curtis, Charlotte. FIRST LADY. 1st Pyramid, 1962. Wrs. Many details of JBK's life as wife to the President.

Dareff, Hugh. JACQUELINE KENNEDY: Portrait in Courage. (Juv.) Parents Mag. Pr., 1965.

Dariaux, Genevieve A. ELEGANCE. D'day, (1964). Ref. to JBK.

Lester, David. THE LONELY LADY OF SAN CLEMENTE. The Story of Pat Nixon. 1st Crowell, 1978. Comparison with JBK.

EBONY. "Glamorous First Ladies - Mrs. Houphouet-Boigny and Jackie Kennedy," Aug. 1962: 21-24ff. Both on cover.

Exman, Eugene. THE HOUSE OF HARPER. 1st H&R, 1967. The Manchester affair; books by JFK and RFK.

Fairchild, John. THE FASHIONABLE SAVAGES. 1st D'day, 1965. Chap.16: "Her Elegance." (JBK)

THE FIRST LADIES' COOK BOOK. Favorite Recipes of All the Presidents of the U.S. Parent's, 1966. JFK and JBK: 207-211.

Fletcher, Adele Whitney. "Her Friends Reveal the Jackie Kennedy Nobody Knows," LADY'S CIRCLE, Sept. 1967: 20-21ff.

Friedman, Stanley P. THE MAGNIFICENT KENNEDY WOMEN. 1st Monarch, 1964. Wrs.

Gallagher, Mary Barelli, ed. by Frances Spatz Leighton. MY LIFE WITH JACQUELINE KENNEDY. McKay, 1969. TLS Mar.28, 1974. TLS HALLMARK re JBK's Christmas card drawings. "My Boss, Jackie Kennedy" L.H.JRNL, July, 1969: 61-68. Postscript to "My Life with Jackie Kennedy," Nov. 1969: 84ff.

GOOD HOUSEKEEPING. "Jacqueline Kennedy: the Future of a Noble Lady," by Wm. Shannon, April, 1964: 76-81ff. "Jackie Kennedy and Her Children One Year After Tragedy," by Shannon, Nov., 1964:80ff. "How Jackie Kennedy and Other Young Widows Have Rebuilt Their Lives," by Alan Levy, Mar., 1965: 96-99ff. "Jackie Kennedy: What People Close to Her Think About Her Now," by Helen Dudar, Oct., 1967: 90-91ff.

Granton, E. Fannie. "The Lady in Black. U.S. Negroes Look With Nostalgia on Former First Lady's White House Reign," EBONY, Feb. 1964: 81-82ff.-

Haines, Aubrey B. "First Lady in Her Own Right," TORCH, Nov.1963: 16-19. -

Hall, Gordon L. and Ann Pinchot. JACQUELINE KENNEDY. Fell, 1964. Also 1st Signet, 1966, wrs.

JACQUELINE KENNEDY

Writings About Jacqueline Kennedy

Harding, Robt.T. and A.L.Holmes. JACQUELINE KENNEDY: A Woman for the World. Ency. Enterp., 1966. Photos from UPI. Four of JBK's paintings reproduced.

HARPER'S BAZAAR: 100 Years of the American Female. 1st Random, 1967. Full page photo of JBK.

Heller, Deane and David. JACQUELINE KENNEDY: The Complete Story of America's Glamorous First Lady. 1st Monarch, 1961. Wrs. New enlarged edition, Monarch, 1963.

JACQUELINE KENNEDY. Country Wide, 1964.

"Jacqueline Kennedy -B.B.C. (Brains, Beauty and Charm)." READER'S DIGEST: 157-158, condensed from "Topics," in N.Y.TIMES July 17,62.-

JACQUELINE KENNEDY, WOMAN OF VALOR. Macf.-Bartell, 1964. Wrs.

Johnson, Lady Bird. A WHITE HOUSE DIARY. 1st HR&W, 1970. Includes relationship with JBK, RFK's death, personal reactions to events.

Jones, Candy. LOOK YOUR BEST. H&R (1964). Praise for JBK.

Kittler, Glenn D. "A Profile in Faith: Jacqueline Kennedy," CORONET, April, 1964: 20-25. - JBK on cover.

Klamkin, Marian. WHITE HOUSE CHINA. 1st Scrib.,1972. Social history of personal tastes of each First Lady including JBK.

Klapthor, Margaret B. THE GOWN OF MRS. JOHN F. KENNEDY - as displayed in U.S. National Museum. Smithsonian, 1963. Wrs.

Kluckhohn, Frank L. AMERICA: LISTEN! 1st of rev.enl.ed. Monarch, 1962. Wrs. "Current chaos," but JBK gets A+.

LADIES' HOME JRNL. "Jacqueline Kennedy's New Life," by Virginia T. Stratford, Feb., 1966: 70ff. "The Real Villain's of the William Manchester Book," April, 1967: 60 , by Judith Crist.- "Lord Harlech's Family Talks About the Kennedys," June, 1968: 57-59ff. by Diana Lurie. "Jacqueline Kennedy's Memories: From a Very Private Photo Album," Dec., 1968: 100-101.

Lewis, Wilmarth S. ONE MAN'S EDUCATION. 1st Knopf, 1967. JBK related to author through Auchincloss', visited, read ms.

LIFE. "Jackie Kennedy: A Front Runner's Appealing Wife," Aug.24, 1959: 75-81. JBK and JFK on cover. "Ex-fotog Shoots Her Own Pix of Newsy Vacation," Aug.1, 1960:82-83. "To See Another Jackie You Don't Have to Look Hard..." Jan.20, 1961: 16-22.- "First Lady in World of Carriages and Kids," May 12, 1961: 12-13. "Jackie and the Ambassador's Ladies," Sept., 29, 1961: 58-59. Cont'd 150.

THE KENNEDY FAMILY OF MASSACHUSETTS

Writings About Jacqueline Kennedy

LIFE Cont'd. "A Week in the Life of JFK's Wife," Nov.24, 1961: 32-41. John Jr. on cover. "The Best-Dressed Women," Jan.12, 1962: 44-45. "A First-Rate Junket for a First Lady," (India), Mar. 23, 1962: 42-44. "Jackie Leaves Her Mark on India and Vice Versa," Mar.30, 1962: 24-35. "Jackie Water-Skiing," July 27, 1962: 32-33.- "Fanfare and Flourishes for a Temple of Music," (Lincoln Center). Oct.5, 1962: 100A-104. "Hers Was a Gentle World. As Jackie Expects Her Third..." Apr.26, 1963: 26-33.- "Mrs. Kennedy Says Thank You," Jan.24, 1964: 32B-32C. "On a Birthday, a Family Visit to Arlington," June 12, 1964: 50. "'Congratulations,' Whispered Jackie, 'And Thanks...'" by Shana Alexander, Sept.4, 1964: 30-31. "Jackie at Opera on Callas Night," Apr. 2, 1965: 105-106. "Jackie Kennedy, Conquistador. She Captivates Spain with Her Style," May 6, 1966: 78A-80ff. JBK on cover. "Jackie's Short Skirt Rates Five Stars," Dec.16, 1966: 37.- "Jackie Kennedy in Cambodia, " Nov.17, 1967:97-100ff. JBK on cover.

Lobsenz, Norman M. "How Jacqueline Kennedy Saved a Child's Life" REDBOOK, July, 1963: 47ff. -

LOOK."The Kennedy Women," by Peter Maas, Oct.11, 1960: 93-102. JBK on cover. "Jacqueline Kennedy: What You Don't Know About Our First Lady," by Laura Berquist, July 4, 1961: 61-62ff. JBK on cover. "Mrs. Kennedy's First Cousins," by Edw. Korry, Aug. 29, 1961: 78-82.- "Jacqueline Kennedy Inspires the International Look," June 5, 1962: 73-78. JBK and JFK on cover. "Valiant Is the Word for Jackie," by Berquist, Jan.28, 1964: 72-74ff. JBK on cover. "Jacqueline Kennedy Goes Public," by Berquist, Mar.22 1966: 46ff. JBK on cover. Additional material by Douglas Jones: 42-45. "William Manchester's Own Story," by Manchester, April 4, 1967: 62-66ff. JBK on cover. "Letter to the Editor," by Pierre Salinger (re Manchester's book), May 16, 1967; with Manchester's reply: 8. "Lord Harlech Talks About the Kennedys," Oct.1, 1968: 30-34.

McCALL'S. Letters of Sympathy to Mrs. John F. Kennedy, June, 1964: 82-83. JBK on cover. "Jacqueline Kennedy's Secret Mission in Asia," by Bernard and Marvin Kalb: 60-61ff. JBK and Lord Harlech on cover. "The Painting of the Kennedy Legend," by Aaron Shikler, Mar., 1961: 76-81ff. Twelve paintings including one of JBK on cover.

McConnell, Jane and Burt. OUR FIRST LADIES. Martha Washington to Pat Ryan Nixon. Crowell, 1969, rev.ed. JBK: 335-353.

Manchester, Wm. CONTROVERSY and Other Essays in Journalism 1950 -1975. L-B (1976). JBK: 1-66.

Mead, Margaret. "A New Role for Jacqueline Kennedy?" REDBOOK, June, 1964: 24ff. -

JACQUELINE KENNEDY

Writings About Jacqueline Kennedy

Means, Marianne. "What Three Presidents Say About Their Wives,"
GOOD HOUSEKEEPING, Aug. 1963: 57-61ff. JFK, Truman, Ike. THE
WOMAN IN THE WHITE HOUSE. The Lives, Times and Influence of
Twelve Notable First Ladies. 1st Signet, 1964, Wrs. JBK:253-288.

Mesta, Pearl. "First Ladies I Have Known," McCALL'S, Mar.,1963:
34ff. JBK with Caroline and John on cover.

NEWSWEEK. "First Lady's First Year," Jan.1, 1962: 31-35. JBK on
cover. "The First Lady and the White House," Sept. 17, 1962: 71-
78. JBK on cover. "Caesar's Wife," Oct.28, 1963: 20-21. - "Looking Ahead: JBK Purchase of Georgetown House," Dec.23, 1963: 16-
17. Also "Eulogies for JFK:" 17-18; "Report from FBI:" 19-20.-
"Jacqueline Kennedy - From Memories, a New Mission," Jan.6, 1964:
15-18.- JBK on cover. "Newsmakers: Jacqueline Kennedy," (her ac-
knoledgement of 800,000 condolence messages): 48.- Also "Letters.
Tribute to Jackie:" 2ff. "Controversies: the Best Kennedy Book?"
Sept.5, 1966: 21-22.- "Jacqueline B. Kennedy, Plaintiff..." Dec.
26, 1966: 39-43. JBK on cover. "Jacqueline Kennedy's 'Victory',"
Jan.2, 1967: 16-19.- "The Holiday Spirit," by Kenneth Crawford,
1967: re Manchester.- "Temporary Cease-Fire," Jan.9, 1967: 20-
21.- "Manchester's Own Story," Jan.30, 1967: 21-24.- "Letters -
More on Manchester," Feb.13, 1967:4ff.- "Plane Fact,"Feb.20, 1967:
58.- "The Travels of Jackie," (Cambodia), Nov.20, 1967:76-77.-
"Romance. I Spy," (JBK and Lord Harlech), Mar.4, 1968:23-24.-

ONE DOZEN RED ROSES. The Life Story of Jacqueline Kennedy. Tatler
Publ., 1964.

Porter, Katherine Anne. "Her Legend Will Live," (JBK), LADIES'
HOME JRNL., Mar.,1964: 58-59.-

Sadler, Christine. AMERICA'S FIRST LADIES. MacF, 1963. Wrs.

SALUTE TO JACQUELINE KENNEDY. Matthews Publ., 1964. Wrs.

Sanseveri, Gianna M. "L'Amore Segreto di Jackie," LE ORE, 16 Set-
tembre, 1965: 62-63ff. -

SAT.EVE.POST. "An Exclusive Chat with Jackie Kennedy," by Joan
Braden, May 12, 1962: 85-88. "How Jackie Restyled the White
House," Oct.26, 1963: 42-51. Norman Rockwell portrait. "A Look
at Tomorrow Today," by Richard Armstrong (JBK astrology chart).
Mar.26, 1966: 23-27. JBK on cover. "Jackie Kennedy: A View From
the Crowd," by Alan Levy, Mar.11, 1967: 19-23.-

Schlesinger, Arthur. "History and the Manchester Affair," ATLAN-
TIC, Mar., 1967: 69-74.

Schreiber, Flora Rheta. "What Jackie Learned from Her Mother,"
GOOD HOUSEKEEPING, Oct., 1962: 74-75ff.

Writings About Jacqueline Kennedy

Sidey, Hugh. "The First Lady Brings History and Beauty into the White House, LIFE, Sept.1, 1961: 54-65. JBK on cover.

Storm, Irene. "Jacqueline Kennedy: the Women Who Like Her...the Women Who Don't," TV RADIO MIRROR, Feb., 1963: 52-53ff.

Thayer, Mary Van Rensselaer. JACQUELINE BOUVIER KENNEDY. D'day, 1961. "Dear Mrs. Kennedy," (Children's letters), May, 1963: 76ff. LADIES HOME JRNL. JACQUELINE KENNEDY: THE WHITE HOUSE YEARS. L-B, 1971. 1st ed.

TIME. "Jackie," illus. with painting by JBK, Jan.20, 1961: 18-26. JBK on cover.-"JBK on Goodwill Tour to India and Pakistan," Mar. 16, 1962: 37. "Big Year for the Clan," (JBK's pregnancy), Apr. 26, 1963: 23-24. "Art - Toward the Ideal," Sept.6, 1963:61-67. (White House Project).- "Jackie Kennedy," (carved inscription on mantel of presidential bedroom), Jan.17, 1964: 34.-

TOWN AND COUNTRY. "1967 Society Sweepstakes," by Geo. Christy: 68-69. Mention also of Stephen and Jean Smith.

U.S.NEWS... "First Lady Gives a Lesson in Diplomacy," Jan.1, 1962: 52-53.- "On Tour in Asia with U.S.First Lady," Mar.,1962:58ff.- "Mrs. Kennedy's Tour," Mar.19, 1962: 70-71.- "A New Home for Jacqueline Kennedy and Children," Dec.9, 1963: 18.- "A Year of Mourning Set by Mrs. Kennedy," Dec.23, 1963: 8.-

West, J.B. with Mary Lynn Kotz. UPSTAIRS AT THE WHITE HOUSE. My Life with the First Ladies. C,McC & G, 1973. Most space to JBK. Ibid. LADIES HOME JRNL. Sept. 1973:50ff.

Wolff, Perry. A TOUR OF THE WHITE HOUSE WITH MRS. JOHN F. KENNE-DY. D'day (1962). Also 1st Dell, 1963, wrs.

(Recording) Portrait of a Valiant Lady...Jacqueline Kennedy. Research Craft Corp. Includes JBK's "Thank You," message. RC1600.

JACQUELINE ONASSIS
Writings of Jacqueline Onassis

"A Dream Realized," LADIES' HOME JRNL. Sept., 1971: 113ff. The opening of the JFK Center for the Performing Arts.

"The Bright Light of His Days," McCALL'S, Nov. 1973: 81-82.

"Being Present," in The Talk of the Town section of THE NEW YORKER Jan.13, 1975: 26-29. Unsigned. International Center of Photography.

"Interview," to Bill Roeder of NEWSWEEK, Sept.29, 1975:80-81. Occasion: as consulting editor for Viking Press.

Writings of Jacqueline Onassis

Editor, with the cooperation of the Metropolitan Museum of Art, IN THE RUSSIAN STYLE. 1st Viking Penguin, 1976.

"A Visit to the High Priestess of Vanity Fair." In VANITY FAIR brochure of the Metropolitan Museum of Art exhibition catalog, 1977. JKO interview with Diana Vreeland. "Vanity Fair," N.Y. TIMES MAG., Dec.11, 1977: 151ff. Excerpted from exhibition brochure.

Writings About Jacqueline Onassis

Beman, Lewis. "The Reality Behind the Onassis Myth," FORTUNE, Oct. 1975: 130-135ff.

BILLY BALDWIN REMEMBERS. 1st HBJ, 1974. Chapter 10: Jacqueline. "Jacqueline Kennedy Onassis: a Memoir," McCALL'S, Dec.,1974:24ff.

Birmingham, Stephen. JACQUELINE BOUVIER KENNEDY ONASSIS. G&D, 1978. "The Public Event Named Jackie," N.Y.TIMES MAG., June 20, 1976: 10-11ff.

Brady, James. SUPERCHIK. 1st L-B, 1974. Chapter 9: "Jackie & Co."

Brothers, Joyce. "The Happy, Second Widowhood of Jackie Onassis." GOOD HOUSEKEEPING, Jan.,1976: 32ff.

Cafarakis, Christian. THE FABULOUS ONASSIS. His Life and Loves. Morrow (1972). Meretricious. With the collaboration of Jacques Harvey. "The Fabulous Onassis," McCALL'S, Mar.,1972: 75-76ff. JKO on cover.

Friedman, Bruce Jay. "Why Won't Jackie Onassis Leave Galella Alone?" ESQUIRE, Mar. 1972: 94-95ff. JKO on cover.

Frischauer, Willi. ONASSIS. 1st Meredith, 1968. "Onassis: the Yachtsman Who Has Had Them All Aboard," L.H.JRNL.,Mar. 1968: 90ff. Review of ONASSIS by Paul D. Zimmerman, NEWSWEEK. - "Christina Onassis: the Happiness Money Can't Buy," L.H.JRNL, Mar, 1975:40ff. "Jackie and Onassis - What Really Happened," GOOD HOUSEKEEPING, Aug., 1975: 34ff.

Galatopoulos, Stelios. CALLAS: LA DIVINA: Art that Conceals Art. Ldn.House, 1970. Eulogistic account.

Galella, Ron. JACQUELINE. S&W, 1974. Tells how and why he became "compelled" to photograph JKO.

ILLUSTRADA. "El Escandolo de las Fotos de Jacqueline," GACETA, 14 enero, 1973: 16-19. JKO on cover.

Joeston, Joachim. ONASSIS - A Biography. A-S (1963).

Writings About Jacqueline Onassis

Kelly, Katie. THE WONDERFUL WORLD OF WOMEN'S WEAR DAILY. Sat.
Rev.Pr., 1972. Autographed. WWD's frequent mention of "Jackie O."

LIFE. "Jackie's Wedding," Nov.1, 1968: 18-25. Wedding photo on
cover.- "Occupation: Jackie-Watcher," Feb.12, 1971: 32-37. JKO
on cover. "Parting Shots. One Man's Running Battle with Jackie,"
Mar.31, 1972: 64-68. JKO on cover.

Lilly, Doris. THOSE FABULOUS GREEKS: Onassis, Niarchos and Liv-
anos. 1st Cowles, 1970. "Jackie's Fabulous Greek," LOOK, June 30,
1970: 30-36ff. JKO and Onassis on cover. "Portrait of Jackie:
What She's Really Like," FAMILY CIRCLE, July 10, 1976: 4ff.

LONDON SUN.TIMES Team. ARISTOTLE ONASSIS. 1st Lipp.,1977.

McCALL'S. "How Jacqueline Onassis Is Shaping Her Children," by
Stephen Birmingham," Jan. 1973:80-81. Caroline and John on cover.
"Jacqueline Onassis at 45," by Gloria Emerson, July, 1974:90-91ff.
"Onassis," by Helen Dudar, April, 1975: 88-89ff. "Christina On-
assis: A New Life," Sept., 1975: 62ff. "Jacqueline: Behind the
Myths," July, 1975: 79ff. JKO on cover. "The Surprising New Life
of Jacqueline Onassis," by Vivian Cadden and Helen Market, Feb.,
1976: 26ff. JKO on cover. "Jacqueline Kennedy, the Trash and the
Truth," by Gloria Emerson.

McLendon, Winzola. "The New Jackie," L.H.JRNL., Jan.,1976:34ff.
JKO on cover.

Nadel, Gerry. "The Score from New Hampshire: Democracy 1, Onassis
0." ESQUIRE, July, 1964: 106-109.

NEWSWEEK. "Jackie Kennedy Onassis," By Kenneth Auchincloss, Oct.
28, 1968: 38-42. JKO on cover. "Trials of an Heiress," by David
Pauly with Scott Sullivan (includes Onassis' will: 59), July 28,
1975: 56-60ff.

N.Y.TIMES MAG. "Feminism's Effect on Fashion," Aug.28, 1977, Pt.2,
91-92; and "Diana Vreeland...Defines the 70's Style," Pt.2, 120ff.
JBK as the only First Lady to have an effect on the style of the
country.

PEOPLE. "Jackie: Twice Widowed, Rich Beyond Counting - and Alone
Again," by Liz Smith. Mar.31, 1975: 6-8. "Jackie's New Life on
Her Own," by Letitia Baldridge, April 18, 1977: 26-33; also Annemarie Huste interview: 32. (ANNEMARIE'S PERSONAL COOKBOOK, Gram-
ercy, 1968. Former chef of the household of Jacqueline Kennedy.)

Phillips, Quentin. "Special Report on Jackie and Onassis," CORO-
NET, Oct., 1970: 32-40.

Schreiber, Flora R. "How Jacqueline Onassis Keeps Trim," FAMILY
CIRCLE, May, 1969: 12ff.

Writings About Jacqueline Onassis

Smith, Liz. "Jackie Onassis," L.H.JRNL., July, 1975: 34ff.

Sparks, Fred. THE $20,000,000 HONEYMOON. Geis, 1970. Much third-hand reporting. "The $20,000,000 Honeymoon of Jackie Onassis," LH JRNL. July, 1970 :122-124.

TIME. "Jackie's Marriage. From Camelot to Elysium (Via Olympic Airways)." Oct.25, 1968: 19-24. JKO on cover.

Valeri, Odette. "Les Gens. Jackie Ne Se Cache Plus Depuis Le Reglement De Son Heritage," PARIS MATCH, Jan.,1978: 14-17.

Vlachos, Helen. HOUSE ARREST. 1st Gambit, 1963. Refers to Onassis; photo of JBK in Mykonos, 1963.

VOGUE. "The Everything-Room: Focused on Family," June, 1973: 148-149.

Walters, Barbara. HOW TO TALK WITH PRACTICALLY ANYBODY ABOUT PRACTICALLY ANYTHING. 1st D-day, 1970. Onassis: xi-xiii.

Collection of 44 articles (1962-1973) from fan magazines that print "sensational" stories about the former First Lady. For analysis of such materials: "Hollywood's New Cover Girl," TIME, January 22, 1965.- "...tasteless outside, nondelivery inside." Irving Shulman "JACKIE": THE EXPLOITATION OF A FIRST LADY, Trident,1970. The professional gossipmongers and their "Jackie" factories and a look at the "fans" who could make such an industry successful.

LEE BOUVIER RADZIWILL

(Writing by) "A Conversation on Manners," L.H.JRNL. Feb.,1962:50ff. "Fancy Speaking," ESQUIRE, Dec.1964: 159-161ff. "Opening Chapters," L.H.JRNL. Jan.,1973: 79-83ff. SUDDENLY ONE SUMMER, op.cit.

Coleman, Terry. "Lee Radziwill: Stay Tuned for the Princess," S.E.P., Dec.16, 1967: 28-29.

Curtis, Charlotte. "Lee Radziwill in Search of Herself," McCALL'S Jan., 1975: 39-40.

LOOK. "The Public and the Private Lee," Jan.23, 1968: 36-40.

Radziwill, Michael. ONE OF THE RADZIWILLS. Murray, 1971.

Steinem, Gloria. "...And Starring - Lee Bouvier!" McCALL'S, Feb., 1968: 78-80ff.

SECTION TWO

ROBERT FRANCIS KENNEDY

ETHEL SKAKEL KENNEDY

PART ONE. ROBERT F. KENNEDY

WRITINGS OF ROBERT F. KENNEDY

Books, Articles, Speeches, Interviews

Earlier writings from the BOSTON POST on the Palestine situation
reproduced in full in the Appendix of WHY ROBERT KENNEDY WAS KILL-
ED, by Godfrey Jansen, Third Press, 1970: "British Hated by Both
Sides," June 3, 1948:259-264; "Jews Have Fine Fighting Force,"
June 4, 1948"264-269; "British Position Hit in Palestine," June
5, 1948: 269-274; "Communism Not To Get Foothold," June 6,1948:
275-278. Four articles written by RFK on a visit to Palestine
just before he graduated from Harvard.

Letter from RFK to N.Y.TIMES Jan.26, 1954 on Treaty-making and
Yalta (and reply by Arthur Schlesinger Jr. Feb.4, 1954, refuting
him) published in TALKING BACK TO THE NEW YORK TIMES, Kalman
Seigel, ed., Quad.,1972. Also reproduced, letter from Richard
Nixon re RFK's position on the right to freedom of speech.

"Hoffa's Unholy Alliance," LOOK, Sept.2, 1958:31-32.

THE ENEMY WITHIN. 1st Harper, 1960. A report on the work of the
McClelland Committee on Improper Activities in the Labor and Man-
agement Field. Also 1st Popular, July, 1960, wrs. Condensation
READERS' DIGEST.-

"Robert Kennedy to Peter Maas. Robert Kennedy Speaks Out." LOOK,
Mar.28, 1961: 23-26.

Address at the Law Day exercises of the University of Georgia Law
School, Athens, Ga., May 6, 1961 in Appendix to MR. KENNEDY AND
THE NEGROES, op.cit.:98, by Harry Golden: 290-300.

Twelve lines of RFK's speech in West Berlin Feb. 1962 in BERLIN
IM SPIEGEL special issue 1962. "Address to the Free University
of Berlin," in VOICES OF CRISIS, Floyd W. Matson ed., Odyssey,
1967: 95-104.

"Buying It Back from the Indians," LIFE, Mar.23, 1962: 17ff.
Effort to right the wrongs of early days in U.S. history.

JUST FRIENDS AND BRAVE ENEMIES. 1st H&R, 1962. A report on RFK's
30,000 mile trip with Ethel in 1962 - round-the-world, with some
thoughts on the responsibilities of freedom. "The World Needs
the Truth about America," (adapted from the book), SEP, Aug.25-
Sept.1, 1962: 17-21. Also 1st Popular ed. of book, 1963, wrs.

"Robert Kennedy Speaks His Mind," interview on the first two
years of the Kennedy Administration. U.S.NEWS...Jan.28,1963:54-
65.

WRITINGS OF ROBERT F. KENNEDY

Books, Articles, Speeches, Interviews

"A Free Trade in Ideas," SAT. REV., Feb.16, 1963: 43-44. Adapted from a talk before the National Workshop of the Council on Student Travel.

"Address" at the annual meeting of the Missouri Bar Assn., Kansas City, Sept.27, 1963: 301-307 in appendix to Golden's MR. KENNEDY AND THE NEGROES, op.cit. 98. Necessity of making our legal system responsive to legitimate grievances.

"Robert Kennedy Defines the Menace," N.Y.TIMES MAG., Oct.13, 1963: 15ff.- The private government of organized crime.

"Tribute to JFK," Dec.18, 1963. In a TRIBUTE TO JOHN F. KENNEDY, Salinger and Vanocur eds., op.cit.:135.

THE PURSUIT OF JUSTICE. 1st H&R, 1964. Twelve essays dealing with problems that most occupied RFK as Attorney General, edited by Theodore J. Lowi. Central theme: the role of the individual in search of his own dignity. Also 1st Perennial, 1964, wrs.

"Robert Kennedy Answers Some Blunt Questions," interview with Orianna Fallaci. LOOK, Mar.9, 1965: 60ff.

"Our Climb Up Mt. Kennedy," LIFE, Apr.9, 1965:22-27. RFK cover.

"Counterinsurgency. Political Action Required," VITAL SPEECHES, Aug.15, 1965: 649-652. Delivered before the graduating class, International Police Academy, Wash.,D.C., July 9, 1965.

"The Urban Ghetto and Negro Job Problems: a Diagnosis and a Proposal," in NEGROES AND JOBS, ed. by Louis A. Forman et al.,U.of Mich.,1969: 256-271. From a statement given before the Senate Subcommittee on Executive Reorganization Aug.15, 1966.

"Suppose God Is Black," LOOK, Aug.23, 1966: 44-46ff. RFK cover.

FEDERAL ROLE IN URBAN AFFAIRS. Hearings Before the Subcommittee on Executive Reorganization of the Committee on Government Operations, U.S.Senate, 89th Cong., 2nd sess. GPO, 1966-67. 18 vols. (Pts. 7,8 missing), wrs. Cf.Pt.1: RFK on the city as the central problem of American life:25-59; Pt.10: RFK "The War On Poverty..." Exhibit 157:2172-77; Pt.13: RFK on Bedford-Stuyvesant, Exhibit 197: 2831-37; Pt.14: Exchange between RFK and Martin Luther King Jr.: 2987-94; also questioning of witnesses.

"What Can the Young Believe,?" NEW REPUBLIC, Mar.11, 1967: 11-12. Also published in NATURAL ENEMIES, Alexander Klein ed., Lipp. 1969: 446-450. Remarks made at an ADA dinner in Philadelphia, Feb.24, 1967, published in part in article, in full in Klein volume.

THE KENNEDY FAMILY OF MASSACHUSETTS

Books, Articles, Speeches, Interviews

"Government Injustice to Business," NATION'S BUSINESS, June,1967: 7072ff. RFK on cover.

"Industrial Investment in Urban Poverty Areas," in RACE AND POV-ERTY; The Economics of Discrimination, John F. Kain, ed. P-H,1969: 153-163. Encouragement to profit-making firms to invest in the ghetto. From a speech to the U.S.Senate July 12, 1967.

"Crisis in Our Cities," CRITIC, Oct.-Nov.,1967: 60-63.

Hall, Sue G. and Staff eds. THE QUOTABLE ROBERT F. KENNEDY, 1st Droke, 1967. "The definite reference book on where RFK stands."

Adler, Bill, ed. THE WASHINGTON WITS. 1st Macm., 1967. Examples of wit of RFK, EMK, Sargent Shriver et al.

TO SEEK A NEWER WORLD, 1st D'day, 1967. From travel and experi-ence as Attorney General and U.S. Senator on youth, race, Alli-ance for Progress, nuclear control, China policy, Vietnam. Also 1st Bantam, 1968, wrs., in which RFK expanded and updated the chapter on Vietnam and added portions of his formal announcement of candidacy for Presidency. Review: NEW REPUBLIC, Dec.2, 1967: 29-30ff. by Gilbert A. Harrison. "What Our Young People Are Re-ally Saying," L.H.JRNL., Jan., 1968: 35ff. Excerpted from book.

"Bobby Kennedy on the War," NEWSWEEK, Feb.19, 1968: 24.

"Kennedy on Vietnam," U.S.NEWS... Feb.19, 1968: 10.-

"On Business, Antitrust, Taxes, the Urban Crisis and Lost Youth," FORTUNE, Mar., 1968: 115ff.

"Conflict in Vietnam and at Home," address delivered Mar. 18,1968 Kansas State Univ., in ISSUES, 1968 ed. by Wm.W. Boyer. Univ. Pr. of Kansas, 1968: 29-45. "...our policy there (Vietnam) is bank-rupt."

"A Ripple of Hope. Quotations from RFK," NEWSWEEK, June 17, 1968: 3.- RFK on cover.

Interview as a presidential candidate with David Frost in THE PRESIDENTIAL DEBATE 1968, S&D, 1968: 112-126.

THE ROBERT F. KENNEDY WIT. Bill Adler ed. Berkeley Medallion, 1968. Wrs.

AMERICA THE BEAUTIFUL. Country Beautiful Corp., 1968. His public statements which convey "the primary concerns to which he dedica-ted his life."

A NEW DAY. Bill Adler ed. Signet 1st prtg., 1968, wrs. Positions on domestic and foreign policy with dates and places.

WRITINGS OF ROBERT F. KENNEDY

Books, Articles, Speeches, Interviews

ROBERT F. KENNEDY: APOSTLE OF CHANGE. Trident, 1968. The public
record of RFK drawn from speeches, interviews and press conferences on Vietnam, civil rights, cities, poverty, crime and more,
edited by Douglas Rose.

THE SPIRIT OF ROBERT F. KENNEDY. G&D (1968) wrs. Compiled by
Sue G. Hall from his speeches.

THIRTEEN DAYS: A Memoir of the Cuban Missile Crisis. 1st Norton,
1969. Introductions by Robt. McNamara and Harold Macmillan.
Also Signet 1st prtg., 1969. "Thirteen Days: the Story About
How the World Almost Ended," McCALL'S, Nov., 1968:6-9ff. -
"Complete and exclusive, published for the first time anywhere."
Review of THIRTEEN DAYS, by Robert Kennedy, THE UNFINISHED ODY-
SSEY OF ROBERT KENNEDY, by David Halberstam, 85 DAYS by Jules
Witcover, ROBERT KENNEDY A MEMOIR, by Jack Newfield; reviewer:
Alexander M. Bickle, NEW REPUBLIC, July 5, 1969: 26-28.

I DREAM THINGS THAT NEVER WERE AND SAY, WHY NOT? Quotations of
RFK selected by Jane Wilkie and Rod McKuen. Stanyan Books,1970.

(Recording) "WELCOME TO THE LBJ RANCH!" Includes the voice of
RFK. Comedy interview, Robin-Doud. Capitol Record W2423.

Forewords and Introductions

One of 2 forew ard statements to YEAR 1964 encyclopedia news annual: events of the year 1963. Op.cit.:60.

Foreword to THE EFFECTIVENESS OF A PRISON AND PAROLE SYSTEM by
Daniel Glaser, 1st B-M, 1964, wrs.

Introduction to revised and enlarged A NATION OF IMMIGRANTS by
John F. Kennedy op.cit.:1.

Foreword to Memorial Edition of PROFILES IN COURAGE by John F.
Kennedy, op.cit.: 1. "Tribute to JFK," LOOK, Feb.25, 1964:37-38ff.
with "Brothers in Courage," by editors of LOOK: 42. "Foreword to
a Book," CATHOLIC DIGEST, Aug., 1964:45-47.-

Introduction to William D. Rogers' THE TWILIGHT STRUGGLE: the
Alliance for Progress and the Politics of Development in Latin
America. Random, 1967. RFK:"...we have made a commitment ...We
cannot turn back." This book a review of history and politics of
the Alliance.

Foreword to WORDS TO REMEMBER (JFK's quotations) op.cit.: 9.

Foreword to Wm. Crofut's TROUBADOUR: a Different Battlefield.
Dutton, 1968. Praise for two young American men who toured 29
countries in eight years with a banjo and guitar.

Forewords and Introductions

Preface to Norman Dorsen's FRONTIERS OF CIVIL LIBERTIES. 1st Pantheon, 1968. First Amendment Rights, due process and discrimination - contemporary issues in civil liberties.

WORKS ABOUT ROBERT F. KENNEDY
General Biography

American Heritage eds. RFK. HIS LIFE AND DEATH. 1st Dell, 1968. Wrs. Narrative by Jay Jacobs. Eyewitness account of the last 36 hours by Kristi N. Witker.

DeToledano, Ralph. RFK - THE MAN WHO WOULD BE PRESIDENT. 1st Signet, 1967. "This is not a biography - it's a mugging." Newfield.

Heuvel, Wm. vanden, and Milton Gwirtzman. ON HIS OWN: RFK 1964-1968. 1st D'day, 1970. The Senate years, the tragic campaign. RFK:..."a voice of compassion and concern toward those...hurt by society..."

Hudson, James A. RFK - 1925-1968. 1st Scholastic, 1969, wrs.

Lasky, Victor. ROBERT F. KENNEDY: The Myth and the Man. Trident, 1968. "Let's just say that Victor's good humor and his conscience are equally expansive," Murray Kempton.

Newfield, Jack. ROBERT KENNEDY: A MEMOIR. 1st Dutton, 1969. Chronicle and analysis of RFK's politics and character and the changes in America 1963-1968. "...the one politician of his time who might have united the black and white poor into a new majority for change..." Also 1st Bantam, 1970, wrs.

Nicholas, Wm. THE BOBBY KENNEDY NOBODY KNOWS. Fawcett (1967) Wrs. Written by Nick Thimmesch & Wm. Johnson and published under their collective name. Up-date of ROBERT KENNEDY AT 40.

Schaap, Dick, with Michael O'Keefe, picture editor. R.F.K. 1st NAL, 1967. More than 250 photos. Also 1st Signet, 1968, wrs.

Schlesinger, Arthur M. Jr. ROBERT KENNEDY AND HIS TIMES. 1st H-M, 1978. A definitive study.

Shannon, Wm.V. THE HEIR APPARENT: Robert Kennedy and the Struggle for Power. 1st Macm., 1967.

Stein, Jean (Interviews) and George Plimpton (editor). AMERICAN JOURNEY: the Times of Robert Kennedy. 1st HB&J, 1970. Cf. also interview with George Plimpton in PEOPLE, Apr.18, 1977:30.

Swinburne, Laurence. RFK: THE LAST KNIGHT. 1st Pyramid,1969.Wrs.

Thimmesch, Nick and Wm. Johnson. ROBERT KENNEDY AT 40. 1st Norton, 1965.

WORKS ABOUT ROBERT F. KENNEDY

General Biography

Thompson, Robt.E. and Hortense Myers. ROBERT F. KENNEDY: The Brother Within. Macm.,1962. "The major defects...in those passages that try to catalog him. Robert Kennedy has a unique capacity for growth." Wm. O. Douglas.

Robert F. Kennedy Pre-1960

Cohn, Roy. McCARTHY. Lancer, 1968. Wrs. Account of relationship with RFK. Chap.5: "The Kennedys."

Douglas, Wm. O. RUSSIAN JOURNEY. 1st D'day, 1956. Trip through Russia accompanied by RFK.

LIFE. "Teamster's Union Projects Turn Up a Tilt or Two as Senators Hear of Involvements with Pinball Monopolies and Politics," Mar.11, 1957:31-37. Includes RFK questioning racketeer Jas.Elkins.

Petro, Sylvester. POWER UNLIMITED. A Report on the McClelland Committee Hearings. Ronald, 1959. Summary of 39 vols. of the McClelland Committee disclosures. Chief Counsel RFK quoted many times - with excerpts of his questions and answers given.

Straight, Michael. TRIAL BY TELEVISION: The Army-McCarthy Hearings. Beacon Pr. (1954). RFK vs. Roy Cohn included.

TIME. "Labor: Torch Without Song," Aug. 18, 1958: 14-15. Hoffa and RFK.

U.S.NEWS... "Background of Hoffa Case - Was Race a Factor?" Aug. 16, 1957: 78-80.-

Velie, Lester. LABOR U.S.A. A Candid Look at American Labor Today... 1st Harper, 1959. References to RFK and Hoffa.

Attorney General Robert F. Kennedy

Ajemian, Robert. "Robert Kennedy's Week to Reckon," LIFE, July 3, 1964: 24-31. Editor's note: a reunion of two classmates - Bob Kennedy and Bob Ajemian. RFK with four of his children and Caroline and John on cover.

AMERICA. "Mr. Kennedy's Crusade," June 20, 1964: 841-842.- RFK and the search for even-handed justice as Attorney General.

ATLANTIC. "Atlantic Report on Washington," Nov., 1961: 4ff. RFK and organized crime, civil rights, new Federal judges.

Baldwin, James. THE FIRE NEXT TIME. Dell, 1963, wrs. Quotes RFK re possibility of a Negro president in 40 years.

THE KENNEDY FAMILY OF MASSACHUSETTS

Attorney General Robert F. Kennedy

Carawan, Guy and Candy. WE SHALL OVERCOME. Oak Publ., 1963. Wrs. Songs of the Southern Freedom Movement compiled for SNCC. Adaptations of musical idiom of Negro spirituals with new words geared to new thrust for freedom. Many addressed to RFK.

Childs, Marquis. "Bobby and the President," GOOD HOUSEKEEPING, May, 1962: 80-81ff.

Cipes, Robert M. "The Wiretap War," (RFK, LBJ and FBI), NEW REPUBLIC, Dec.24, 1966: 16-22. THE CRIME WAR, NAL, 1st, 1968. Critical of RFK's methods re Jimmy Hoffa.

Clark, Ramsey. CRIME IN AMERICA, 1st S&S, 1970. Includes the work of RFK to combat organized crime, reform pre-trial detention.

Cook, Fred. THE FBI NOBODY KNOWS, Macm., 1964. Demonstrates the Bureau often overstepped the bounds of propriety. Touches on RFK's difficulties with J. Edgar Hoover.

Cressey, Donald R. THEFT OF THE NATION. The Structure and Operations of Organized Crime in America. 1st H&R, 1969. RFK as Atty. Gen. launching a "coordinated drive" on organized crime.

Drinan, Robt. F. "Human Rights in the Sixties," CATHOLIC INTERRACIAL COUNCIL, n.d. 2p. folder.

Fuller, John G. THE GENTLEMAN CONSPIRATORS. The Story of the Price-Fixers in the Electrical Industry. Grove, 1962. Sentences pronounced in 1961 with support of RFK.

Gardner, Joseph L. LABOR ON THE MARCH. The Story of America's Unions. 1st Amer.Heritage Jr.Lib., 1969. RFK, Beck and Hoffa.

Goldberg, Arthur J. EQUAL JUSTICE. The Warren Era of the Supreme Court. 1st Noonday, 1972. Wrs. Racial equality into legal reality. RFK's Committe on Poverty and administration of Federal criminal justice.

Green, Mark J. THE OTHER GOVERNMENT: The Unseen Power of Washington Lawyers. Grossman/Viking, 1975. Refs. to RFK, EMK.

HARPER'S. "The Choice for Vice-President," Aug.1964: 95ff.-

Hoffa, James R. THE TRIALS OF JIMMY HOFFA. Autobiography as told to Donald I. Rogers. Regnery, 1970. RFK's "vendetta." HOFFA:THE REAL STORY as told to Oscar Fraley. 1st S&D, 1975.

Horne, Lena and Richard Schickel. LENA. 1st D'day, 1965. Autobiography. Best account of what really happened at meeting with Atty.Gen. RFK, James Baldwin and prominent Negroes.

WORKS ABOUT ROBERT F. KENNEDY

Attorney General Robert F. Kennedy

Hughes, Langston. FIGHT FOR FREEDOM, The Story of the NAACP. Berkeley Med.,1962, wrs. Mention of RFK's action to ban segregation in interstate bus transportation and terminals.

Hugo, Grant. APPEARANCE AND REALITY IN INTERNATIONAL RELATIONS. 1st Columbia U., 1970. Chap.2. RFK on JFK and missile crisis.

Knebel, Fletcher. "Bobby Kennedy: He Hates to Be Second," LOOK, May 21, 1963:91-94ff. RFK, Mary Kerry, David on cover.

Kraft, Joseph. "Riot Squad for the New Frontier," HARPER'S, Aug. 1963: 69-75. How RFK transformed the Justice Department "into the yeastiest office in Washington." "The Ambitions of Bobby Kennedy," LOOK, Aug.25, 1964: 22-28ff. RFK on cover.

Leonard, George B. THE MAN AND WOMAN THING: and Other Provocations. 1st Delacorte, 1970. "RFK - Ross Barnett:" 55-63.

Lewis, Anthony. "What Drives Bobby Kennedy," N.Y.TIMES MAG., April 7, 1963: 34ff.- GIDEON'S TRUMPET. Random (1964). The case of Clarence Earl Gideon. Describes RFK's efforts two years before the Gideon case to provide for the indigent in Federal courts.

LIFE. "The President's Brother Takes a Trip," (RFK and Ethel in the Ivory Coast). Aug.28, 1961: 28-33. "The No.2 Man in Washington - Robert Kennedy," by Paul O'Neil, Jan.26, 1962: 76-78ff. RFK on cover. "Dr. Kennedy's Goodwill Wave in Tokyo," Feb. 16, 1962: 2-3. RFK and Ethel on cover. "Bobby Irks Texas," Feb.23, 1962: 38-39. RFK in Japan and Indonesia. "The 50-Mile Walk," by Robert Wallace, Feb.22, 1963: 72A-77. "Bobby Kennedy Trades Compliments with Some Indians," Sept.27, 1963: 44D. Editorial: "Hold Your Nose at Bobby Kennedy's Pork. But Listen to His Canary, Oct. 18, 1963:4. "Journey Out of Grief: RFK's Mission to Asia"(with Ethel), Jan. 31, 1964: 32-33.- "All the Way with LBJ and Who?" The Democratic vice-presidential scramble. May 8,1964: 94B-98. - "Inside Hoffa's Savage Kingdom (and The Plot to Kill Robert Kennedy)" by Edward G. Partin, May 15, 1964ff. "When Polish Eyes Are Smiling," July 10, 1964:34B. RFK, Ethel in Warsaw. "People's Choice for LBJ's V.P.," by Ernest Havemann, Aug.14, 1964: 68-70ff. Roper poll: 47% for RFK.

McCarry, Chas. CITIZEN NADER. Sat.Rev.Pr. (1972). Ref. re RFK.

McGill, Ralph. THE SOUTH AND THE SOUTHERNERS. 1st L-B, 1963. Moral dilemma of 150 years. RFK and Voting rights of Negroes, James Meredith.

McGrory, Mary. "Having Wonderful Time...Bobby," AMERICA, Feb. 24, 1962: 674.-

Attorney General Robert F. Kennedy

Maas, Peter. THE VALACHI PAPERS. Putnam (1968). RFK urged V. to write history of his underground career - gave first concrete evidence that COSA NOSTRA exists, names names, revealed structure.

Moffet, Toby. THE PARTICIPATION PUT-ON. Reflections of a Disenchanted Washington Youth Expert. 1st Delacorte, 1971. Inspired by RFK to enter government service.

Mollenhoff, Clark R. STRIKE FORCE. Organized Crime and the Government. P-H (1972). Chaps. 5, 6 and 16 - RFK and Hoffa.

Navasky, Victor S. KENNEDY JUSTICE. 1st Atheneum, 1971. The clash between RFK "the maximum Attorney General" and J. Edgar Hoover "the ultimate bureaucrat." "Robert F. Kennedy, Martin Luther King Jr., J. Edgar Hoover: Who Did What to Whom," ATLANTIC, Nov.1970: 43-52. Navasky book "indispensable for an understanding of Robert Kennedy as Attorney General," Schlesinger.

NEWSWEEK. "Diplomacy: the Kennedy Touch," Feb.3, 1964.- "A Vice-Presidential Skirmish," Mar.4, 1964: 27-28.- Also "The Verdict on Hoffa:" 30-31.- "Europe: Tour Time," July 13, 1964: 34.- RFK, Ethel and children in Poland. "The Hoover-Kennedy Bug-Passing Feud," Dec.26, 1966: 19-20. Also "Hoffa's Funeral:" 20-21, Supreme Court upholds 1964 Hoffa conviction.

N.Y.TIMES MAG. "'Someone the President Can Talk To,'" by Robert Manning, May 28, 1961: 22ff. "Front Runners for '72," by Warren Weaver Jr., May 22, 1962: 26-27ff. RFK on cover with others. "Room 5115: Civil Rights G.H.2," July 7, 1963: 8-9.- "What Future for Robert Kennedy?" May 24, 1964: 6. RFK on cover.-

Raskin, A.H. "The Power of Jimmy Hoffa," ATLANTIC, Jan., 1964: 39-45.

Sale, Kirkpatrick. S.D.S. (Students for a Democratic Society) Ten Years Toward a Revolution. 1st Random, 1973. RFK as more popular with members on chapter level than with leaders.

Salerno, Ralph and John Tomkins, "After Luciano," Chap. 6 in MAFIA U.S.A. Nicholas Gage ed. Playboy, 1972. RFK and his war on organized crime.

Sheridan, Walter. THE FALL AND RISE OF JIMMY HOFFA. SAT.REV.PR. (1972). Hoffa as a satellite of organized crime; RFK as dedicated prosecutor, Richard Nixon as Hoffa's protector. Documented.

TIME. "Civil Rights: the Gauntlet," Oct.25, 1963: 29. RFK's appearance before House Judiciary Committee. "The Truth About Hoover," Dec.23, 1975: 14-21.

Turner, Wallace. GAMBLERS' MONEY. The New Force in American Life. H-M, 1965. RFK as greatly feared by Nevada gamblers.

WORKS ABOUT ROBERT F. KENNEDY

Attorney General Robert F. Kennedy

U.S.Congress, House Judiciary Committee. IMPEACHMENT OF RICHARD
M. NIXON PRESIDENT OF THE UNITED STATES. 93d Congress, 2d sess.
1974. Report No. 93-1305. Autographed by John Doar, Special Coun-
sel, Committee on the Judiciary. TLS from Doar Oct.9, 1974.
"John Doar Is Satisfied With the Process," (impeachment of Pres.
Nixon) by James M. Naughton in N.Y.TIMES "Week in Review," Sept.
15, 1974. Cf.Guthman WE BAND OF BROTHERS and Dorman WE SHALL
OVERCOME re Doar's work with RFK.

U.S.Congress. Senate Report 94-755. Supplementary Detailed
Staff Reports on Intelligence Activities and the Rights of Americans. Book III. FINAL REPORT OF THE SELECT COMMITTEE TO STUDY
GOVERNMENTAL OPERATIONS RE INTELLIGENCE ACTIVITIES April 23,
1976. GPO, wrs. Case study of MLK (79-184) esp. RFK and wire-
taps, and FBI attempts to discredit King.

U.S.NEWS... "Opportunity - Or Trouble - For President's Brother?"
Jan.9, 1961: 40-42. - "Role of Robert Kennedy; No.2 Man in Washington," July 10, 1961: 42-45. "'Bobby' Kennedy: Is He the "Assistant President?" Feb.19, 1962: 48-52. "Robert Kennedy: Grass-
Roots Ambassador to Everywhere," Mar.5, 1962: 45-46.- "Fun on
the 'New Frontier:' Who Fell and Who Was Pushed?" July 2, 1962:
40.- "How Robert Kennedy Sizes Up His Future," Dec.16, 1963:24.-
"'Bobby' Kennedy on LBJ's Ticket?" Mar.23, 1964: 42-44. "Bobby
Kennedy's Future," July 13, 1964: 36-38.

Valenti, Jack. A VERY HUMAN PRESIDENCY. Norton (1975). LBJ as
President including his conflict with the Kennedy myth and the
reality of Robert Kennedy. TLS - 19 lines - from Ivan Sinclair
Assistant to LBJ, "explaining" the President's decision not to
recommend to the Convention as a candidate for the Vice Presidency any members of the Cabinet or any of those who meet regularly
with the Cabinet. The White House, August 22, 1964.

Whitehead, Don. ATTACK ON TERROR: The FBI Against the Ku Klux
Klan in Mississippi. 1st F&W, 1970. The murders of three civil
rights workers in 1964. Role of RFK, JFK initiating struggle.

Winter-Berger, Robt.N. THE GERALD FORD LETTERS. Stuart, 1974.
Includes 4p.+ letter re Alexander Guterma and RFK and the indict-
ments and convictions during RFK's tenure as Attorney General.

Wright, Richard O., ed. with Wm.K. Lambie. WHOSE FBI? Open Court
Publ., 1974. Defense of FBI. Daniel Joy, John Snyder,with eds.
re RFK.

> "It is not easy to give institutional shape
> to love; it means transforming it into
> justice."
>   - James McBride Dabbs

U.S. Senator Robert F. Kennedy of New York

Alexander, Holmes. "RFK: How He's Building His Own Party,"
NATION'S BUSINESS, July, 1966: 38-39ff. RFK on cover.

Alsop, Stewart. "Robert Kennedy and the Liberals," S.E.P., Aug.
28, 1965: 18.

Armstrong, Richard. "Bobby Kennedy and the Fight for New York,"
S.E.P., Nov.6, 1965: 29-31ff.

Asinof, Eliot. PEOPLE VS. BLUTCHER. 1st Viking, 1970. Black
men and white law in Bedford-Stuyvesant at the time John Doar
was appointed executive director of a corporation set up to
redevelop this part of Brooklyn - one of two such corporations
founded by Senator RFK.

Baus, Herbert M. and Wm. B. Ross. POLITICS BATTLE PLAN. 1st
Macm. 1968. Includes RFK's senatorial campaign in New York.

Bohn, Dorothy and Louis J. Ryan. HUMAN RESOURCES SURVEY: East
Central Citizens Organization (ECCO), 1967. Unpublished ms.
Newspaper clipping "Kennedy, Ribicoff Praise ECCO Program,"
tipped in.

COMMONWEAL. RFK Wants Out (of Vietnam). Mar.17, 1967:668-9.-

CRITIC. Dec.'65 and Jan.'66 cover: photographs of "the fifteen
most important Catholics in the USA," JBK and RFK included.

Davidson, Bill. "What Has Tragedy Meant to Bobby Kennedy?"
GOOD HOUSEKEEPING, July, 1964: 56-57ff.

EBONY. "Dr. King Carries Fight to Northern Slums," April, 1966:
94-96ff.-

Fallaci, Oriani. "Dean Martin Talks About His Drinking, the
Mafia, Frank Sinatra, Women, and Bobby Kennedy," LOOK, Dec. 26,
1967: 78-83ff.-

Feiffer, Jules. "A Matter of Conscience," COMMENTARY, Dec.,1964:
52-54. RFK - Keating senatorial campaign.

Gardner, Gerald. ROBERT KENNEDY IN NEW YORK. The Campaign for
the Senate. 1st Random, 1965. A sparkling account.

Kahin, George McT. and John W. Lewis. THE UNITED STATES IN VIET-
NAM. 1st Dial, 1967. RFK's efforts for peace.

Kiker, Douglas. "Robert Kennedy and the 'What If' Game," ATLAN-
TIC, Oct., 1966: 66-70.

Knebel, Fletcher. "Las Vegas...Fights the Bobby Kennedy Vendetta"
LOOK, Dec.27, 1966: 75-78ff.

WORKS ABOUT ROBERT F. KENNEDY

U.S.Senator Robert F. Kennedy of New York

Kopkind, Andrew. "He's a Happening. Robert Kennedy's Road to
Somewhere. NEW REPUBLIC, April 3, 1966: 18-21.

Kotler, Milton. NEIGHBORHOOD GOVERNMENT: The Local Foundation
of Political Life. B-M, 1969, wrs. East Central Citizens Organization of Columbus, Ohio,(ECCO), as example of neighborhood
movement; also RFK and Bedford-Stuyvesant.

LIFE. Index: Vols. 56-57, 58-59, 60-61: Jan.1964-Dec.,1965;
Vol.66-67: Jan.-Dec., 1969. "Bob Kennedy's Senate Bid," Sept.4,
1964, 1964: 32-32A. "Keating...Kennedy...in a Ripsnorter That
Has Everything," Oct.9, 1964: 32-37. "Bobby on Mt. Kennedy,"
Apr.2, 1965: 46-47. Photograph: "The Perils of Touring Diplo-
macy," Nov.26, 1965:42. Sec'y of State Rusk and RFK in S.America.
"Bobby and the Political Battle Between the Generations," July 1,
1966: 34D, by Hugh Sidey. "What Is Robert Kennedy Up To? The
Drive Toward the "Restoration." "His Truce with LBJ," by Hugh
Sidey; "The New Kennedy Identity and How He Uses Power," by Penn
Kimball, Jan.2, 1967: 34-43ff. "Robert Kennedy - la Fuerza de
Una Leyenda en Su Futuro Politics," LIFE in espanol, 2 de Enero
de 1967:4-20. Con articulos de Hugh Sidey y Penn Kimball.

Lowenstein, Allard K. BRUTAL MANDATE, 1st Macm., 1962. Journey
to South West Africa. RFK and Lowenstein first met in May, 1966,
when L. came to brief him on South Africa before his visit there.

McGrory, Mary. "A Kennedy in New York Politics," AMERICA, Sept.
19, 1964: 284.-

Maas, Peter. "What Will RFK Do Next?" S.E.P., Mar.28, 1964:17-
21. "Can Kennedy Take New York?" S.E.P. Oct.21, 1964: 32-32.

Morgan, Thomas B. "Requiem or Revival? What's Next for the Civil
Rights Movement?" LOOK, June 14, 1966: 71-73ff.

Newfield, Jack. "A Few Rags of Hope. Bedford-Stuyvensant's Critical Experiment with 450,000 People and 500 Square Blocks," LIFE,
Mar.8, 1968: 83-85ff. RFK's part in the experiment.

NEW REPUBLIC. "Will Bobby Kennedy Run in New York?" by Murray
Kempton, June 6, 1964:7-8.- Letter re the letters on the Kennedy-
Keating campaign (Oct.3) by Arthur Schlesinger Jr. Oct.10,1964:29.

NEWSWEEK. "Robert Kennedy and New York: Decision Point," Aug.24,
1964: 22-24.- RFK on cover. "LBJ: 'I Ask for a Mandate to Begin:'"
15-31 - includes RFK and filmed memorial to JFK: 27-29; entrance
into Senate race from New York: 29, Sept.7, 1964. "Keating vs.
Kennedy: High Stakes for New York," Oct.12, 1964: 35ff.- "The
Senators Kennedy," Jan. 18, 1965.- "Headless in Albany," (RFK vs.
Mayor Robt. Wagner) Jan.25, 1965: 26.- "Congress: the 99th Senator," Mar.15, 1965: 29-30.- "Campaign Tour (RFK in Latin America)
Nov.22, 1965: 39-40.-

Cont'd p. 168

U.S. Senator Robert F. Kennedy of New York

NEWSWEEK cont'd. "Development: Litany of Woe," May 23, 1966:71.-
RFK as champion of Latin American democratic left in position
paper in Senate. "Africa: the Favorite American," June 27, 1966:
53-54.- RFK and Ethel: two week trip through Africa. "Making of
the President, 1972," Sept.5, 1966: 17-18. LBJ vs. RFK. "How to
Lose a War," Feb.6, 1967: 34-35.- "Bobby Abroad," Feb.13, 1967:
34-35.

N.Y. TIMES MAG. "Keating vs Kennedy," Sept.13, 1964: 22.-

Roberts, Steven V. "Bobby Kennedy's Shadow Cabinet," ESQUIRE,
Sept., 1966: 168-169ff.

Rustin, Bayard. "The Lesson of the Long Hot Summer," COMMENTARY,
Oct., 1967: 39-45.

Scheer, Robt. "A Political Portrait of Robert Kennedy," RAMPARTS,
Feb., 1967: 11-16. RFK on cover.

TIME. "Democrats: the Shadow and the Substance," (RFK) Sept. 16,
1966: 32-36. RFK on cover.

U.S.NEWS..."The Kennedy Brothers' Dream," Sept.14, 1964: 33-35.
"RFK in New York Senate Race," Oct.5, 1964: 72-74. "Will Bobby's
Friends Trip Up LBJ in '68?" April, 1967: 53-54.

Weaver, Warren. "Will the Real Robert Kennedy Stand Up?" N.Y.
TIMES MAG. June 20, 1965: 8-9ff. Assessment after RFK's six
months in Senate. RFK on cover.

Whiteside, Thomas. THE INVESTIGATION OF RALPH NADER. General
Motors vs. One Determined Man. Arbor, 1972. Includes RFK's participation in the hearings on auto safety by the Senate Subcommittee on Executive Reorganization. Also 1st Pocket Bks. 1972,
wrs. For RFK and Nader on federal role in traffic safety cf.
Buckhorn, Robt.F. NADER; The People's Lawyer, P-H, 1972.

Wolfinger, Rayomnd E. Chap.3. "Some Consequences of Ethnic Politics," in THE ELECTORAL PROCESS ed. by M. Kent Jennings and L.
Harmon Ziegler, P-H, 1966. RFK's use of ethnic appeal.

Presidential Campaign 1968

Adelman, Clifford. NO LOAVES, NO PARABLES. Liberal Politics and
the American Language. 1st Harper's Mag.Pr., 1974. RFK as example of "populist style" of communication.

Arlen, Michael J. LIVING-ROOM WAR. Viking (1969). TV in our
lives. "McCarthy in Wisconsin:" 196-201 and "Kennedy in California:" 207-222.

WORKS ABOUT ROBERT F. KENNEDY

Presidential Campaign 1968

Baker, Russell. OUR NEXT PRESIDENT. The Incredible Story of What Happened in the 1968 Elections. (Fiction). 1st Athen.,1968.

Bird, Robert S. "Robert F. Kennedy: At Home with the Heir Apparent," S.E.P., Aug.26, 1967: 28-35. RFK and sons on cover.

Brown, Stuart Gerry. THE PRESIDENCY ON TRIAL. Robert Kennedy's 1968 Campaign and Afterwards. U.of Hawaii, 1972. The politics of presidential leadership.

Buchwald, Art. HAVE I EVER LIED TO YOU? Putnam, 1968. 4 Essays.

Chester, Lewis et al. AN AMERICAN MELODRAMA: The Presidential Campaign of 1968. Viking (1969).

Cleaver, Eldridge: POST PRISON WRITINGS AND SPEECHES, Robt. Scheer, ed. Random (1969). "Robert Kennedy's Prison," 21-22.

Davis, Lanny J. THE EMERGING DEMOCRATIC MAJORITY. 1stS&D, 1974. Good insight into McCarthy-RFK campaign.

DeToledano, Ralph. RFK: THE MAN WHO WOULD BE PRESIDENT. 1st Putnam, 1967. A knife job without corroborating references. Also 1st Signet, 1968, wrs.

English, David et al. DIVIDED THEY STAND. P-H (1969) British view of American presidential election of 1968.

Felker, Clay, ed. THE POWER GAME. 1st S&S, 1969. Breslin, Steinem, Wolfe on RFK and power. Other references JBK and JFK.

Gregory, Dick. WRITE ME IN! 1st Bantam, 1968, wrc.

Hacker, Andrew. "The McCarthy Candidacy," COMMENTARY: Feb., 1969: 34-39.

Halberstam, David. "Politics 1968 - McCarthy and the Divided Left," HARPER, Mar.1968: 32ff. "Travels with Bobby Kennedy," ibid., July, 1968: 51-61ff. THE UNFINISHED ODYSSEY OF ROBERT KENNEDY. Random (1968). Also 1st Bantam ed., 1969, wrs. "The Man Who Ran Against Lyndon Johnson," ibid. Dec. 1968: 47-62ff. (Allard K. Lowenstein).

Hamill, Pete. IRRATIONAL RAVINGS. Putnam, 1971. Includes account of RFK's presidential campaign and eye-witnessing of his death.

Hastings, Max. THE FIRE THIS TIME. America's Year of Crisis. Taplinger, 1969. Written for the English about the events of 1968. Reports on travel with RFK as well as assassination.

HERE AND NOW, a Christian Jrnl. of Opinion. Front cover feature of RFK by "Krumm," May-June, 1968.

Presidential Campaign 1968

Kimball, Penn. BOBBY KENNEDY AND THE NEW POLITICS. P-H (1968).
Reliance on personal organization in preference to party machin-
ery. Critical of RFK. Numerous quotes but no references.

LADIES HOME JRNL. "The Real Robert F. Kennedy," Feb., 1967:75ff.

Laing, Margaret. THE NEXT KENNEDY. A Woman's View of Robert F.
Kennedy as Prospective President. C-McC., 1968. Ethel included.

Larner, Jeremy. "Inside the McCarthy Campaign," HARPER, Part I.
Apr. 1969: 62-72ff.; Part II., May, 1969: 71-94. Cartoons.

Leitch, David. GOD STANDS UP FOR BASTARDS. 1st H-M, 1973. Autobiography. Unsympathetic account of RFK in Calif. and his death.

LIFE. "They All Love Gene Until He Takes the Stump," by Gerald
Moore, Jan.19, 1968: 50B=53.- "Serious New Hampshire Madness,"
Mar.22, 1968: 56A-57.- "All Together Now, I Wanna Hold Your
Hand," (Gene McCarthy Campaign) Mar.29, 1968: 26-31.- "Kennedy's
Search for a New Target," Apr.12, 1968:34-35, by Jack Newfield.
"The Star-Spangled Look of the '68 Campaign," (who the entertain-
ers support)May 10, 1968: 64A-69. "Candidates On the Road West,"
May 17, 1968: 72-79; articles by Philip Kunhardt, Shana Alexander,
Loudon Wainright. Campaign in Indiana, Nebraska, Oregon, Calif.
"The Primary Players in Oregon," by Shana Alexander, June 7, 1968:
34-41. "1968 Democratic Convulsion," Sept.6, 1968:18-31.

McCarthy, Eugene. THE YEAR OF THE PEOPLE. D'day (1969). Discuss-
es his relation with RFK and his aides. Lowell's poem "RFK:" 175.
Part memoir, part commentary, part testimonial. Review of book:
Harrison, Gilbert A. "McCarthy On His Campaign," NEW REPUBLIC,
Oct.25, 1969: 21-23.

McGinnis, Joe. THE SELLING OF THE PRESIDENT. Trident (1969).
Nixon's 1968 campaign "the first electronic election." Refers to
RFK's supporters and death.

Mailer, Norman. MIAMI AND THE SIEGE OF CHICAGO. An Informal History of the Republican and Democratic Conventions of 1968. World,
1969. Many references to RFK and EMK. "Miami Beach and Chicago"
HARPER, Nov.1968: 41-52ff. Meeting with RFK, his death.

Manning, Robert. "Campaign 1968," ATLANTIC, Nov., 1968: 4ff.

NEW REPUBLIC. "Kennedy's Quandry," Jan.27, 1968:7. "Welcome
Aboard, Bobby," Mar.23, 1968: 7-8. "In View of Kennedy," Mar.30
1968: 5-6. "McCarthy and Kennedy," by David Riesman, April 13,
1968: 21-23. Included: "Why I Am for McCarthy," by Robert Lowell:
22. "Why I'm for Kennedy," by Arthur Schlesinger Jr. May 4, 1968:
19-23. "Kennedy and McCarthy," by Robt. Yoakum, May 11, 1968:23ff.

Presidential Campaign 1968

NEWSWEEK. "Men at War: RFK Vs. LBJ,"Mar. 13, 1967: 33-34.- "'That Man' and 'That Boy'," Mar.20, 1967:25-26.- (On Vietnam). "Why Is McNamara Leaving? - And a Sum-Up," Dec.11, 1967:25-30. "JBK and RFK at Democratic Fund-Raiser," Dec.25, 1967:40.- "Bobby's Dilemma: To Be or Not To Be,: Jan.29, 1968: 18-19. "And From the White House - Silence," Mar. 18, 1968:45-46.- (RFK's opposition to the Vietnam war). "Bobby on the Run. Mobilizing the Kennedy Mafia," Apr.1, 1968:24ff. Includes Wisconsin campaign. "The Democrat's New Ball Game," Apr.15, 1968:44ff.- Includes "Why He Did It - What Now:" 42-43. LBJ's withdrawal. "Eye on the Candidates," Apr.22, 1968:90ff.- "Can Hubert Humphrey Stop Bobby Kennedy?" Apr.29, 1968: 23-24ff. "This One Counts," (Indiana Primary); May 6, 1968: 27-29A.- Also Kenneth Crawford, "The Indiana Blitz:" 32; Louis Harris "The Newsweek Poll Shows RFK Ahead:"28-29.- "RFK:'It's Much Better to Win.' Louis Harris Analyzes the Indiana Primary, May 20, 1968:34-36ff. "A Domino Falls for RFK," May 27, 1968:32-33.- Nebraska Primary. "Perils of the Primaries," June 10, 1968:25-26. Campaign in Oregon.

Paolucci, Henry. WAR, PEACE AND THE PRESIDENCY. A Classical ConservativeViews America's Great Dilemma. 1st McG-H, 1968.

Reeves, Richard. "Kennedy - The Making of a Candidate," N.Y.TIMES MAG., Mar.31, 1968: 25-27ff. RFK and EMK on cover.

Reichley, A. James. "Bobby Kennedy: Running Himself Out of the Race. What He Thinks of Business, Antitrust, Taxes, the Cuban Crisis, etc." FORTUNE, Mar., 1968: 112-114ff.

REALITIES. "Qui Gouvernera L'Amerique?" Fev., 1968:32-40. The presidential candidates.

S.E.P. "The Revolt Against LBJ," by Roger Kahn, Feb.10, 1968: 17-21. "The Picking of the President," by Russell Baker, Mar.9, 1968: 19-23ff. "How Bobby Plans to Win It," by David Wise, June 1, 1968: 23-27ff. RFK on cover. "The Decline and Fall of the Democratic Party," by Murray Kempton, Nov.2, 1968: 19-21ff. An account of the Chicago convention with expression of attitude re RFK.

Scammon, Richard and Ben J. Wattenberg. THE REAL MAJORITY. An Extraordinary Examination of the American Electorate. C-McC,1970. Election of 1968; RFK, JFK, EMK as candidates.

Schecter, Wm. COUNTDOWN '68. Profiles for the Presidency. Fleet, (1967). Eight men, including RFK.

Sheed, Wilfred. THE MORNING AFTER: Selected Essays and Reviews. 1st F.S.& G., 1971. RFK: 105-120.

Sherrill, Robert G. "The Faith of Eugene McCarthy," NATION, Dec.4, 1967: 589-591.

Presidential Campaign 1968

Sherry, Gerard E. "Cesar Chavez," OUR SUNDAY VISITOR, Sept.1, 1968: 10-11.

Stout, Richard T. PEOPLE. The Story of the Grass-Roots Movement That Found Eugene McCarthy...1st H&R, 1970. The primary battles between McCarthy and RFK.

Sullivan, Leon H. BUILD BROTHER BUILD. Macrae Smith, 1969. The bloodless revolution of jobless black workmen in Philadelphia. RFK: 134.

TIME. "Three's a Crowd. The Johnson-Kennedy-McCarthy Fight." Mar. 22, 1968: 11-19. "Democrats: Tarot Cards, Hoosier Style," May 17, 1968: 21-22. Indiana primary. "The Politics of Restoration," May 24, 1968: 22-27. RFK on cover. TIME CAPSULE/1968. A History of the Year Condensed from the Pages of TIME. Time-Life, 1969.

U.S.NEWS... "Kennedy and '68 - the Odds, the Problems," Mar.25, 1968:21.- "Latest Gallup Poll - RFK Leads LBJ," Apr.1, 1968: 10.- "What the Candidates Would Do About Vietnam," Apr.8, 1968: 44.- "Who Will It Be In November?" Apr.15, 1968:35-38.- "RFK the Choice in Poll of Democrats," Apr.22, 1968: 14.- "Kennedy Moves Up - the Race Ahead," May 20, 1968:34-35.- In Indiana. "Robert Kennedy's Chances: What a Survey Shows," June 3, 1968: 48-50.-

VanGelder, Lawrence. THE UNTOLD STORY: Why the Kennedys Lost the Book Battle. 1st Award, 1967, wrs. Claims attempts to stop publication of Manchester's book wrecked RFK's political timetable.

White, Theodore. THE MAKING OF THE PRESIDENT 1968. Athen. (1969). Review: Aug.1, 1969, TIME:70ff.-

Vidal, Gore. "the Best Man - 1968," (RFK), ESQUIRE, Mar., 1963: 59-62.- RFK on cover.

Witcover, Jules. "The Indiana Primary and the Indianapolis Newspapers - a Report in Detail," COLUMBIA JRNLISM REV. Summer, 1968: 11-17. "The Last Day of the RFK Campaign," N.Y.T.MAG., Nov.13, 1977:85ff. 85 DAYS. The Last Campaign of Robert Kennedy," Putnam, 1969. Direct quotations of RFK's campaign speeches. Excellent political reportage in depth. Also 1st Ace Bk., 1969, wrs.

Yoakum, Robt. "Drew Pearson and Jack Anderson and Martin Luther King and Robert Kennedy and..." COLUMBIA JRNLISM. REV. Summer, 1968, op.cit. 18-19. Four days before the Oregon primary and 11 days before the Calif. primary Pearson and Anderson charged RFK "ordered a wiretap put on the phone of the Rev.Dr. Martin Luther King Jr." The allegations were never documented.

> "...the quiet gentleness of the personal man... his singular promise as a man of reconciliation in a time of racial polarization..."   Jules Witcover.

WORKS ABOUT ROBERT F. KENNEDY

Assassination of Robert F. Kennedy

Associated Press. THE WORLD IN 1968. History As We Lived It.
N.P., 1969. RFK: 114-121.

Bremer, Arthur H. AN ASSASSIN'S DIARY. Harper's Mag.Pr., 1973.
Four references in diary to Sirhan, accused of RFK's murder.

Chastain,Wayne R. "The Assassination of the Reverend Martin Luther King Jr. and Possible Links with the Kennedy Murders,"
Parts 1 to 11. COMPUTERS AND PEOPLE, Feb. to Dec.1974. Eleven
issues.

COMPUTERS AND AUTOMATION. "The Assassination of Senator Robert
F. Kennedy," Aug., 1970: 48-55. Includes text of suit against
the L.A. Police Dept. seeking disclosure of information with
suspected assassin named.

Corson, Wm.R. PROMISE OR PERIL: The Black College Student in
America. 1st Norton, 1970. Reaction to the death of RFK.

Divale, Wm. Tulio with James Joseph. I LIVED INSIDE THE CAMPUS
REVOLUTION. 1st Cowles, 1970. Profile of Sirhan, "best friend"
to author's room-mate. Author: FBI informer. Claims Sirhan
as lone assassin of RFK.

Frank, Gerold. AN AMERICAN DEATH. The True Story of the Assassination of Dr. Martin Luther King Jr. and the Greatest Manhunt of
Our Time. D'day (1972). Includes discussion of JFK and RFK. Conclusion: no conspiracy in MLK's death.

Freed, Donald. THE KILLING OF RFK. 1st Dell, 1975, wrs. Asks:
Who were the men who found the assassin they needed, recruited,
trained and used him?

Hall, Jay Cameron. INSIDE THE CRIME LAB. The Untold Story of
How Police Scientists Detect the Guilty. 1st P-H, 1974. Includes
"how simple sloth and official pressure bungled the forensic investigations of both Kennedy assassinations." Claims evidence of
a second gun - a second assassin - who was RFK's actual killer.

Harris, Richard. THE FEAR OF CRIME. Praeger, 1969. Example of
RFK and MLK deaths, and the Omnibus Crime Bill.

Hough, John T. Jr. A PECK OF SALT. L-B, 1970. Reaction from
the ghettos of Chicago and Detroit to RFK's death.

Houghton, Robt. A. SPECIAL UNIT SENATOR. The Investigation of
the Assassination of Senator Robert F. Kennedy. 1st Random, 1970.
Collaborator: Theodore Taylor. Claims no conspiracy. For critique of this investigation cf. Kaiser, RFK MUST DIE, to follow.
Index to SPECIAL UNIT SENATOR: COMPUTERS AND AUTOMATION, Oct.,
1970: 56-60ff.

THE KENNEDY FAMILY OF MASSACHUSETTS

Assassination of Robert F. Kennedy

Jacobs, Jay and American Heritage eds. RFK: HIS LIFE AND DEATH. 1st Dell, 1968.

Jansen, Godfrey. WHY ROBERT KENNEDY WAS KILLED. The Story of Two Victims. Middle East conflict. Op.cit.: 156

Kaiser, Robert. "Sirhan in Jail," LIFE, Jan.17, 1969: 20-25. "R.F.K. MUST DIE!" Dutton, 1970. A history of the Robert Kennedy assassination and its aftermath. Claims the police turned away from evidence pointing to a possible conspiracy. Also 1st Evergreen Black Cat ed, 1971, wrs. Book bonus "R.F.K. Must Die," L.H.JRNL. May, 1970: 163-170ff. Review: NEWSWEEK, by Geoffrey Wolfe, Oct.19, 1970: 114ff.

Klagsbrun, Francine and David C. Whitney, eds. ASSASSINATION: ROBERT F. KENNEDY 1925-68. Cowles, 1968. Memorial to RFK based on U.P.I.'s news and picture coverage of the five days from the shooting through the day of national mourning with a section on events and pictures of his life and family.

Langman, Betsey and Alexander Cockburn. "Sirhan's Gun. The Books Are Not Yet Closed on the Second Kennedy Assassination. HARPER'S, Jan. 1975: 16-18ff.

Leek, Sybil and Bert R. Sugar. THE ASSASSINATION CHAIN. Corwin, 1976. Review: by Harry R. Harris in CONTINUING INQUIRY, 4/22/77.

Lester, Julius. REVOLUTIONARY NOTES. 1st Evergreen Black Cat, 1970, wrs. The political meaning of the death of RFK.

LIFE. "The Death of Robert Kennedy," by Loudon Wainwright, June 14, 1968: 32-37. Also Paul O'Neil, "Kennedy Family's Tragic Fate" 75-84ff. and Theodore White, "The Last Wearing Weeks and a Last Precious Day:" 38-42C. "The Accused Ray and Sirhan," June 21, 1968: 24-35. "Incredible '68. Special Issue," Jan.10, 1969.

Lowenstein, Allard K. "Flaws in RFK-Sirhan Case Cry for Fresh Look," WASHINGTON STAR, 1975. Reprinted in CONGRESSIONAL RECORD May 21, 1975, under sponsorship of Christopher Dodd. Reprint. "More Questions About Robert Kennedy's Murder," THE PLAIN DEALER March 14, 1977: 19A. "The Murder of Robert Kennedy. Suppressed Evidence of More Than One Assassin?" SAT.REV. Feb.19, 1977:6-10ff. RFK on cover.

Mehdi, M.T. KENNEDY AND SIRHAN - WHY? New World, 1968, wrs. Cf. Kaiser op.cit. which casts doubt on this argument that Sirhan did it for his country.

Mollenhoff, Clark. "Behind the Plot to Assassinate Robert Kennedy," LOOK, May 19, 1964: 49-50ff.

174.

WORKS ABOUT ROBERT F. KENNEDY

Assassination of Robert F. Kennedy

Moynihan, Daniel P. "The Democrats, Kennedy and the Murder of Dr. King," COMMENTARY, May, 1968: 15-16ff.

NEWSWEEK. "Once Again...Once Again," June 17, 1968: 20-21.- "Bobby's Last, Longest Day:" 22-32ff. "A Flame Burned Fiercely:" 36-43. "Understanding Violence:" 43-46. "What the Doctor's Found" 68ff. "The Long Watch:" 102-103. "Chronicling Kennedy:"104. RFK on cover. "The Assassination: Sirhan Denies Guilt," Aug.12, 1968: 29. "Trials: Round One," Feb.3, 1969:33.- L.A.: Sirhan; New Orleans: Clay Shaw. "All the Elements," (Sirhan's trial), Mar.10, 1969: 36ff. - "Trials: Verdict on Sirhan," Apr.28, 1969: 41ff.- "The Jury vs. Sirhan," May 5, 1969:34ff.- "The Letter and the Law" (Sirhan), June 2, 1969:33.- "The Assassins: Who Did It and Why?"Mar.24, 1969: 28-29, with Coretta King and Ethel Kennedy: 38-39.- RFK and MLK on cover. "Testing the RFK Murder Gun," by James R. Gaines with Anthony Morrow, Sept. 29, 1975: 45.

NEW YORKER. "The Talk of the Town:"RFK's Assassination, June 22, 1968: 19.

Seigenthaler,John, et al. A SEARCH FOR JUSTICE. Aurora, 1971. Trials of Clay Shaw, Sirhan Sirhan, James Earl Ray.

Shannon, Wm. V. "Said Robert Kennedy, 'Maybe We're All Doomed Anyway," N.Y.TIMES MAG., June 16, 1968: 7ff. Headline front cover.

Sprague, Richard E. "The Conspiracy to Assassinate Senator Robt. F. Kennedy and the Second Conspiracy to Cover It Up," COMPUTERS AND AUTOMCATION, Oct. 1970: 52ff. "The Assassination of Senator Robert F. Kennedy: Proofs of Conspiracy and of Two Persons Firing," ibid., Sept., 1972: 24-27.

TIME. " Robert Kennedy," June 14, 1968: 15-22. RFK on cover.

Tributes, Memorials and Assessments

Adler, Bill ed. DEAR SENATOR KENNEDY. D-M, 1966. Selected letters from young and old after the assassination of JFK.

Berry, Jason. AMAZING GRACE: With Charles Evers in Mississippi. Sat.Rev.Pr., 1973. The strong influence of RFK.

BOBBY. Macfadden-Bartell, 1968. Authors represented: Pete Hamill, Louis Sabin, Jimmy Breslin.

BUSINESS WEEK. "A Shock of Violence Hits the Campaign," June 8, 1968: 38-42. RFK on cover.

Drew, Elizabeth. "Bobby Books," ATLANTIC, July, 1969: 98-101.-

Evers, Charles. EVERS. 1st World, 1971. Autobiography.

THE KENNEDY FAMILY OF MASSACHUSETTS

Tributes, Memorials and Assessments

Goodwin, Richard. "A Day in June - a Sentimental Tribute to Robert Kennedy," McCALL'S, June, 1970: 38ff. RFK's last day.

Guthman, Edwin. WE BAND OF BROTHERS: A Memoir of Robert F. Kennedy. 1st H&R, 1971. The catastrophes and occasional victories of seven years of our national life.

(Kennedy) ROBERT FRANCIS KENNEDY Eulogy Delivered at St. Patrick's Cathedral, New York City, by Senator Edward M. Kennedy, June 8, 1968. Autographed by EMK 1972. ALS re above undated.

(Kennedy) ROBERT FRANCIS KENNEDY, Memorial Edition. M.F. Enterprises, 1968.

LIFE. "The Kennedys. Special Edition," 1968, wrs.

Lowell, Robert. "R.F.K. (1925-1968)." NEW REPUBLIC, June 22, 1968: 27. 14 line poem. NOTEBOOK 1967-1968. F.S.& G., 1969. Poems either directly or obliquely on RFK's presidential campaign and murder included.

McCarthy, Eugene, "Kennedy's Betrayal," N.Y.TIMES MAG., Nov. 13, 1977: 90ff.

McGinness, Joe. HEROES. Viking (1976). Chapters on RFK, EMK.

Newfield, Jack. ROBERT KENNEDY: A MEMOIR. 1st Dutton, 1969, op.cit.: 161. Review: NEWSWEEK, June 23, 1969: 98ff.- BREAD AND ROSES TOO. Reporting About America. 1st Dutton, 1971. Two chapters of memories of RFK. With Jeff Greenfield - A POPULIST MANIFESTO. The Making of a New Majority. Praeger, 1972. Dedication: "This One Is For Robert Kennedy."

NEW REPUBLIC. Editorial "The Kennedy Cause," June 15, 1968:3-4.

NEWSWEEK. "Kennedys: A Mass for RFK," June 16, 1969: 35.-

PLAYBOY. "RFK the Statesman," by Arthur Schlesinger Jr.:176-178ff. and "RFK the Man," by Bud Schulberg: 176-178ff., Jan., 1969.

Roddy, Joseph, "McCarthy Talk," LOOK, Apr.1, 1969: 19-21.

Rogers, Warren. "The Administration of Robert F. Kennedy," INTELLECTUAL DIGEST, June, 1972: 14-17. What might have been. RFK on cover.

Rovere, Richard H. "The Sixties: 'This Slum of a Decade'." N.Y. TIMES MAG., Dec. 14, 1969: 25-27ff. RFK, JBK, JFK on cover.

Salinger, Pierre, Edwin Guthman, Frank Mankiewicz and John Siegenthaler eds. "AN HONORABLE PROFESSION," A Tribute to Robert F. Kennedy. 1st D'day, 1968. 77 eulogies, statements, memories.

WORKS ABOUT ROBERT F. KENNEDY

Tributes, Memorials and Assessments

Schlesinger, Arthur M., Jr. THE CRISIS OF CONFIDENCE: Ideas, Power and Vigilance in America. 1st H-M, 1969. "In Memory of Robert Francis Kennedy."

TIME. "For Perspective and Determination" (the death of RFK), June 14, 1968: 15-22. RFK on cover.

U.S.Congress, Memorial Tributes. ROBERT FRANCIS KENNEDY 1925-1968 Late a Senator from New York. GPO, 1968. Memorial tributes delivered in Congress incl. newspaper editorials, poems from constituents, magazine articles, communications from officials and private citizens.

(Recording) ROBERT FRANCIS KENNEDY - A MEMORIAL. Two 12" records "RFK in His Own Words," and "Funeral Service for RFK." Columbia Records D2S792.

(Recording) ROBERT FRANCIS KENNEDY (1925-1968), with EMK's Eulogy to this brother in St. Patrick's Cathedral and RFK's major addresses. Premier Albums Inc.

(Recording) ROBERT F. KENNEDY - A Tribute. Includes voices of RFK, Ethel, EMK. WNEW Radio in N.Y., Fleetwood Recording Co.

Memorabilia

Ohio Democratic dinner menu and program with picture of RFK, Oct. 8, 1966. Also ticket for same, #59.

RFK Speech List, 52 mimeo. pp. in John F. Kennedy Library. A 3 page Reading List, Jan. 1974, ibid.

Presidential Campaign 1968: 5x7 photo of RFK with campaign pledges on back. Campaign poster 38"x24". Portrait in charcoal matted and framed 11x14½ unsigned. Flyers: "I run for the Presidency because I want the United States to stand for the reconciliation of men..." 4p. "The youth of our nation are the clearest mirror of our performance." 2p. Memorial card with prayer in Italian, second in English.

United Farm Workers Calendar 1970 with photo of RFK with quotation; Cesar Chavez on cover. Delano,CA UFWOC, AFL-CIO

Poster of United States postage stamp honoring RFK Jan.12, 1979.

> Robert F. Kennedy "need not be idealized, or enlarged in death beyond what he was in life,to be remembered simply as a good and decent man, who saw wrong and tried to right it, saw suffering and tried to heal it, saw war and tried to stop it." EMK June 8, 1968

WORKS OF AND ABOUT ETHEL KENNEDY

Autographs

ALS on Hickory Hill stationery July 27, 1962: one page hand-written, one page typed - both signed, describing the Hickory Hill
Seminars.

Franked envelope with four memorial prayer cards of RFK, June 6,
1968.

Presentation copy"...with warm wishes, Ethel Kennedy June, 1980"
on RFK's TO SEEK A NEWER WORLD, op.cit.:158. This copy has
Michael Kennedy's signature also appended.

Presentation, signed"...with warm wishes Ethel Kennedy June 1980"
on EMK's DECISIONS FOR A DECADE (described in EMK section).

Writings About Ethel Kennedy

Birmingham, Stephen. "Ethel Kennedy: A Surprisingly Happy Woman,"
McCALL'S, June, 1974: 94-95ff. Ethel on cover.

David, Lester. ETHEL. The Story of Mrs. Robert F. Kennedy. 1st
World, 1971. Lively portrait of an admirable woman. Also 1st
Dell, 1972, wrs. "Ethel: Bravest of the Kennedys," GOOD HOUSEKEEP-
ING, Nov. 1970: 92-95ff.

Hamill, Pete. "The Woman Behind Bobby Kennedy," GOOD HOUSEKEEPING
Apr. 1968: 96-99ff. -

LADY'S CIRCLE. "A Mother's Day Tribute to Ethel Kennedy," May,1973:
20-21. Ethel on cover.

LIFE. "Full Life of a Famous Wife - Ethel Kennedy and Her Children," Nov.10, 1961: 81-86ff. "Life Goes to Christening of Bobby
Kennedy's Son," Aug.9, 1963: 87-89. (Christopher George).

LOOK. "Ethel's Kennedys: How She Manages Them," June 25, 1968:
30-37. Ethel and children on cover.

McCALL'S. "Ethel Kennedy: Profile in American Courage," by Anne
Chamberlin, Aug. 1968: 111-113.

Marvin, Susan. THE WOMEN AROUND R.F.K. Lancer, 1967, wrs.

NEWSWEEK. "'Laughter Is Better Than Tears'," (Ethel) June 17,
1968:39. Op.cit. p.176.

Sheehan, Susan. "The Lady of Hickory Hill," N.Y.T.MAG., Nov.30,
1969: 30-31ff. Ethel on cover.

CHILDREN OF ROBERT AND ETHEL KENNEDY

Writings About Ethel Kennedy

THREE MOTHERS. Macf.-Bart., 1968, wrs. Ethel, JBK, Coretta King.

TIME. "The Kennedy of Hickory Hill," (Ethel), Apr. 25, 1969: 46-48ff.- Ethel on cover.

CHILDREN OF ROBERT AND ETHEL KENNEDY

Berquist, Laura. "Kathleen Kennedy: the Daredevil Girl," REDBOOK: Jan., 1973: 70-71ff.

David, Lester. "Robert Kennedy's Oldest Son Grows Up," GOOD HOUSEKEEPING, Oct., 1972: 34ff. Joseph Kennedy III.

Gorey, Hays. "Joe Kennedy Comes of Age," N.Y.TIMES MAG., May 29, 1977: 6-11ff. Joseph Kennedy III on cover.

Kennedy, Robert F. Jr. JUDGE FRANK M. JOHNSON JR. Putnam, 1978. Intro. by John Doar. Biography developed from Robert's senior thesis at Harvard on the Southern individualist who changed the life of Alabama against the opposition of George Wallace. In part, about the civil rights cases RFK, Atty. General, brought or joined in before Judge Johnson.

LIFE. "Bobby Jr. in Africa," Feb.14, 1969: 42-49.

Peter, Viviane and Connecticut Walker. "Joseph Kennedy III - Bobby's Son Grows Up," PARADE, Sept. 13, 1970: 4-5.

Quindlen, Anna, "A Kennedy's Son's Grim Struggle with Drugs," (David), McCALL'S, Apr., 1980: 83ff.

SIGN. "Bob Kennedy's Family Grows Up," July, 1961: 15-21. - RFK with Ethel and seven children on cover.

What though the radiance which was once so bright
Be now for ever taken from my sight,
    Though nothing can bring back the hour
Of splendor in the grass, of glory in the flower;
    We will grieve not, rather find
    Strength in what remains behind;
    In the primal sympathy
    Which having been must ever be;
    In the soothing thoughts that spring
    Out of human suffering;
    In the faith that looks through death,
In years that bring the philosophic mind.

                        - William Wordsworth

SECTION THREE

EDWARD MOORE KENNEDY

JOAN BENNETT KENNEDY

PART ONE. EDWARD M. KENNEDY

WRITINGS OF EDWARD M. KENNEDY

Autographs

TLS Feb.5, 1971, re contest for Assistant Majority Leader, 10 lines.

Autograph note, together with copy of Congressional Record, Jan.19, 1972, with address by Senator Kennedy to the Washington Press Club on the Vietnam Policy of the Administration, with other domestic and foreign policies.

Autographed copy (1972) of Eulogy of Robert Francis Kennedy by Senator M. Kennedy, June 8, 1968.

TLS - 11 lines: "...unable to respond sooner...Enclosed is material for your use," May 7, 1980. Enclosed with package dated May 13 1980, includes campaign 1980 speeches and press releases.

Books, Articles, Speeches, Recordings by EMK

"A Fresh Look at Vietnam," LOOK, Feb.8, 1966: 21-23.

"Ellis Island," ESQUIRE, Apr., 1967: 118-119.

DECISIONS FOR A DECADE. Policies and Programs for the 1970's. 1st D'day, 1968. Inscribed op.cit.: 178. Re military service, dissenting youth, the control of crime, the racial crisis at home; abroad: detente with Russia, the perils of overcommittment in Asia, an approach to Latin America, aid to poor nations to win their fight against poverty. Also 1st Signet, 1968, wrs.

CHINA POLICY FOR THE '70's. No. 33 in the Sidney Hillman Reprint Series. Adapted from speech in New York City, March, 1969.

"The Value of a United States Initiative," (re Chinese representation in the United Nations) in ASIAN DILEMMA: U.S., Japan and China a Center Occasional Paper: 163-165. Wrs. Center for the Study of American Democratic Institutions, October, 1969.

"The Responsibility of Government for Leadership in Health Care:" in MEDICINE IN THE GHETTO, John C. Norman ed., A-C-C, 1969. EMK gave six proposals for action by Congress.

EMK letter on National Health Plan, July 10, 1970, to the N.Y.TIMES published in TALKING BACK TO THE NEW YORK TIMES by K. Seigel, op. cit.: 156.

Edward M. Kennedy on the Presidency. MEMORIAL TRIBUTES DELIVERED IN CONGRESS: Dwight David Eisenhower, G.P.O. 1970: 14-15. Harry S. Truman, G.P.O., 1973: 177-178. Lyndon Baines Johnson G.P.O., 1973: 192-193. Texts of Civil Rights Act of 1964 and the Voting Rights Act of 1965 added at request of EMK.

WRITINGS OF EDWARD M. KENNEDY

Books, Articles, Speeches, Recordings by EMK

"The Future Is Now for the 18-Year-Old Vote," SCHOOL & SOCIETY, Mar., 1972: 151-155.

IN CRITICAL CONDITION. The Crisis in America's Health Care. 1st S&S, 1972. Indictment of the American health industry on the basis of testimony heard by EMK as Chairman of the Senate Health Subcommittee.

"It Is Time To Normalize Relations with Cuba: a Scene that Senator Kennedy Would Like to See," N.Y.TIMES MAG., Jan. 14, 1973: 16-17ff.

"Face to Face on the Issues," LIFE, June 30, 1972:33-37. Debate on the economy by EMK for the Democrats and John Connally for the Republicans.

"Ted Kennedy's Conversation with Theodore Sorenson - Memories of JFK," McCALL'S, Nov. 1973: 88ff.

"The Persian Gulf: Arms Race or Arms Control?" FOREIGN AFFAIRS, Oct., 1975: 14-35.

"My Mother, Rose Kennedy," L.H.JRNL., Dec., 1975: 68-69ff.

"Meeting the Challenge of Preventive Medicine," FAMILY HEALTH, Jan., 1976: 40-42ff. EMK on cover.

With Charles Morgan Jr. and Christopher H. Pyle, "'Legal' Bugging?" Pros and Cons of S.3197. THE NATION, July 31-Aug.7, 1976: 72-74.

OUR DAY AND GENERATION, edited by Henry Steele Commager with a foreword by Archibald MacLeish. 1st S&S, 1979. Collection of extracts from EMK's public speeches on the problems of the nation.

Campaign 1980:
Announcement of Candidacy, Faneuil Hall, Boston, Nov.7, 1979.
Statement on Soviet Aggression in Afghanistan, Jan. 7, 1980.
"The Rights of Women and the Future of the Family," Portland, Maine, Feb.1, 1980.
Press Release: Policy Paper on Energy, Feb.3, 1980. Policy Paper: "Enhancing America's Energy Security by Ending Our Petroleum Paralysis," Feb.3, 1980. Press Release: Policy Paper on Energy, Feb.7, 1980. Policy Paper: "A Program for America's Economic Recovery."
Press Release: On Carter Administration Proposed 1981 Budget, Feb.12, 1980. Statement on the Carter Administration Budget for Fiscal Year 1981, Feb.12, 1980.
Address to the Forum JFK School of Government, Harvard University, Feb.12, 1980: "On the Institution of the Presidency."
Press Release: On Equalify and Justice for Women," Feb. 16, 1980.
Policy Paper: "Equality and Justice for Women." Cont'd p.182.

THE KENNEDY FAMILY OF MASSACHUSETTS

Books, Articles, Speeches, Recordings by EMK

Press Release: On Elderly, Feb.20, 1980. Policy Paper:"The Eld-
erly in America," Feb.20, 1980.
Address: Franklin Pierce Law Center, Concord, N.H., Feb.20, 1980,
"The Nuclear Question."
Address: City Hall Auditorium, Dover N.H. Feb.23, 1980. "The En-
vironment."
Address: City Club of Chicago, "Myths of Economic Politics,"
March 7, 1980.
Remarks: Illinois Mineworkers Annual Legislative Conference,
Detroit, March 10, 1980.
Press Release: On the Environment," Mar. 15, 1980. Policy Paper:
"Protecting the Environment for the Next Generation, Mar.15, 1980.
Address: To the Nat'l Assn. of Neighborhoods, Chicago, Mar.13.
Statement for the National Housing Conference, March 18, 1980.
Address: Columbia University Mar.20, 1980. On Foreign Policy.
Statement: On Receiving the Endorsement of American Federation
of Teacher Affiliates. April 15, 1980.
Address: On the Carter Doctrine to Defend the Persian Gulf Area;
Other Foreign and Domestic Issues. N.d.
            This material issued through EMK Campaign Hdqtrs.

(Recordings) Op.cit.: 17, 177.

Forewords and Introductions by EMK

Introduction to JOHN F. KENNEDY, MAN OF THE SEA byTazewell Shep-
hard Jr. Morrow, 1965. Author served as Naval Aide to JFK.

With Eunice Shriver, forewords to THE CHALLENGE OF THE RETARDED
CHILD by Sister Mary Theodore of St. Coletta School. St. Meinrad,
rev.ed., 1969, wrs.

Introduction to STILL HUNGRY IN AMERICA, by Robert Coles, 1st
World, 1969. An expression of the moral disgrace of the hunger
and malnutrition pinching the lives of many folk as felt by EMK
on the U.S.Senate Subcommittee on Employment, Manpower and Poverty, July 11th, 1967. Dedication: "In memory of Robert Francis
Kennedy and the millions of people like those in this book for
whom he spoke and worked."

Introduction to WHO WILL DO OUR FIGHTING FOR US? by George E.
Reedy, 1st World, 1969. For: an army of all citizens raised by
draft-by-lottery; against: an all-volunteer professional army
manned by the poor and the black.

Introduction to DON'T GET SICK IN AMERICA by Daniel Schorr.
Aurora, 1970. Based on two-part CBS television broadcast.

> "...there are still children who feel pain and get no
> relief from it; who fall sick and get no medicine; who
> suffer accidents and learn to clench their fists and
> grit their teeth or cry long and hard - to no avail."
>   —EMK

WRITINGS ABOUT EMK

Biographies

Associated Press. THE WORLD IN 1969. History As We Lived It.
Western Publ.,1970. THE WORLD IN 1970. Ibid.,1971.

Burns, James MacGregor. EDWARD KENNEDY AND THE CAMELOT LEGACY.
1st Norton, 1976.

Cadden, Vivian. "The Burdens of Ted Kennedy," McCALL'S, Feb.,
1974: 48ff. "What Happened at Chappaquiddick," Aug., 1974: 79-
81ff. "The Recurring Doubts about Chappaquiddick."Ibid., Nov.
1975: 46ff.

David, Lester. TED KENNEDY: Triumphs and Tragedies. 1st G&D,
1972. Based on "hundreds of interviews," including EMK. "Ted
Kennedy: His Triumphs and Tragedies," L.H.JRNL., Jan., 1972:
77ff. "The Ted Kennedys Begin Again," GOOD HOUSEKEEPING, July,
1975: 74-75.

Dye, Thomas R. WHO'S RUNNING AMERICA? Institutional Leadership in the United States. 1st P-H, 1976, wrs. EMK among the
elites discussed, named "The Crown Prince."

Hersh, Burton. THE EDUCATION OF EDWARD KENNEDY. A Family Biography. 1st Morrow, 1972. "The Survival of Edward Kennedy,"
WASHINGTONIAN, Feb., 1979: 91-103.

Honan, Wm. H. TED KENNEDY: Profile of a Survivor. 1st Quad-
rangle, 1972.

Howar, Barbara. "Ted Kennedy Since Chappaquiddick," L.H.JRNL.
Aug., 1974:79ff.

LIFE. Brower, Brock. "Incident at Dyke Bridge," Aug.1, 1969:
16B-25. EMK on cover.

Lippman, Theo, Jr. SENATOR TED KENNEDY. The Career Behind
the Image. 1st Norton, 1976. Work and accomplishments as a
United States Senator. Review: N.Y.TIMES BK.REV. By Raymond
A. Schroth, Jan.11, 1976: 3ff.

McCALL'S. Kopechne, Mrs. Joseph, as told to Suzanne James.
"The Truth About Mary Jo," Sept., 1970: 65-67ff.

McGinness, Joe. HEROES. op.cit.: 176. Chapter on EMK.

Morgan, Thomas B. SELF-CREATIONS: 13 IMPERSONALITIES. 1st
H.R.& W., 1965. 13 portraits including EMK at thirty.

News Front/ YEAR Editors. YEAR - 1971. Covering Events of
1970. Year Inc., 1970.

EMK Biographies

Olsen, Jack. THE BRIDGE AT CHAPPAQUIDDICK. 1st L-B, 1970.

Reybold, Malcolm. THE INSPECTOR'S OPINION: the Chappaquiddick Incident. 1st Sat.Rev.Pr./Dutton, 1975.

Rogers, Warren. "Ted Kennedy Talks About the Past and His Future," LOOK, Mar.4, 1969: 38-46. EMK on cover.

Sherrill, Robert. "Chappaquiddick + 5," N.Y.TIMES MAG., July 14, 1974: 8-9ff. "...a suppurating editorial corpse, oozing speculative gases, worm-riddled with inaccuracies," - Burton Hersh. THE LAST KENNEDY, 1st Dial, 1976. EMK of Massachusetts.

TIME. "People," June 18, 1965: 36.- EMK and family nurse Luella Hennessey. "The Mysteries of Chappaquiddick," Aug.1, 1969: 11B-12. EMK on cover. "Jack Anderson: the Square Scourge of Washington," Apr.3, 1972:40-44. Note mention of Chappaquiddick "the biggest story on which Anderson erred:" 43. TIME ANNUAL. 1969: The Year in Review. Time/Life, 1970.

The Senate Years of Edward M. Kennedy (1962-　.)

Alpern, David M. "Kennedy Pulls a Sherman," NEWSWEEK, Oct.7, 1974: 35-38. EMK bows out of 1976 Presidential race.

Alsop, Stewart. "What Made Teddy Run?" SAT.EVE.POST, Oct.27, 1962. 1962 Senate race in Massachusetts.

Archer, Jeffrey. SHALL WE TELL THE PRESIDENT? 1st Viking, 1977. Novel about EMK that prompted JKO to resign her editorial position at Viking.

Behr, Edward. "A Day of Joy and Sadness," SAT.EVE.POST, July 11-18, 1964: 35ff.- EMK in Ireland.

Bernstein, Carl and Bob Woodward. ALL THE PRESIDENT'S MEN. 1st Warner, 1975, wrs. Revelation of the persistence needed to unravel the Nixon Administration dissimulation and crimes. EMK and his Subcommittee on Administrative Practice and Procedure which he ordered to investigate allegations of White House sponsored sabotage and spying in October, 1972. Howard Hunt's investigation of EMK. JFK and forged message re Diem murder.

Buchwald, Art. THE ESTABLISHMENT IS ALIVE AND WELL IN WASHING-TON. Putnam, 1969. Many references, two columns each EMK and Jacqueline.

Cameron, Juan. "Ted Kennedy in the Wake of Watergate," FORTUNE, Oct. 1974: 140-143ff. James Wyeth drawings.

WRITINGS ABOUT EMK

The Senate Years of Edward M. Kennedy (1962-   )

Campaign Hdqtrs. 1980. "A Record of Leadership and Accomplish-ments."

Carlson, Joel. NO NEUTRAL GROUND. Crowell, 1973. South Africans, victims of a racist society. Help given in 1966 by RFK,EMK.

Coughlan, Robert. "Three Clans in a Hot Political Chowder, The Senate Seat Scramble in Massachusetts," LIFE, June 29, 1962: 59-63ff. EMK on cover.

Drew, Elizabeth. AMERICAN JOURNAL: The Events of 1976. 1st Random, 1979. The issues and the election of 1976. Many references to EMK.

English, David et al. DIVIDED THEY STAND. op.cit.: 169. EMK's near-miss at being nominated.

ESQUIRE. "New Faces '72," Feb., 1970: 55-59ff. Profiles of 10 candidates including EMK. "The Selling of a Candidate," June, 1970: 87-99. EMK on cover.

Greeley, Andrew M. AMERICAN POLITICS IN THE 1970s. Watts, 1974. Wrs. Dedicated to EMK, with many allusions to JFK, RFK, EMK.

Hargreaves, Robert. SUPERPOWER. A Portrait of America in the 70s. St.Martin's, 1973. EMK's presidential prospects, JFK's foreign and domestic policy, RFK, the Mafia and Hoover.

HARPER'S. "Kennedy, Agnew and Black America," May, 1973: 42. A poll taken by HARPER'S.

Harris, Richard. DECISION. 1st Dutton, 1971. EMK's active role among others in the case of G. Harrold Carswell, Nixon's nominee to the Supreme Court.

Honan, Wm. H. "Will He Say: 'Help Me Finish What My Brothers Began'?" N.Y.TIMES MAG., Nov.28, 1971: 27ff.-

Howe, Russell W. and Sarah H. Trott. THE POWER BROKERS: A Reveal-ing Account of Foreign Lobbying in Washington. 1st D'day, 1977. Includes EMK and lobby legislation control efforts.

Leamer, Laurence. PLAYING FOR KEEPS IN WASHINGTON. 1st Dial, 1977. Position of majority whip: EMK vs. Robert Byrd.

Levin, Murray B. KENNEDY CAMPAIGNING. The System and the Style as Practised by Senator Edward Kennedy. 1st Beacon, 1966. Refers mainly to 1962 campaign for Senate.

LIFE. "Congress Opens. Teddy's At Work," Jan.18, 1963: 34-37. Photo: Sen. Edward Kennedy with broken back in orthopedic bed, Oct.30, 1964: 37ff.   Cont'd: 186

The Senate Years of Edward M. Kennedy (1962-   )

LIFE Cont'd. "Ted Kennedy's Recovery," Jan.15, 1965: 28-35.
EMK on cover. Includes Robert Ajemian's "He Did More Than Just
Get Well." "The Kennedy Center's Gala Debut," June 11, 1971: 26-
33. EMK and Joan on cover. "Kennedy's Searing Tour," Aug.29,
1971: 26-29. Trip though grim Pakistan refugee camps in India.
"The Wallace Shooting."A Photographic Record of the Assassination
Attempt by Arthur Bremer."Ted Kennedy Hears the News," by David
Maxey. Editorials. May 26, 1972:4-11ff.

Lindley, Ernest K. "Will Kennedy Run for President?" in Vol.4
of AMERICA: An Illustrated Diary of Its Most Exciting Years.
Stonehouse Pr., 1973.

Lukas, J. Anthony. NIGHTMARE: The Underside of the Nixon Years.
"Us vs. Them," - the White House battle plan, with the first of
'Them': EMK. Also numerous mention of JFK and RFK.1st Viking,'76.

McCarthy, Joe. "One Election JFK Can't Win," Nov.6, 1962: 23-27.
EMK's first Senate race.

Magruder, Jeb Stuart. AN AMERICAN LIFE; One Man's Road to Watergate. Athen.,1974. Includes Nixon's preoccupation with EMK.

Mailer, Norman. ST. GEORGE AND THE GODFATHER. 1st Signet, 1972,
wrs. Democratic and Republican Conventions of 1972.

Mankiewicz, Frank. U.S. VS. RICHARD M. NIXON; The Final Crisis.
1st Quad.,1975. Engrossing account of the vindication of the American political system through the legal institutions. EMK as
first using the word "impeachment;" as recommending John Doar
for the position of chief special counsel.

Massie, Robert K. "The Youngest Lions," USA1,May 1962: 24-27.
EMK's first campaign for the Senate.

Nader, Ralph: Congress Project. Robert Schwartzman , author.
EDWARD M. KENNEDY, Democratic Senator from Massachusetts. 1st
Grossman, 1972. 2000 c. printed. Wrs. Non-partisan profile of
legislative activity of EMK.

NEW REPUBLIC. "Draft-Kennedy Conclave," Oct., 11, 1972.

NEWSWEEK. "Rendevous," June 29, 1964: 20.- EMK and plane wreck.
"One for Old Joe," Oct.11, 1965: 33-34.- "Is Teddy's 'No' the
Last Word?" Aug.5, 1968: 13-16ff. EMK on cover. "'No Safety In
Hiding'," Sept.2, 1968: 28-32. Also EMK's prescription for Viet-
nam peace by Kenneth Crawford: 33. "Teddy Kennedy Cracks the
Whip," Jan.13, 1969: 13-16. EMK on cover. "Teddy on the Stump"
June 2, 1969: 33.-

New York Times Staff. THE END OF A PRESIDENCY. H.R.& W., 1974.
Nixon and surveillance of EMK, the "preliminary inquiry" into
Watergate.   186.

WRITINGS ABOUT EMK

The Senate Years of Edward M. Kennedy (1962-   )

Page, Joseph A. "The Precocious Ted Kennedy," NATION, Mar.10, 1962: 212-214.

Press Release: 27 Foreign and Defense Policy Leaders Support Kennedy's Proposal for Select Commission on National Security Policy, March 20, 1980.

Redman, Eric. THE DANCE OF LEGISLATION. S&S, 1973, wrs. Traces the drafting and passing of S.4106, the Nat'l Health Service Bill sponsored by Senator Warren Magnuson; co-sponsor EMK.

Reeves, Richard. CONVENTION. 1st H.B.J., 1977. Democratic National Convention 1976: Jimmy Carter nominated, EMK in sub-dued role.

Roddy, Joseph. "Coming Up Strong in the Senate: Ted Kennedy on His Own," LOOK, July 13, 1965: 29-35.

Rogers, Warren. "Kennedy's Comeback: Will He or Won't He?" LOOK, Aug.10, 1971: 13-20ff. EMK on cover.

Sampson, Anthony. THE SOVEREIGN STATE OT ITT. S&D, 1973. The 8th biggest corporation in America and the biggest American company in Europe. EMK as member of Senate Judiciary Committee studying ITT's role in political gift to Nixon-Kleindeinst.

Shannon, Wm.V. "The Emergence of Senator Kennedy," N.Y.TIMES MAG. Aug.22, 1965: 16-17ff. EMK on cover.

Sheehan, Edward R.F. "Massachusetts: Rogues and Reformers in a State on Trial," SAT.EVE.POST, June 5, 1965: 25-35ff. EMK cover.

Smith, Judith G. ed. POLITICAL BROKERS: People, Organizations, Money, Power. Liveright/ Nat'l Jrnl. Book, 1972. Some of the most important pressure groups - EMK's ratings with them.

TIME. "Ted and Kennedyism," Sept. 28, 1962: 14-18. EMK on cover. EMK's race for the Senate.- "The Ascent of Ted Kennedy," Jan.10. 1969: 12-17. EMK on cover. "The Non-Candidacy of Edward Moore Kennedy," Nov.29, 1971: 16-18ff. EMK on cover. "George McGovern Finally Finds a Veep," Aug.14, 1972: 15-20. EMK's refusal.

U.S.NEWS. "Will Edward Kennedy Now Move Up?" June 24, 1968: 40-42.- "Can Ted Kennedy Be Drafted?" Aug.5, 1968: 14ff.- "Ted Kennedy's Chances Now," Nov.3, 1969: 30-34. Senate re-election in 1970.

U.S.Senate (EMK) Room 431 Russell Office Bldg. Wash.D.C. "Report to Massachusetts:" On Elderly and New Jobs... Nov.3, 1972; Food, Fuel...J.F.K.Library, Nov., 1973; Soviet Trip...June, 1974; Leg-islative Record, 1974, 1975-1976.

THE KENNEDY FAMILY OF MASSACHUSETTS

The Senate Years of Edward M. Kennedy (1962-   )

Weil, Gordon L. LONG SHOT. George McGovern Runs for President. 1st Norton, 1973. With details of EMK's refusal to run as V-P.

White, Theodore M. THE MAKING OF THE PRESIDENT - 1972. Athen., (1973). Nixon, McGovern, EMK. Also mention of JFK, RFK.

Winter-Berger, Robt.N. THE WASHINGTON PAY-OFF. A Lobbyist's Own Story of Corruption in Government. 1st Stuart, 1972. EMK as one of the leaders of crusade for full disclosure and public funds for elections. The Kennedys as avoiding political debts.

Witcover, Jules. MARATHON: The Pursuit of the Presidency 1972-1976. 1st Viking, 1977. Chapter 9. EMK

Witker, Kristi. HOW TO LOSE EVERYTHING IN POLITICS (Except Massachusetts). 1st Mason & Lipscomb, 1974. References to EMK.

For Senate Years cf. also Writings of EMK and Biographies op.cit.

Presidential Campaign - 1980

Brown, Gene, ed. THE KENNEDYS: A NEW YORK TIMES Profile. 1st Arno, 1980. The family as reported, analyzed and photographed by the N.Y.TIMES. Published as EMK's presidential campaign advanced to March 27, 1980. The TIMES' slants apparent.

CITIZEN PARTICIPATION. "The Presidential Candidates on Citizen Participation," Mar/Apr., 1980: 3ff. EMK and other candidates answer eight questions on issues.

Clymer, Adam. "Stalking Iowa's Crop of Candidates," N.Y.TIMES MAG., Jan.20, 1980: 30ff. "Carter's Vision of America," ibid., July 27, 1980: 14ff.

COLUMBUS DISPATCH. "Carter Reasoning Labeled Hogwash," Feb.3, 1980: A-6. Carter's refusal to debate EMK.

Kramer, Michael. "The National Interest: The Three-Party System?" NEW YORK, April 7, 1980: 12-13. "Teddy time."

Hebers, John. "The Democrats in Disarray," N.Y.TIMES MAG., Aug.10, 1980: 26-29ff.

Lerner, Max. TED AND THE KENNEDY LEGEND: A Study in Character and Destiny. 1st St.Martin's, 1980.

McGrory, Mary. "In New York Before the Fall," BOSTON SUNDAY GLOBE, Mar.30, 1980.-

NEWSWEEK. "Kennedy's Ragged Start," Dec.10, 1979:56ff. "Kennedy's Blooper," Dec.17, 1979:46ff.   Cont'd page 189.

Presidential Campaign 1980

NEWSWEEK cont'd. "Newsweek Poll: The Drag on Kennedy," Jan.14, 1980: 38-39. "Can Kennedy Hang On?" (After Iowa) Feb.4, 1980: 47ff. "Ted Tries, Tries Again," (Georgetown speech) Feb.11, 1980: 29ff. "Sinking Feeling in Camelot," Feb.18, 1980: 46. "A Bitter Personal Vendetta," (Carter and EMK) Feb.25, 1980: 28ff. "Last Chance for Kennedy," (11 point loss in New Hampshire) Mar.10, 1980: 36ff. "Kennedy Woos the Jewish Vote," Mar.24, 1980: 39. "Carter Is In Trouble Again," (EMK's victories in New York and Conn.) Apr.7, 1980: 22-25. "Carter vs. Kennedy: No Peace Pipe," June 16, 1980: 22-24. "Kennedy Going Fishing?" July 7, 1980: 21-22. "Ronald Reagan Up Close: A Special Report," July 21, 1980: 24ff. "The Mutinous Democrats," Aug.4, 1980: 21ff. "The Dump-Carter Movement," Aug.11, 1980: 18-25. "A New Ted Kennedy?" by Allan J. Mayer et al.: Aug.25, 1980: 31-33. EMK on cover.

NEW YORKER. "The Talk of the Town," (1980 Democratic Nat'l Convention): 19-23.

NEW YORK TIMES. June 1, 1980: "Kennedy and Carter in Tight Race in New Jersey Primary," by Joseph L. Sullivan: 28. July 27, 1980: "Kennedy Backers Have Renewed Hope of Winning Nomination," by Stephen V. Roberts: 22. "Carter's 'Guarantee Rule," (background of attempt to control delegate procedure at Democratic Convention 1980) by Tom Wicker: E21. Aug.17, 1980: "Kennedy Indicates His Zeal for Ticket Depends on Carter," by B. Drummond Ayres: 1, 22.

PUBLIC OPINION. Westerville, Ohio, Nov.29, 1979. Full page ad: "Stop Teddy for Presidency:" 11.

Roberts, Steven B. "Ted Kennedy: Haunted by the Past," N.Y.TIMES MAG., Feb.3, 1980: 54ff.

Shoup, Laurence H. "Who's Behind John Anderson?" INQUIRY, Aug. 4 and 18, 1980: 12-16.

Sidey, Hugh and John Stacks. "That Which We Are, We Are: Kennedy Goes Out in Style - and Looks Ahead," TIME, Aug.25, 1980: 24-26.

TIME. "In New Hampshire They're Off!" Feb.25, 1980: 10ff. "Kennedy's Startling Victory," Apr.7, 1980: 14-15ff. Also same issue: "Press- Rough Ride on the Primary Trail:" 91-92.

WASHINGTON POST. "Playing 'Get Teddy:' The Anti-Kennedy Bias in TV News Reporting," by Tom Shales, Jan.30, 1980: B1,11.- "The Carter Campaign," Four Part Series by Martin Schram, June 8-11, 1980.- "Kennedy Strikes Chord Before NAACP," by Herbert Denton, July 3, 1980: A3.- "The Artful Dodge," (Artists for Kennedy) by T.R.Reid, July 21, 1980: A1-A2.- "The Founding Mother: Rose Kennedy at 90," by Donnie Radcliffe, July 21, 1980.- "Candidates: Intractable and Proud," by Martin Schram: A1, A6.- Important for description of first meeting between EMK and Carter in 1974.

THE KENNEDY FAMILY OF MASSACHUSETTS

Presidential Campaign 1980

WASHINGTON STAR. "Massachusetts Is Prodded Into the Carter Fold,"
by Mary McGrory: A4-; "Split Ohio Delegation Never Bound Wounds"
by Mary Thornton: A4-; "The Politics of Bitterness," by Richard
Reeves: A11-. All Aug. 15, 1980.

Memorabilia

Campaign 1980 letters April 3, 23, May 15, June 20, July 30, Sept.
12, signature stamped "Ted Kennedy." July 30 communication includes reprint of an article by Ted Wicker "What Is a Delegate?"
N.Y.TIMES July 11, 1980. Sept.12 letter includes colored photo
of EMK with Joan and text of address by EMK to the Democratic
Nat'l Convention 1980. Campaign flyers: "You Do Have a Choice,"
"Where Senator Kennedy Stands on the Issues." Miscellaneous letters from George McGovern, Peter Rodino, John B. Anderson, League
of Women Voters, Democratic National Committee. Notice of Historic
Handgun Control Legislation introduced March 20, 1980.

Bumper stickers 1980; Campaign buttons 1980; comparison of EMK
with Carter on labor issues, on health care, 1980.

Committee for Fifteen: EMK with Jonathan Bingham and Morris Udall
campaign letter June-July and Sept 5, 1974, for 15 men who can
make a difference, with biographies.

Crummere, Maria Elise. "Vogue's Horoscope: Edward Kennedy,"
VOGUE, Feb.15, 1971: 33.-

Democratic Party, Ohio. THE STATE DINNER 1972. N.P., folio, wrs.
EMK main speaker with portrait.

Leek, Sybil. ASTROLOGICAL GUIDE TO THE PRESIDENTIAL CANDIDATES.
Abelard-Schuman (1972) Includes EMK.

PART TWO. JOAN BENNETT KENNEDY

WORKS OF AND ABOUT JOAN KENNEDY

Articles and Interviews By Joan Kennedy

"Tells Her Own Story," McCALL'S, Aug., 1978: 120-121,ff.

"Does Kennedy Really Want It?" BOSTON GLOBE,Feb.10, 1980.- Ellen
Goodman interview with Joan Kennedy.

"Teddy the Underdog Flies Into the Maine Event," WASH. POST, Feb.
10, 1980: H1-3. Myra MacPherson interview with Joan Kennedy.

WORKS ABOUT TED KENNEDY JR.

Joan Kennedy: Articles and Interviews

"'Win or Lose, I Win.'" Interview with Myra MacPherson in
McCALL'S, June, 1980: 28ff. Joan on cover.

Works About Joan Kennedy

David, Lester. "Joan - the Reluctant Kennedy," GOOD HOUSEKEEPING,
June 1972: 76-79ff. JOAN: THE RELUCTANT KENNEDY, 1st F&W, 1974.
A biographical profile.

Hoffman, Betty H. "What It's Like to Marry a Kennedy," L.H.JRNL.,
Oct., 1962: 60-62ff. "Joan Kennedy's Story," L.H.HRNL., July,
1970: 57-59ff. "Joan Kennedy Today," L.H.JRNL., Aug., 1970: 82-
83ff.

Kevles, Barbara. "An Intimate Portrait of Joan Kennedy," GOOD
HOUSEKEEPING, Sept., 1969: 76-79ff. Joan on cover.

L.H.JRNL. "Joan Kennedy: Woman Under Pressure," by Kandy Stroud,
Sept., 1974: 58ff. "My Friend, Joan Kennedy," by Mieke Tunney,
Oct., 1974: 66ff.

LIFE. "Joan Kennedy Plays Tennis," Sept.8, 1972: 10-11.

NEWSWEEK. "'A Born Again Politician,'" April 7, 1980: 25.

N.Y TIMES. "The Wives Finding Rewards on the Campaign Trail," by
Leslie Bennetts, Feb.24, 1980: 14.-

Sadler, Christine. "The Coming of Age of Joan Kennedy," McCALL'S,
Feb., 1965: 126-127ff.

Seay, Sue. "A New Mrs. Kennedy in Washington," LOOK, Feb.26, 1963:
21ff. Joan on cover.

Smith, Liz. "Joan Kennedy: the Life That Put Her Into Silver
Hill," PEOPLE, June 24, 1974: 4-9.

TIME. "The Non-Candidate's Wife " Nov.29, 1971: 23, op.cit. 187.
"The Relentless Ordeal of Political Wives," (Pat Nixon, Betty Ford,
Joan Kennedy). Oct.7, 1974: 15-15ff. Three women on cover.

WORKS ABOUT TED KENNEDY JR.

Articles

David, Lester. "How the Ted Kennedys Handled Their Son's Crisis,"
L.H.JRNL., Feb., 1974: 92-93ff. "Teddy Jr. - the Bravest of the
Kennedys," GOOD HOUSEKEEPING, Oct., 1974: 104-105ff.

Rivera, Geraldo. "Teddy Kennedy Jr." in A SPECIAL KIND OF COURAGE:
Profiles of Young Americans. 1st S&S, 1976: 189-214.

SECTION FOUR

OTHER MEMBERS OF
THE KENNEDY FAMILY

WRITINGS BY AND ABOUT OTHER MEMBERS
OF THE KENNEDY FAMILY

JOSEPH KENNEDY JR.

Writings About Joseph Kennedy Jr.

Morison, Samuel Eliot. "Death of a Kennedy," (Joe Jr.). LOOK, Feb.27, 1962: 105-106ff.

Olsen, Jack. APHRODITE: Desperate Mission. Putnam, 1970. The World War II mission that cost the life of Joe Kennedy Jr.

Searls, Hank. THE LOST PRINCE: Young Joe, the Forgotten Kennedy. World, 1st prtg., 1969.

EUNICE KENNEDY SHRIVER

Writings by Eunice Kennedy Shriver

"Hope for Retarded Children," SAT.EVE.POST, Sept.22, 1962: 71-75.

Interview with Jane Berdes. "Useless People: All They Need Is Love, Love," U.S.CATHOLIC, Jan., 1974: 6-11. The work of the Kennedy Foundation.

R. SARGENT SHRIVER

Writings by R. Sargent Shriver

"America, Race and the World," in CHALLENGE TO RELIGION, edited by Mathew Ahman. Regnery, 1963: 142-152, wrs.

"...And Your Brother Shall Live With You," INTERRACIAL REVIEW, June, 1959: 120-122. Address as President Chicago Board of Education and Chicago Catholic Interracial Council before National Council of Christians and Jews Feb.3, 1959.

National Council of Catholic Women. "Highlights of Conference on Religion and Race, Jan., 1963. Mimeo. Excerpts from R.S.Shriver.

JFK appointed Shriver as the first Director of the Peace Corps. Shriver's writings about the Peace Corps have been cited in JFK Foreign Policy: 80.

"The War on Poverty: Toward Economic Equality," AFRICAN FORUM, Fall, 1966: 111-118.

Writings About Sargent Shriver

Liston, Robert A. SARGENT S HRIVER: A Candid Portrait. 1st Farrar Straus, 1964.

OTHER MEMBERS OF THE KENNEDY FAMILY

Writings About Sargent Shriver

TIME. "George McGovern Finally Finds a Veep," Aug.14, 1972: 15-20. Shriver's photo on cover. Op.cit. 187.

STEPHEN EDWARD SMITH

Writings About Stephen Edward Smith

Berquist, Laura. "The Inscrutable Mr. Smith. A JFK Brother-in-law Takes on the Task of Reelecting the President," LOOK, Sept. 24, 1963: 29-30ff.

* * * * * *

For other members of the Kennedy family cf. Sable, A BIO-BIBLIOG-RAPHY OF THE KENNEDY FAMILY, op.cit.: 11. Rose Marie: 246; Kathleen Kennedy Cavendish: 247; Patricia Kennedy Lawford: 259-60; Jean Kennedy Smith: 296.

INDEX

195.

INDEX

ONASSIS, JACQUELINE KENNEDY, writings of,152-153; writings about, 153-155.
ORGANIZATION OF AMERICAN STATES, 76.

PAKISTAN, 75, 186.
PALM BEACH, 19, 20.
PANAMA CANAL, 76.
PEACE, 2, 5, 6, 64, 71, 73, 103.
PEACE CORPS, 8, 49, 66, 77, 79-81.
PERSIAN GULF, 181, 182.
PHOTOGRAPHS, PORTRAITS, 58-60.
POETRY, 33, 140, 170.
POLAND, 163, 164.
POST OFFICE, 109.
POSTAGE STAMPS, 95, 142, 177.
POVERTY IN UNITED STATES, 36, 37, 38, 143, 157-162 passim, 182.
PRESIDENT'S ADVISORY COUNCIL ON THE ARTS, executive order, 95.
PRESIDENT'S COMMISSION ON CAMPAIGN COSTS, 104, 111.
PRESIDENT'S COMMISSION ON THE STATUS OF WOMEN, 103.
PRESIDENT'S COMMITTEE ON JUVENILE DELINQUENCY 1962, 94.
PRESIDENTIAL POLITICS, 2, 3, 4, 5, 11, 109-111.
PRESS CONFERENCES, 8, 9.
PT109, 11, 20.
PUBLIC OPINION SURVEYS, 49, 171, 172, 189.
PUERTO RICO, 75.

RADZIWILL, LEE, 56, 147; writings of, 155; writings about, 155.
RECORDINGS of and about JFK, 10, 17, 25, 62, 130, 137; Kennedy family, 58; JBK, 152; RFK, 159; EMK, 17, 177.
REGIONAL DEVELOPMENT ACT, 76.
REGIONAL POLITICAL STUDIES, 111
RELIGIOUS GROUPS, 6, 23-34 passim, 49, 53-55, 62, 68, 98, 132.
REPUBLICAN PARTY, 109, 110, 111, 145, 170, 186.
RIGHTISTS, 7, 48-49, 62, 66, 68, 71, 113, 118, 144.
ROOSEVELT, ELEANOR, 43, 44.
ROOSEVELT, FRANKLIN D. 10, 14.
RULES COMMITTEE, 104.
RUSSIA, 8, 72, 81-85 passim, 161, 180, 181, 187.

SARAWAK, 80.
SCIENCE AND SCIENTIFIC ELITE, 65, 67, 68, 70, 112.
SECRET SERVICE, 111, 129, 130.
SENATE, 41, 42, 44, 45, 86, 125, 128, 136, 165, 181, 185; cf. also CONGRESS.
SHRIVER, EUNICE KENNEDY, writings by, 182, 192; writing about,15.
SHRIVER, R. SARGENT, writings by, 80, 192; writings about, 15, 79, 80, 81, 133, 158, 193.
SILVER PURCHASE ACT OF 1963, 63.
SMITH, JEAN KENNEDY, 15, 193.
SMITH, STEPHEN EDWARD, 15, 193.

ABOUT THE COMPILERS

DOROTHY RYAN is associated with L. J. Ryan Scholarly Books. Her articles have appeared in *The Catholic World.*

LOUIS J. RYAN is the owner of L. J. Ryan Scholarly Books. He is coauthor of *Preface to Happiness.*